Praise for *BAD INDIANS BOOK CLUB*

"*Bad Indians Book Club* is a compendium of worlds. From a lifetime of reading, there emerges a marriage of tapestry and map, a vision of the literary canon not as some secret handshake of the correctly educated but as a living, growing organism. . . . There's a dangerousness to a book like this. It's not enough to define the Good Indian, the Grateful Immigrant, the Untroublesome Minority. Nor is it enough to simply reject these designations. One must interrogate how they came to hold so much power, how they offer the willing participant so many crumbs of reward from colonialism's table."

—**Omar El Akkad**, award-winning journalist and author of *American War* and *What Strange Paradise*

"*Bad Indians Book Club* is full of good medicine—challenging us to ask questions and bringing us home to ourselves. As Patty Krawec guides us into the deep wisdom wells of many people who journey in kinship, we consider how to hold the curiosity of care and stories, and what it means to imagine and create a future that integrates all our stories into a web of healing. Please buy this book, and celebrate the power of story in a weary yet flourishing world."

—**Kaitlin B. Curtice**, award-winning author of *Native* and *Living Resistance*

"With *Bad Indians Book Club*, Patty Krawec gifts us a compelling investigation into the power of not just reading books but also doing so in community. Krawec makes the case for building your circle through reading, as a way of being in better relations with all our kin, including the land. Thinking deeply alongside other books, *Bad Indians Book Club* is a needed guide at a moment when books are under attack. Books are not just written culture; they are also oral culture, and Krawec illuminates this beautifully."

—**Dr. Chanda Prescod-Weinstein**, theoretical physicist and author of *The Disordered Cosmos*

"This genre-crossing, shape-shifting, imagination-expanding book is for all who love to, and also need to, read. We tell stories to live, and this enlivening book reflects on all kinds of stories, each page suffused with Patty Krawec's unmistakable voice and generous, timeless wisdom."

—**Astra Taylor**, documentary filmmaker and author of several books, including *Remake the World* and *The Age of Insecurity*

"In *Bad Indians Book Club*, Patty Krawec provides critical space for the ne'er-do-wells, disrupters, red sheep, box-busters, tricksters, and all of us rowdy relatives defying expectations. Indigenous people have always been proverbial thorns in the sides of colonizers, and this piercing book does an incredible job of letting the air out of today's imperialist narratives."

—**Taté Walker**, award-winning Two Spirit Lakota storyteller and community-builder

BAD INDIANS BOOK CLUB

BAD INDIANS BOOK CLUB

READING AT THE EDGE OF A THOUSAND WORLDS.

FOREWORD BY OMAR EL AKKAD

PATTY KRAWEC

Broadleaf Books
Minneapolis

BAD INDIANS BOOK CLUB
Reading at the Edge of a Thousand Worlds

30 29 28 27 26 25   1 2 3 4 5 6 7 8 9

Library of Congress Control Number: 2024951607 (print)

Cover design: Faceout Studio

Print ISBN: 978-1-5064-9912-3
eBook ISBN: 978-1-5064-9913-0

Printed in India.

For Kerry, without whom none of these conversations would have been possible,

and Kyle, who asked a silly question.

It's not about blood and it never has been. It's about how you arrive and build a relationship with the land you're on. And once you're there, it's also about how you receive others.

—Natalie Diaz (Mojave/Akimel/O'odham)

Other nations take these things into account, and in doing so they reinforce something we, with our fixation on blood, have forgotten: bending to a common purpose is more important than arising from a common place.

—David Treuer (White Earth Ojibwe)

CONTENTS

FOREWORD

It's not common knowledge that Georgetown University maintains a small satellite campus in the tiny Arabian Gulf nation of Qatar. In the fall of 2024, I was offered a month-long residency at the campus. I grew up in Qatar, and while the prospect of flying halfway around the planet for work became less and less appealing as I got older, I couldn't pass up the opportunity to see high school friends and visit the site of my childhood.

It ended up being a good residency; it has been one of the few instances when I've taught a creative writing workshop where most of the students weren't white westerners. Toward the end of my stay, I stopped by the campus bookstore and bought a school hoodie.

Since I've returned to North America, that hoodie has become a kind of real-time sociology experiment. There's nothing particularly unusual about it—it simply states the name of Georgetown University in English and Arabic. But the Arabic script is larger, running bold across the chest. I've come to recognize a particular kind of reaction whenever I wear it in this part of the world: a passing glance that notices the Arabic script and then does a double-take, something like consternation in the eyes. Brows then furrow at the words *Georgetown University* in English below, joined to the name of some faraway place. Sometimes, in these fleeting interactions, the final expression on the other's face is one of open hostility. Most often it's just disorientation.

I imagine this phenomenon must have something to do with all the other times people in this part of the world tend to see Arabic script: on ISIS flags in the news; on the storefronts of disheveled set-piece towns in American action movies, soon to be made ruins by one kind of cinematic violence or another; on election pamphlets dispensed throughout "ethnic" neighborhoods; and on those "Everyone's Welcome" murals where, because not a single person involved speaks the language, the letters appear backwards and disjointed. These looks I get, wearing what should be an utterly innocuous hoodie, are not because people haven't heard stories told in and about my mother tongue, but precisely because they have. It's just that someone else has been doing the telling.

Language is never enough. Any discrete collection of words and grammar captures the analog reality of human experience no better than a net captures water. We are all of us made of stories half-told, half-understood, changed each time in that lawless space between the saying and the listening. In this way, to read a book, to take in a story, is to unshackle oneself from the obligation of complete understanding—to instead participate in a different kind of communion, one in which failure is a revelatory thing, a prelude to a more honest relationship with the world.

I first met Patty Krawec as a consequence of my own failure. She'd read my debut novel, a book called *American War*, set in the ruins of a future United States. She reached out to ask where, in my imagining, were the descendants of the people who'd first walked and tended to this land, the people who'd been erased from so much of this continent's cultural output over the centuries. I had intended the novel to be an inversion of erasure, a means of superimposing the stories of the part of the world I came from onto the heart of the superpower. And yet I had, by way of the obliviousness that so often accompanies self-perceived righteousness, engaged in another kind of erasure, too.

The conversations Patty and I had since then have been some of the most reorienting I've ever had about my own work. At the time, much of the critical assessment of my novel centered on the book as literary prophecy, a depiction of some ruinous American future, when I had intended no such thing. Patty read something entirely different, saw another world in the pages.

Bad Indians Book Club is a compendium of worlds. From a lifetime of reading, there emerges a marriage of tapestry and map, a vision of the literary canon not as some secret handshake of the correctly educated but as a living, growing organism.

Perhaps the most straightforward assessment of this book centers on the text as a kind of recommended reading list, a collection of titles chosen by the author to achieve some rhetorical or ideological goal. Certainly, Patty's kaleidoscopic literary appetite easily allows for such an assessment, and there is enough here to construct the most refreshing contemporary syllabus. But this reading alone does the work a disservice. So does a reading focused on agreement, the relative distance between the reader's opinion of these various texts, and the author's. In many cases, I found myself at odds with Patty's interpretation of some work we'd both read, and these moments of friction—of noticing the same light passing through different prisms—were among the most enjoyable.

But again, it's insufficient. Instead, something else entirely forms the narrative backbone of *Bad Indians Book Club*, makes it most vital: the connective tissue. Decades of reading across cultures, across histories, across worlds, presents itself as a web of passages from one people's experiences to another's. From the ongoing obliteration (both physical and rhetorical) of Palestinians to the complexities of Indigenous identities within Appalachia, and the centuries-long refusal of the colonial project to recognize them. From the Native Hawaiian relationships with land to the Haitian diaspora's relationships with home. There begins to build, page by page, a sense of solidarity born not of unquestioning unanimity or orthodoxy but the sharing of many stories outside the suffocating flatness of empire. An *us that includes you*.

Perhaps the longest-resonating aftereffect of reading *Bad Indians Book Club* is the realization that the default mode of living under colonialism and its capitalist machinery is the exact inverse of this lateral solidarity: a perpetually walled-off existence, an *us* over here, a *you* elsewhere.

Many years ago, I read the memoir *Good-bye to All That* by Robert Graves. Toward the end of that book, Graves, having survived the

First World War, travels to Egypt to teach English. There, he laments the inherent hopelessness of students with names like "Mahmoud Mohammed Mahmoud" and "Mohammed Mahmoud Mohammed," and how desperately he "wished to protect Shakespeare from them."

I was reminded of that glib, plainly racist vignette while reading a section in *Bad Indians Book Club* where Patty describes publishing a magazine article, for which a photograph of her and her son was commissioned:

> *There isn't anything real about this picture. The photographer staged it, and it represents her idea of how we should look rather than who I actually was. When the photographer arrived, I had been wearing a purple dress with a full skirt that I liked because of the way that it moved when I danced at the powwows I attended . . .*
>
> *You can imagine my confusion when the photographer's first words were to ask where my traditional clothes were. She wanted the whitestream vision of Pocahontas—braids and buckskin—not a young mother with bobbed hair and a purple dress. I was not yet confident enough to push back, so I accepted my place as a Good Indian.*

There's a dangerousness to a book like this. It's not enough to define the Good Indian, the Grateful Immigrant, the Untroublesome Minority. Nor is it enough to simply reject these designations. One must interrogate how they came to hold so much power, how they offer the willing participant so many crumbs of reward from colonialism's table.

And on the other side of that interrogation, perhaps, an alternative way of being emerges: one based on the strength of our relationships, the only language enough to hold the whole of living.

—Omar El Akkad

AANIIN

I am trying to urge you toward something new—not simply against their myths of conquest, but against the urge to craft your own.

—Ta-Nehisi Coates

AANIIN, BOOZHOO. Wabanan Anangonkwe n'dishnakaaz. Adik n'dodem. Obishkokaang n'doonjibaa. Ojibwe Anishinaabekwe n'daaw.

Hello. I was taught to introduce myself with my name, clan, community, and nation, so that people would know the location I speak from, the communities I belong to. An introduction is where we set our intentions. We call in the past, present, and future generations to remind us that while our words may live in the present, they are rooted in what came before and lay the groundwork for what is yet to come.

Where we are from is a fraught question, particularly at this moment when it is being used to justify the worst kind of violence against anyone deemed to be out of place. In this context, where we are from determines where we are supposed to be and gives government—as well as those it deputizes formally and informally—the right to remove whoever it decides belongs someplace else. I hear this all the time when I bring up Land Back, as if restoring the land to itself would mean replicating the racial categories and hard boundaries of our current world. Used in this way, "Where are you from?" is a question of suspicion rather than curiosity. But this is all very recent, and it doesn't have to be that way. Where are you from can be the beginning of relationship and understanding of what you bring with you into this place.

For millennia, people have moved and lived in ways that shared space without having to determine through blood or politics if you belonged. As Natalie Diaz says in the opening epigraph, it was never about blood. It was about how you arrive and build relationship; and then, having established yourself there, it is about how you welcome others as well. David Treuer reminds us that bending toward a common purpose is what makes a community. Our relatives matter, and the places where our ancestors became a people matter, because the land is my ancestor as surely as any of my human relatives are. But human ancestry is not the only relation that determines who we are and what we are building, and as Ta-Nehisi Coates (Black) says in his book to young writers, *The Message*, we must resist the temptation to find belonging by crafting our own narratives of conquest and all the borders and violence they require.[1] Bad Indians know that we survive together or not at all.

Understanding these relations is important. Deborah Miranda (Ohlone/Costanoan-Esselen), author of *Bad Indians: A Tribal Memoir*, says that knowledge of who is telling the story is critical information that you, the reader, need in order to understand the stake they have in telling you a story. "Who," she asks in the context of reading about history, "is inventing me, for what purpose, with what intentions?"[2]

So let me tell you who I am, my purpose, and set some intentions about this book club we are embarking on. I am a member of Lac Seul First Nation in northwestern Ontario, several hours north of Lake Superior, although I've never lived there. I tend to say that I *belong* there rather than that I am *from* there, in part because it is a legal belonging, not the place I ought to be as if I am currently out of place. It is where my father and his father, myself and my sons were and are registered as Indians under the Indian Act in Canada. That's a piece of legislation from the late 1800s that has been amended many times and continues

---

1 Ta-Nehisi Coates, *The Message* (Penguin Random House, 2024), 35.

2 Deborah A. Miranda, *Bad Indians: A Tribal Memoir* (Heyday Books, 2024), xx.

to shape and control the lives of Indigenous people within Canada's borders. In the United States, that kind of legal belonging is determined by the tribe itself, although the state or federal government retains the authority to legally recognize the tribe. Federally that authority rests with the Bureau of Indian Affairs, located within the Department of the Interior.

I belong to Lac Seul through kinship relations as well—a dense network of cousins covering the land and cities north and west of Lake Superior. My father and his family were far away and seemingly out of reach, but their existence was never hidden from me. In many ways my life has been a search for people and stories that could help me put flesh on the relatives and ancestors I knew only through photographs. I grew up in the 1970s and '80s, so the stories I found about Indians were written by white historians and anthropologists, then projected by Hollywood into our homes and onto me. They were invented stories, told with purpose and intention. In the stories told in books and film, there were, and often still are, Good Indians: those who rescue white heroes so that they can in turn be saved. And in these stories, there are Bad Indians, too: those who refuse to rescue settlers or to be saved themselves.[3]

Finding my father, almost by accident, in the early 1990s sent me looking for Native people rather than just stories about them. Until I found my father living relatively close to me rather than two thousand

---

3 *Indian* can and does also refer to people from the Asian subcontinent and parts of the Caribbean, diverse communities subsumed under the label "Indian" that was created in the fourteenth century to describe the people of the Indus River. This was not a label they chose for themselves, but there, as here, it stuck because of who has the authority to make such things stick. We are diverse communities subject to being seen as good and bad, depending on our support of the nation-state in which we live or how we live out our "Indianness." Although the political details are far beyond the scope of this book, I would recommend seeking out the work of Harsha Walia, Arundhati Roy, Siddhartha Deb, Edwidge Danticat, and V. S. Naipaul. Our struggles are truly connected.

kilometers away near the small town where he and my mother met, I had believed that Native people simply didn't live where I was. It's not that absurd an idea, really; decades later I still meet people who are surprised that we exist at all.

The Native Canadian Centre of Toronto and the Native Women's Resource Centre of Toronto, not too far from where I lived at the time, were hubs I could join and bring my children to. We found some Good Indians, those who rescued white people and then allowed themselves to be saved, through religion or politics or other ways to belong that relied on the displacement of others. Many of these Good Indians found a way to survive in a world that didn't want them to, and, in their own ways, many held onto language and story amid everything else.

But it was the Bad Indians to whom I felt drawn—and still do. I had grown up in the apocalyptic visions of evangelical Christianity, so I was used to thinking about worlds ending. It was these Bad Indians who offered me a vision of new worlds being born—worlds rooted in differences that bring balance and life, not differences that play out in hierarchies and power. Like the faith in which I grew up, Hollywood's apocalyptic stories rely on The One, with everybody else a bit player whose purpose is to ensure the survival of The One. As I said, Bad Indians know that we survive together or not at all.

So I followed these Bad Indians into protest and ceremony, the round dances of Idle No More, a kind of contemporary ghost dance with which we could call forth our ancestors to help us sing and dance new worlds into being. We had no interest in rescuing this system or creating a kinder and more inclusive nationalist project that could save us from ourselves while it benefits from our displacement. My children's earliest memories are walking the streets surrounded by Bad Indians, who refuse to accept political crumbs and demand that promises be kept.

The dominating society loves to categorize people as good and bad depending on whether or not they support the existing system. In his own memoir, film and culture critic Jesse Wente (Anishinaabe) writes about being keenly aware that he is the kind of Indian that residential schools were designed to produce. Made tolerable and acceptable by the system whose intention was to erase and destroy. It is not, he says, an identity to which he aspires and is one that he fights against. He asks himself, working in the midst of colonial systems, "Are you going to be the Acceptable One, or are you going to raise hell and find a way to weaponize your privilege against the very place that's given it to you?"[4]

In her book *Bad Jews*, which examines the history of Jewish people in America, Emily Tamkin (Jewish) calls anti-Semitism "the conviction that Jews are forever foreign or alien to whatever population they happen to be in, and often have designs on corrupting that population."[5] This sounds familiar to me; those of us who are pushed into the margins, into the mashkiig—the swamp—are also seen as foreign or alien to whatever place we find ourselves in. We can try to be good, try to fit in, but in the end it doesn't matter. This world wasn't made for us, and our presence is seen as a threat. Assimilating to that world means negating our history, our ancestors, our selves. Bad Indians refuse this rootlessness.

Following the paths onto which Bad Indians led us, my children and I found others who refused to be saved: people from communities who, like us, have been pushed violently to the margins and people who refused the offer of rescue through compliance with the system that rejected them in the first place.[6] They have also refused the false promises of assimilation that cut them off from their history, their ways of knowing and being in the world. Too often people accept the explanation that we were rejected because of something we did, so we change

---

4 Jesse Wente, *Unreconciled: Family, Truth, and Indigenous Resistance* (Penguin Random House, 2021), 116.

5 Emily Tamkin, cited by Shane Burley and Ben Lorber, *Safety through Solidarity* (Melville House, 2024), 17.

6 So much gratitude to Robyn Maynard (Black), whose emphasis on the violence of marginalization is echoed every time I think about those who are pushed there. Active voice matters. We didn't put ourselves at the margins. Someone pushed us there, often through violence. Miigwech, Robyn.

the things we do in the hopes of being accepted and given a place at a table built on stolen land.

But Bad Indians know that it wasn't anything we did; we're rejected because of who we are.

These paths led me farther and farther into the woods and away from colonial futures. My people are bush Indians. Biskaabiiyang means to return to yourself, and it carries the idea of going into the woods. The Ojibwe Anishinaabe live in the forests and swamps north of Lake Superior, and even though I grew up thousands of kilometers from the place I call home, something of that must linger in my blood or memory to be passed on to my children. When our children were young and we went hiking together, our oldest son, Ben, would frequently follow breaks in the bush. Pushing through shrubbery, following what we came to call "Ben trails," we inevitably found something beautiful—something that those who stayed on the conventional paths would have missed. His younger brothers do this too, scaling rock faces, hiking, and exploring new places. Following my children, now adults—on hikes and across oceans into the communities they find and become part of—has expanded my world as surely as anything I have read.

In a world that is increasingly polarizing along religious, racial, and ethnic lines, it is becoming critical for our survival to talk to each other and think beyond the political categories that keep us apart. Reading groups or book clubs have a long history of exploring new ideas. Indeed, the power of this kind of collective reading is such that during the years of chattel slavery, Black people were not allowed to read at all. Reading groups proliferated in the 1970s as a mechanism for consciousness-raising, and they continue to be sources of grassroots education across a range of racial and political categories. There is a reason, after all, why more and more people seek to ban the books that point us toward collective liberation.

Bad Indians Book Club emerged from a series of conversations I had with friends and authors, some of which became podcasts, about books read and written. As happens in any good book club, ideas about how we could live differently emerged from the connections between us: readers and writers from a variety of backgrounds who are no longer seeking inclusion into a house that is on fire.[7]

I write this as the world is awash in protest, people raising hell, as Wente puts it, all of which is being done wrong according to Good Citizens. We're too loud, too inconvenient, too demanding, too everything. Demanding something other than genocide, violence, and extreme inequity, *we're* the bad ones. I'm okay with that—with being one of many Bad Indians who challenge the stories we tell about the society in which we live, because the things we believe have consequences that are often borne by others, consequences we may not see. My first book, *Becoming Kin*, challenged the myths and stories that Canada and the United States tell about their history. But history isn't the only story we tell about our encounters with the worlds around us. This book is an invitation to join me in challenging all the stories. I hope that you can begin challenging the stories you encounter—stories that, like the colonialism in which they are rooted, serve to displace and erase other ways of knowing.

We live in a culture that romanticizes certain kinds of outlaws, and I don't want to do that, but we should pay attention to how marginalized people are spoken of when we refuse to take our place.

To remind us of what's at stake, of how we are seen and spoken of when we refuse to behave, memoirist Deborah Miranda writes a "Novena to Bad Indians," a novena being an urgent nine-day prayer petitioning for grace or favour. She offers gratitude and intention to those who are called names and painted as violent. She petitions those who refused to accept their position in social and gendered hierarchies. She asks for grace from women whose sexual agency and

---

7 James Baldwin wrote, "Do I really *want* to be integrated into a burning house?" in *The Fire Next Time* (Vintage International, 1962), 94.

reproductive choices were and are seen as threatening. She honours those who refused to convert to a Christianity that arrived hand in glove with empire and those who later recanted. "Illuminate the dark civilization we endure," she implores, "teach us to love the untamed, inspire us to break rules."[8] And remember, she says: "Even dead Indians are never good enough."[9]

Bad Indians Book Club is a novena of sorts: nine chapters of public prayer to Bad Indians and those like them who refuse to be left in their special interest section. Bad Indians know that you learn best when you push aside the dust and detritus you have become accustomed to and make room for new ideas and new ways of thinking about things. Bad Indians take the life around us seriously, even when it is life we don't understand. Bad Indians return to themselves through histories told by those who have a different stake in those stories. We are experts at refusal and creating hostile spaces, and we tell our own stories, even when they aren't pretty. Bad Indians wield stories like weapons in the war against imagination. We pick medicine with the things that go bump in the night, and we know that we have a future despite everything that has been stolen, buried, and burned.

There is something defiant about being a Bad Indian, about leaning into these negative stereotypes. Something adolescent and feral. If I'm going to get into trouble anyway, I might as well deserve it. This book is, ultimately, a book about refusal: refusing political categories and the borders and violence that comes with them, refusing to assimilate by becoming the kind of person the state cannot assimilate. It's written by a Bad Indian who doesn't just want to survive this current

---

8 The cover of this book features a painting of Wanada Parker by Comanche artist Nahmi A Piah. She was the daughter of Comanche chief Quanah Parker and his principal wife Wekeah OldBear, a complicated woman who, in many ways, exemplifies the Bad Indians Miranda is beseeching in her Novena. For more on Wanada, see the *Note About the Cover* provided by her great-great niece Weyodi OldBear.

9 Miranda, *Bad Indians*, 113–15.

apocalypse. I want to join with others—Bad Indians and more—to midwife new worlds into being.

• • •

That is my introduction, my intentions. But we should all—not just those who are marginalized by their race or write from other borderland places—connect the past and present of our lives. If settler colonialism, and the national projects that evolved from it, separates us from our history and the relationships contained there, then grounding ourselves in these relationships to place and people can be a way to refuse that separation.[10]

You need to think about your own grounding, belonging, the places you are from and who you bring with you so that you understand the relationships you form with the books that you read. Max Liboiron (Métis) extends this grounding in their writing by marking the people they cite according to how they introduce themselves in the context of land relations, as I did at the beginning.

In these pages, if somebody's writing does not offer me that kind of introduction and I lack the relationship to ask, like Liboiron, I will use the term *unmarked*. Unmarked doesn't mean the person is white; it just means that I haven't found that kind of introduction in their online presence—although, as Liboiron says, you may notice a pattern.[11] I'll generally do this the first time I mention their name, but if it's been a while or it is particularly relevant to what I'm citing, I'll repeat it. These introductions or markers offer a way to think about the relatives and histories the person brings with them, a place where you can begin to think about the stake *they* have in telling you a story.

---

10 Thank you, Sam, for this description of how settler colonialism acts on us! It is so helpful.

11 Max Liboiron, *Pollution Is Colonialism* (Duke University Press, 2021), Introduction, footnote 10.

Sara Ahmed (Pakistani, British), the author of so many books about feminism, has a citational practice of not quoting any white men. Citation is a kind of relationship; we point to the path we are following by citing those who came before us.[12] When Hana Burgess (Māori) tweeted out her intention to do a PhD without citing any white men, her mentions filled with complaints that she would be excluding experts in the field—an interesting assertion since she hadn't said what she was studying. White men are clearly the experts on all topics. As she progressed in her work, challenging the stories being told about the Māori through public health policy, she found others who were also challenging those stories. Locating her work within a liberatory perspective increasingly meant locating her work within those relationships between all of us who exist in the margins and refuse to be saved.[13] Rather than thinking along exclusively racial lines, Burgess looks to those who bend with her toward a common purpose, people often pushed to the edges, the mashkiig, for wisdom she can lift up.

I find it helpful to think of *Indigenous* the way my friend Troy Storfjell (Sámi)[14] has described: as an analytic or political category rather than an identity. Like *citizen*, *migrant*, *refugee*, and others, it describes

---

12 Sara Ahmed, *Living a Feminist Life* (Duke University Press, 2017), 15.

13 Kerry Goring and I spoke with Burgess about this on the podcast *Medicine for the Resistance*. Her tweet intrigued me so I invited her into conversation about it. Several years later, I'm still thinking about that conversation. Miigwech, Hana, for transformative conversation. https://medicinefortheresistance.substack.com/p/doing-a-phd-with-no-white-men-with-f58#details.

14 On January 20, 2021, Troy Storfjell (Sámi) posted a tweet that changed my life. He wrote that "Indigeneity is an analytic, not an identity. . . . It describes a certain set of relationships to colonialism, anti-colonialism, and specific lands and places." It is description located in a particular time and political circumstance. Before we were colonised, we were Sámi, Lakota, Anishinaabe. *Indigenous* refers to the people who are in a place when settler colonialism imposed another social and political order on top of their way of life. In chapter 2, we will think more about what this means in the context of "Indigenous land." Miigwech, Troy, for this and much more.

our relationship to the country in which we live.[15] It is, as Daniel Delgado (Quechua/Jewish) says, "an intrinsically political term created in response to colonization." The period of colonization created largely racialized categories to explain who everybody was, what rights they had within the empire, and where they belonged.[16] Increasingly, even being born somewhere doesn't always mean you belong. Throughout the countries that emerged from empire, even after generations of presence, your skin or religion could mark you as belonging elsewhere.

So rather than limiting myself to what amounts to a racial category, invented for a purpose and maintained by systems with questionable intent, we will travel the borderlands, the places where we build relationships with the land we are on, think about how we receive others, and bend toward a common purpose. Being marginalized is another analytic or political category. It is a way of describing groups of people whose stories are pushed aside and written on top of by the dominating society. Marginalized people may or may not think of themselves as Indigenous, but we share the common vocabulary of exclusion, of being on the losing end of national hierarchies.[17]

We at the edges often stay in our groups and relate to each other through the invisible narration of whiteness. We may know that the single story being told about us is untrue, but somehow we find ourselves believing the single stories told about others. Worse, we internalize the stories that are told about us and come to believe that we were primitive, savage, uncivilized, and needed to be rescued from ourselves instead of seeing value in what those who came later disparaged.

---

15 Racial, religious, and ethnic groups are also political categories when we consider how they relate to the state and work to support inequity by keeping us separate from each other. The fact of our difference is not the problem, it is the meaning made of that difference we should be questioning.

16 Daniel Delgado, "Are Jews Indigenous? A Quechua Jew Weighs In," 2024, https://www.lifeisasacredtext.com/indigenous/.

17 Nandita Sharma, *Home Rule: National Sovereignty and the Separation of Natives and Migrants* (Duke University Press, 2020), 20.

It's easy to become Good Indians: those following paved roads toward promises that were broken before they were even made.

So it is that I use Bad Indian as a point of pride—as a refusal to seek belonging in a system that never wanted us.

• • •

A journey into the borderlands is best with a companion. Waawaashkeshi'Kwe—the Ojibwe name often translated as Deer Woman—is a Bad Indian. Stories of Deer Woman's vengeance against those who harm women and children are part of many stories told of her across the eastern woodlands and central plains in the lands that eventually became the Americas. We will travel along with her through the stories offered by others who, like Waawaashkeshi'Kwe, stay in the borderlands and refuse to be civilized.

The world is alive with sentient spiritual beings, and for many land-based people with such beliefs, animists, the lines between human and other-than-human are blurry.[18] There are many stories about shape-shifters and other beings across the world. Our relationship to these stories and the way we understand these beings shifting over time depends on dominant narratives. In these pages we'll come across a few of these other beings. Waawaashkeshi'Kwe and her borderland-dwelling kin refuse easy categorizing.

Waawaashkeshi'Kwe often features in whitestream comic books, pulp fiction, and horror movies, all of which exploit her sexuality and violence and rarely take her seriously as a person or spirit. The FX television series *Reservation Dogs*, set in a Mvskoke community in rural Oklahoma, included Deer Lady as a recurring character who shows up intermittently in the lives of characters from this community. She has a backstory and connections with various community members. The Indigenous-led

---

18 Mari Joerstad, *The Hebrew Bible and Environmental Ethics: Humans, NonHumans, and the Living Landscape* (Cambridge University Press, 2019), 11. I love this phrase, sentient spiritual beings. Miigwech, Mari, for your work and conversations.

production takes Deer Lady, and the community in which she emerges, seriously. This is how stories change when we tell them ourselves.

I don't know if it's just the zeitgeist of this moment or something more personal, but Waawaashkeshi'Kwe has been in my thoughts for a while. I think about her transgressiveness: Female deer do not typically have antlers. Conventionally, it is related to abnormal testosterone levels, but how we define normal and gender can be just as political as biological. Waawaashkeshi'Kwe reminds us that boundaries are more blurred than fixed. I think about her insistence on respect and willingness to fight for others. And I think about the deer who go through my backyard, sometimes in small groups and sometimes alone. Native people say that you should look for the medicine that shows up, and she was showing up. So I started wondering what she might be trying to teach me.

The story I tell of Waawaashkeshi'Kwe, whom I have named simply Kwe, is a story I just thought up. The stories begin in a distant past and move through the history and geographies of the Americas and into the future, just as these chapters do. She begins in the woodlands of Anishinaabe aki, my own homelands, and then runs away until she gets to the ocean. After some time with the Mi'kmaq, she follows the coast to what is now Massachusetts. She lingers in one place for several chapters, spending time with the Wampanoag people in the years before and after the arrival of the *Mayflower*, before following the coastline and rivers all the way to what is now Belize. Elsewhere she moves quickly through hundreds of years. These locations reflect some of my own travel, imagining how she might have experienced these places and the people in them; they remind us of political and trade relationships that covered this continent long before colonization. This form, called flash fiction, is a short story told in one thousand words or less, a limitation but also an invitation to fill in the missing pieces yourself and imagine what is left unwritten.

Kwe's story begins as winter is becoming spring, a gesture to the prohibition that some stories should not be told unless there is snow on the ground. To my knowledge I have not shared any stories with this prohibition, but that sometimes changes from one community to another, and so the first part of her story takes place with some snow still on the ground. I have followed the lead of Vine DeLoria Jr. (Lakota) in sharing only stories that have already appeared in print elsewhere, and even then, when they are printed by authors whose judgement I have reason to trust. A much-simplified West African story of Ananzi, which begins the chapter on fiction, is shared with the permission of the storyteller who shared it with me. It is footnoted with a link where you can hear her tell it more completely.

My thoughts on these topics are my own. They might be consistent with other thinkers, but they do not represent Anishinaabe or Indigenous thought, as if such a goal were even possible. I have tried to be careful, to ask for advice and clarify the things I thought I remembered, but whatever errors you come across are my own. These thoughts are shaped by various podcast conversations, books, and articles—the internal collisions of the ever-expanding piles of books, articles, and conversations that are scattered across my desk, shelves, digital landscapes, and memories.

This journey, with pathways that go through the brush and borderlands, is taken with friends, storytellers, and storytellers who became friends. Like all good journeys, this one has made me a different person. We don't just passively absorb the things we read. Books change us because we engage with them, we wrestle and argue with them. The power of book clubs and reading groups lies not just in who we read but in who we read with, and why.

In *The Message*, Ta-Nehisi Coates writes about the impact of words from his earliest years.[19] I read his book recalling that like Coates, I too laid on my bed at five years old, murmuring phrases from one or another volume of the Childcraft series he mentions, the images and stories haunting my play as works read throughout adolescence and then adulthood would find life in my thoughts and actions. And I too made

19 Coates, *The Message*, 16.

the transition from reader to writer when, in a fit of anger against injustice and false histories, it occurred to me that I could shape the stories being told. Now my words haunt others. *I* stay with *them* throughout their day and into their work. It's a profound and humbling thing to realize this: to realize not only the power that reading, and writing, has to change the world but my own place in this work. It is a political act, this demand to be seen and read across genres on our own terms and not as some sidekick existing only to save the white hero. Coates's book, written as it is to the young writers he teaches, implores them to do their part to save the world. This book is the other side of that relationship, imploring *readers* to do their part. I believe in the power of reading to change the world, because reading has the power to change us.

If we are going to be changed, and then change others, we must read intentionally, but more than intentionally I want to read radically.[20] I want you to feel what is at stake in a world of book bans and alternative facts, to grasp the value of listening to those who are pushed to the edges and the communities we build there. More important than reading these books is protecting them, which means getting involved in the places that control access to them—places like libraries and schools, where the decisions are being made.[21]

Hold events at community centres and independent bookstores. Start your own Bad Indians Book Club in the places where they will least expect it but desperately need it. Don't just read banned books; become engaged in the places where they are being taken off the shelves. And remember, above all, the first rule of Bad Indians Book Club: Always carry a book.

---

20 *Radical* comes from the Latin *radix*, which means "root." It means getting to the root of an issue, pulling something out by the roots, planting new roots. This is how we read. We pull out what no longer serves us, what has never served us, by the roots, and we plant something in its place.

21 Libraries for the People is a US-based toolkit for people wanting to take action on this. Although it is US specific, many of the strategies will be applicable elsewhere. https://www.librariesforthepeople.org/.

Kwe

Thin daylight filtered through the trees in the gathering dusk, but Kwe barely noticed. Her ears strained desperately for the sound of footfalls behind her, anything that could signal her pursuers were gaining on her, while her eyes reached forward trying to keep the path in sight, some of it obscured with the snow that persisted where the black spruce shaded the sun. The forest was dense with trees and undergrowth, lacy branches of tamarack and birch tall against the grey sky, with black spruce filling in the gaps between them. Dogwood and chokecherry reached out to her, plucking at her skirt. Kwe was grateful for her leggings, torn as they were, for the smooth hide protected her shins from these scrabbling branches. The branches tugged and tangled in her black hair as if trying to hold her back, but she pushed through, snapping off the thinner offshoots in her haste. Kwe ran deeper into the woods, bits of the forest now ensnared in her loosening braids.

A swarm of bees arose, blocking the now barely visible trail, and Kwe veered away from them into a grassy clearing. The forest opened briefly onto a vernal pond, the edges limned with ice. Kwe recognized alders and dogwood, water willow and winterberry pushing themselves into and above the waters, a swamp filled with medicines she knew she needed. She stopped for a moment, leaning against a birch and pulling oxygen into her burning lungs in ragged breaths. But she couldn't stay. Kwe didn't hear anything, but sounds were muffled by the fog and forest noises, and what daylight remained was vanishing quickly. She turned and ran.

Last year's fallen leaves hid the rocks and tree roots, and her foot caught on them. She fell, arms outstretched, hands and knees colliding sharply on rocks she couldn't see. Lifting her head she saw a snake, dark green with yellow stripes, that had been sunning itself on a dark stone. It raised itself, and looked directly at her for a few seconds, its tongue darting. Then it lowered itself and turned into the forest, back in the direction from which she had come.

Kwe scanned herself for new injuries, then pushed up and on. It wasn't long before she got tangled in aspen shoots and fell again, landing hard against a fallen tree. She rolled on the soft cushion of leaves and pine needles that had collected in the hollow. Looking up into the small clearing, she decided to lie still, just a moment, and closed her eyes. She heard nothing now but her own ragged breath.

• • •

A young deer and her mother delicately picked their way through the forest. Making their way to a bedding area, they stopped, suddenly alert to an unfamiliar presence and the metallic smell of blood.

It was the fawn who first saw Kwe, asleep in the place they had expected to lie down. Curious, the fawn moved closer and, thinking that this might be a deer from another herd, nudged her. Kwe rolled over soundlessly, and the fawn jumped. This wasn't another deer, although the fawn could be forgiven for thinking so, having seen only Kwe's hide-covered back and tangled hair, branches sticking out in all directions.

Kwe's breathing had settled into a soft, shallow rhythm. She was cold, and there was a damp chill in the night air. The fawn, knowing that sleeping close to her own mother kept her warm, sought to warm the stranger, so she laid down beside Kwe and curled herself against the young woman. The doe also laid down, and the three of them settled into a deep rest.

• • •

When the morning sun burned off the remaining fog, only the doe awoke. Kwe and the fawn were still and cold. She nudged them both to no effect, laid down again to try and bring them warmth, but without any change.

Bereft, the doe went in search of the herd. Turning back she saw only the tall grasses that hid the hollow where they lay.

The day passed. Kwe and the fawn were undisturbed behind the grasses and beneath a fallen and decaying log. As day gave way to evening, the doe returned to her bedding area and laid down again beside her fawn.

Throughout the night a curious warmth came from the hollow beneath the tree. By this time, Kwe and the fawn had settled into the leaf litter that collected in the hollow. The brittle leaves and branches of the forest that had collected there months earlier lost their sharpness over the winter months and had by this time begun to form a soft cushion. Silvery tendrils of mycelium reached out from the mushrooms on the fallen tree and into the soil. They touched Kwe and the fawn, initially recoiling from the violence of Kwe's recent memories, which were also sinking into the soil. The tendrils reached out again and felt the gentleness of the fawn's care that brought peace to Kwe's final hours. This combined story of violence and care is the story the tendrils passed along to other beings who live in hidden places. After listening carefully, those beings passed back instructions.

When the doe woke in the morning, she felt the warmth coming from the hollow beneath the log. Thinking for a moment that her fawn had not died after all, she pushed her nose into the grasses and then pulled back in surprise. What she found looked like a newborn fawn, slick and shiny with the residues of birth, but it was so much bigger.

As she cleaned this foundling, she found arms where she expected legs, hooves where there might have been feet. And when this new being opened her eyes they were at once familiar and strange. The doe stepped back as Kwe unfolded herself and stood on shaky legs, trying to find balance on two small pointed hooves. The doe watched curiously.

In the morning light, Kwe saw the shadow of branches, still stuck in her hair. When she reached a hand to pull them free, she found only antler.

1

DAWISIJIGEM

Our literatures are just one more vital way that we have countered these forces of erasure and given shape to our own ways of being in the world.

—Daniel Heath Justice,
Why Indigenous Literatures Matter

WHY DOES READING matter? More to the point, why does reading specifically *Indigenous* material matter? As Daniel Heath Justice would say, Indigenous literatures matter because *we* matter. Because the things that we write down and the stories we tell are one more way that we push back—against the forces that try to erase us, against the people who try to invent us with a purpose and intention that doesn't serve our needs. Reading does matter, and reading radically with purpose and intention can change your life.

I have friendships based entirely on books. As somebody who has always loved to read, I've read widely and intentionally over the years—friends and family sharing books back and forth. Together we have tried to better understand unfamiliar landscapes. We have looked for new centres to revolve around and extend out from—centres that will help us enact our humanity in ways that do not deny it to others.

Reading in this way—focusing on books from a particular place or people—requires a willingness to clear mental space. This idea is contained within dawisijigem, which is an Ojibwe word that translates into English as to clear space, like clearing off a table before a meal, or moving books off my desk or side tables to make room for new piles.

Like many readers, I often have several books going at one time, layering fiction with nonfiction, or setting conversational books alongside more academic material. This puts the books into conversation with each other, which leads to new ideas or ways of understanding the topics, other ways of reading and understanding familiar texts. We might disagree, but that disagreement is a kind of relationship rather than a point of contention. Through dawisijigem, we clear *mental* space; curiosity encourages us to make room for new ideas to permeate into our thinking rather than to just let them float on the surface.

All of this collided when my friend Kyle (white, Canadian settler) asked me to recommend one or two books that would help them get a better understanding of Indigenous experience and thought. As I stood in front of my disorganized shelves and piles of books, trying to think of what I could recommend, I had a problem. The question Kyle was asking was actually pretty broad. Which experiences? Indigenous thought about what?

There was no one single book I could think of recommending over the others, because there are so many things we think and write about. There are, as Justice says in the epigraph, so many ways that we counter erasure and give shape to our own ways of being in the world. There are many similarities to how we live in the world, many shared values. But how we interpret and live out those values sometimes differs drastically even within communities, let alone through the many languages, cultures, traditions, and more.[1]

So, through dawisijigem, rather than through recommending one or two favourite books, I invited Kyle to push aside what they were expecting and turn toward a variety of writing and writers—to explore not a single Indigenous story but a thousand worlds of writers speaking from the borderlands outside any dominating centre. When we read into unfamiliar communities, there is always the risk

---

1 Lara A. Jacobs, ed., *Indigenous Voices: Critical Reflections on Traditional Ecological Knowledge* (Oregon State University Press, 2025), 31.

that we may misinterpret and misunderstand the unfamiliar landscape. This is why reading many books by many authors across different genres and putting them into conversation with each other is so helpful. Important information that we might have missed or misread becomes clearer.

Kyle asked me this question just as fall was turning into winter, so I began to imagine a yearlong probing of these unfamiliar landscapes. I stood in front of my bookshelves, and in front of the piles of books that seem to accumulate with every conversation I have. I started to group the chaos on my shelves into themes that made sense, according to the month in which I thought they should be read but also according to a kind of progression in which I thought they should be read. We began with an overview provided by Daniel Heath Justice (Cherokee Nation) in his book *Why Indigenous Literatures Matter*. Knowing that our literatures matter because we matter, because our knowledge about how to be human matters, provided a foundation for taking seriously the storytelling that came next. I had intended to build toward some kind of end or resolution, and the books I suggested for that final month focused on Indigenous sovereignty. But in the podcast series that emerged from this list of books, the final conversation never happened.

Maybe that's okay. Indigenous thought rarely moves in a linear way, as if we should begin at the beginning and then come to an end. We go off on tangents and then circle back to our main idea. Sometimes we tell stories that don't seem relevant, but they turn out to be. We tend to be cyclical, and what turned out to be our final conversation is much like our first: Knowing that we matter as Indigenous people means that our stories matter.

I don't think about "sovereignty" anymore anyway, because it's a loaded word rooted in the very hierarchies I want to resist. I think about autonomy—the right to refuse, to be a Bad Indian—and it seems to me that this is what we did. We begin and end with the knowledge that our stories matter—not for how they might rescue a dying world but because we matter, and the worlds we have yet to build also matter.

• • •

I am incapable of doing anything in the simplest way, and things quickly spiraled out of control. The answer to my friend's query became a Twitter thread, which became a book club, which became a series of streaming panel discussions between writers and readers that I called *Ambe: A Year of Indigenous Reading.*[2] With the exception of January, each month offered a handful of books for participants to choose from, so that the discussion would bring the ideas contained within those books together. Participants were also invited to talk about other books they had read, podcasts they listened to, or other sources of knowledge from people pushed to the margins, the topic ultimately being more important than the list I had curated for it. This series of conversations broadened my own understanding of what we think of as Indigenous and the place of our various literatures in the broader world.

Like my friend, we often think about Indigenous issues as a separate topic, one that has little to do with anything else. Justice's *Why Indigenous Literatures Matter* opened us up to a much different way of thinking. Using a wide range of Indigenous writing—from fiction and poetry, politics to history—his book helps us to look to Indigenous thought for answers to questions about what it means to be a good human, a good relative, a good ancestor.

But more important than these particular lessons was that these conversations taught us all how to *have* conversations—how to talk with each other and ask questions, how to speak up and be corrected. In my years of podcasting with my friend Kerry Goring (Afro-mystic), people listened to us learning in real time. These conversations taught us how

2 We streamed on Twitch under the username patty_wbk, where you can still find them. Or in your podcast app, most of the conversations were released in podcast format under *Aambe.*

to notice the gaps in the brush, which could lead us down a Ben trail or scale a rock-face toward something we would have otherwise missed.

Gaps in the things we write about and retain in our bookshelves become trails to follow, borderlands to explore—filled with many voices that included (but were not exclusively for) the people who thought of themselves as Indigenous. In that first conversation, Neil Ellis Orts (queer Texan/German descent) brought up Jewish American poet Muriel Rukeyser's point that "the universe is made of stories, not of atoms," which suggests that the universe is made up not of isolated individuals but of the stories we tell to and about each other.[3] From the vastness of the universe to the smallest of atoms, we exist in a world of mostly space. Introduced to this mystery of quantum physics while sitting in my high school class, I, along with my classmates, surreptitiously moved our hands around our desks, trying to find the exact pattern that would allow them to pass through. But the universe is not made of atoms; it is made of the connections between them. The strength of those connections is what holds us together, just as stories do.

This reminds me of scholar Lawrence Gross (Anishinaabe) and his reflections on language and quantum physics. Indo-European languages are concerned with discrete objects, while Anishinaabe is concerned with the processes between those objects. Gross points out that this is much like the way quantum physics works. We are not simply made of atoms; we are the processes between them.

Reading many books on one topic, rather than just a single book, exposes us to many stories and perspectives on that topic. Rather than allowing us to stand on what we think is the stable ground of a singular expert, reading many books draws us into the mashkiig—the swamp—where the ideas in one book layer with the ideas in another. We tend to approach topics as isolated things with borders between them, but the

---

3 Neil made this comment during the first panel. The poem he refers to is "The Speed of Darkness" and can be found in Janet E. Kaufman and Annie F. Herzog, eds., *The Collected Poems of Muriel Rukeyser* (University of Pittsburgh Press, 2006).

science of geography overlaps with the study of history and the experiences of various people add layers to both. Reading broadly brings us into these layered and transitional places that are also their own unique place. Ecotones are transitional places that are neither forest nor grassland, neither saltwater nor fresh.[4] They are a borderland that contains and separates distinct geographies. Mashkiig is an ecotone, a familiar image to hold in our minds as we think about layered human relationships, the places where our communities overlap.

I haven't stopped thinking about those conversations, so this book about books is a way to take the things I learned further. If *Becoming Kin* challenged people to unforget, to understand history differently so that we can imagine a different world, that year of Indigenous reading taught me how applying the practice of dawisijigem to the *way* that we read could help us do that. In the chapters that follow, I won't strictly follow that year of Indigenous reading; I've collapsed some of the themes and conversations and rearranged them in a way that makes more sense to me now. At the time, it made sense as a way to read through seasons. But grounding it in the ways that these conversations changed me meant organizing things differently. And to my chagrin, we did not focus very much attention on fiction, so that's some mashkiig we'll have to explore together in these pages.

So it is that we embark on a new book club, narrated by a Bad Indian.

• • •

My home is surrounded by wetlands—a swamp, really, what the Anishinaabe call mashkiig. Writing about the birth of Waawaashkeshi'Kwe,

---

4 I am grateful to Tiffany Lethabo King (Black) and her book *The Black Shoals: Offshore Formations of Black and Native Studies* (Duke University Press, 2019) for introducing me to ecotones as a place from which to think about layered relationships, not as static places but places that shift and move in productive and contentious ways. Leanne Betasamosake Simpson does this as well in her book *Theory of Water* (Penguin Random House, 2025), where she thinks about shorelines and what water's relationship with shorelines can teach us.

whom I have simply called Kwe, I imagined her there, becoming entangled with its shadowed inhabitants, saw her sinking down into the soft earth and transforming into something new. That is what I want for us too: that we would allow ourselves to become entangled, to sink down into the mashkiig of marginalized writers and become transformed.

Kwe is an Ojibwe word, translated into English as woman. But as Leanne Betasamosake Simpson (Michi Saagig Nishaabekwe) describes in *As We Have Always Done: Indigenous Freedom through Radical Resistance*, kwe is grounded in an understanding of gender that exists in a language without any male or female pronouns. It is, for Simpson, a framework to think about resurgence and resistance, a refusal of the colonial categories and binaries that contain and control. Kwe has the capacity to include cis and trans experiences, she writes, but that is not her decision to make. It is for those trans and nonbinary relatives to decide if kwe includes them.[5]

We don't know what violence Kwe was fleeing; my friend Lyn tells me that's not part of the early stories.[6] I am also leaving it deliberately vague, because I don't want her flight to become confined to a particular kind of violence. I mention pursuers, but we don't know who they are, how they are travelling, or why they might be chasing her. We don't even know what their intentions are; sometimes we run from those who are trying to help us.

I want to be careful here of dominant ideas about Indigenous writing and those sneaky if flattering tropes that are modern variations of the noble savage. Indigenous writing is really any writing done by Indigenous people, and it covers a wide range of topics. It vexes me to see "Indigenous" as a category on its own—as if we don't have something to say about everything that touches our lives, and as if we did not have a variety of perspectives on those things. As with any category, once you

---

5 Leanne Betasamosake Simpson, *As We Have Always Done: Indigenous Freedom through Radical Resistance* (University of Minnesota Press, 2017), 29.

6 Miigwech to my friend Lyn Trudeau (Anishinaabe). During one full moon we talked about Deer Woman, and Lyn generously shared some of what she knows with me.

create the category you have to police who fits into it, and that can be complicated and contentious. Besides, not all skinfolk are kinfolk.[7] Just as Hollywood teaches us, there are Good Indians seeking salvation by rescuing capitalism and nationalist priorities, and there are Bad Indians who refuse to be saved.

Reading intentionally, reading radically, clears that space too: the space that confines us to categories with edges that separate me from people whose ideas I may share or benefit from. This is the purpose of book bans: to keep us in our categories, to mark some books as dangerous, not for what we passively absorb from them but because of the conversations they provoke. This is why I am increasingly interested in the perspectives of others who refuse the invitations of an inclusion based on our extinction, who enter and welcome and bend toward a common purpose. They hold perspectives that emerge from the mashkiig and other swampy places where many of us, from a range of communities, gather together around shared ideas.

Between the seventeenth and nineteenth centuries, fugitive slaves and Indigenous peoples often fled to the swamps. People who had been pushed violently to the margins formed relationships there and sometimes built entirely new communities of people—the Maroons in Jamaica, the Carolinas and Virginias in the United States, the Mocambos or Quilombos in Brazil, and many more—who lived where they could, and resisted when it was necessary.

Writing is, at its core, a search for self and relationship. How do we become human? What kind of humans do we want to be?

---

7 Zora Neale Hurston, *Dust Tracks on a Road* (Amistad, 1995), 237. I was surprised to learn, on reading this in context, that it was those who had chosen the path of the acceptable ones and achieved financial security denied to their kinfolk who looked at those they now saw beneath them and said, "not my kinfolk, not my skinfolk." Its common usage, in which those who were disparaged make it their own, is more familiar. This is a very Bad Indian thing to do: to lean into it and smile back, agreeing that "not all skinfolk are kinfolk."

Throughout *Why Indigenous Literatures Matter*, Daniel Heath Justice poses this question in a variety of ways, asking how different genres ultimately help us learn to live together. Justice looks deliberately at Indigenous writers, a necessary clearing of space and focusing of intent. I want to follow his pathway but go further into the mashkiig, the swamp, where other relationships wait for us. Our stories are not individual—whether they are stories we make up (fiction) or stories about history, science, or some other part of ourselves. They are connective and collective. We are not atoms floating alone in the world. Our humanity exists in the connections between us, and the stories we listen to shape the kind of humans we become.

As Kwe flees deeper into the woods, the forest itself confuses and obstructs her pathway. Branches pluck at her tunic, bees swarm her path, swamp medicines beckon her, and the rocks themselves force her to finally notice the snake. But she doesn't slow down, and she doesn't listen. There are times when the urgency of a crisis pushes us forward, makes us think that we must act now. But most often, we have time to listen. This is important, because if we don't, we might make things worse. There is an Anishinaabe teaching that when a snake crosses your path, it is leading you away from something that is not meant for you right now. It may not be anything bad; it simply isn't for you right now. Since we take other-than-human beings seriously, we recognize the medicine and wisdom of the snake and take the time to slow down.

Throughout my life, marginalized writers have plucked and swarmed me; they have blocked my path and drawn me in other directions. Their stories have beckoned me toward medicines and, at times, seem to be speaking directly to me. They eventually led me away from the centre and deeper into the borderlands where the clues I follow—or the wake left by those who went before me—lead me to create my own path. That path is intermittently strewn with poetry. If books help us think, then poetry helps us feel. It gives expression to the emotions that rise up in response to the things we see and hear in the world around us.

This poem by Antonio Machado (Spanish), written during the Spanish Civil War, captures the hesitation, and anticipation, of these pathways through the mashkiig.

There Is No Road
Traveler, your footprints
Are the only road, nothing else.
Traveler, there is no road;
you make your own path as you walk.
As you walk, you make your own road,
and when you look back
you see the path
you will never travel again.
Traveler, there is no road;
only a ship's wake on the sea.[8]
Antonio Machado

Abolitionist activist Mariame Kaba (African American) refers to these lines frequently in her work. So often, those who dream of other worlds are asked for a clear path or blueprint. And although there is always a lesson we can learn, and a wake we can follow, each generation exists in a different place and, so, the fact is that there isn't a single path. What there is, as she often says, is a need for a million experiments. We try, and fail, and try again. We make the path by walking it.

Our footprints are the paths we take, the only road, because the other alternative is to stay with what is safe and familiar, literary canons and those lists of 100 Books You Must Read that inevitably reinforce a particular way of seeing the world. And this path will change you as it

---

8 Antonio Machado, excerpt from "There Is No Road" from *There Is No Road*, translated by Mary G. Berg and Dennis Maloney (White Pine Press, 2003). Reprinted with permission of White Pine Press. Machado was not Indigenous, but White Pine Press is owned by a Mohawk man, so clearly this piece speaks across oceans.

changed me, taking us beyond that one particular world and opening us to a thousand waiting to be born. The person who starts is not the same person who finishes. Like my boys who venture off the conventional trails to scramble up rock faces, push into dense brush, and explore the places that we are curious about, we make the path by walking.

I examined the medicines these conversations had strewn along my path. Plants, the medicines that emerge before us, may look like isolated beings. But we know that the roots reach deep below what we see and become entangled with other beings. So, rather than remain invested in the order and divisions that made sense to me as I stood before those piles of books, I decided to think about everything I learned and the places these conversations led me. I decided to think about those tangled roots, the thick mats of community they create, and the often-blurred boundaries between genres.[9] I decided to notice what pushed up through the swamp, what obstacles emerged to slow me down.

• • •

We look first to our relationships to place. Mashkiki—an Anishinaabe word translated to English as medicine—is more like the strength of the land and guides our look at the writing that seeks to structure and explain the natural world. Science writing (as discussed in chapter 2) can be extractive, focusing on what natural resources have to offer us. Or it can be relational, demonstrating how can we exist alongside these other beings.[10] We will be learning to think with Bad Indians who know

---

9 I will apologize here for not adhering to rigid boundaries in these chapters. I do my best, but boundaries are blurry more often than they are fixed. It may be helpful if you think of each topic as a centre with edges that layer with other centres rather than as discrete categories.

10 I got this book far too late to weave in the wisdom it contains: *Indigenous Voices: Critical Reflections on Traditional Ecological Knowledge*, edited by Lara A. Jacobs, contains two dozen essays by a variety of Indigenous people on Traditional Ecological Knowledge and the various ways we live out relationships, reciprocity, and responsibility in our ways of thinking.

that the world is alive in ways that we don't understand, and we will learn to take that life seriously.

In chapter 3, we turn toward our relationship to time; Biskaabiyaang describes the process of returning to ourselves. Bad Indians hold history in their hands, have refused to separate themselves from it. And so we return to ourselves by listening to *their* stories about the past we emerged from. The stories we tell in the present about history shape the futures that seem possible, and Bad Indians centre those marginalized stories and histories.

Bad Indians reject rigid ideas about gender and the colonial binaries they rode in on; we are experts at refusal. Chapter 4 is "Niinwi," which means us but not you. Bad Indians refuse the us-but-not-you of patriarchy and embrace an us-but-not-you that prioritizes the marginalized. Having decided who we are rather than who we are not, in chapter 5, we discuss memoir, or N'dadibaajim, which generally translates as "I tell a story." Bad Indians tell their own stories, on their own terms—as acts of devotion to the ancestors who made their lives possible.

Somebody once asked me if there was an Anishinaabe word for fiction, which is the genre we explore in chapters 6, 7, and 8. The Anishinaabe language does not talk about "truth" in absolute terms. We speak from our hearts or describe the things we have seen. In our truth-telling, we acknowledge that there may be things we don't know. And some Anishinaabe word-forms actually indicate whether I know something firsthand or if I am relying on somebody else's information.

Anishaa dibaajimowinan is a phrase that suggests the stories we just made up or the stories we tell for no reason.[11] After the first set of chapters about nonfiction, during which we follow Kwe through a developing awareness of her place in the world, it is in chapter 6 that

11 I have to give credit to my son Ben Krawec and his partner, Angela Easby, whose proficiency in Anishinaabemowin has made them valuable teachers, and I am deeply grateful for their advice and take responsibility for any mistakes . . . Miigwech!

we begin to look at fiction. We have always made up stories about the world around us. Bad Indians know that these stories are powerful.

In chapter 7, we turn toward horror. Horror, or dark fiction (zegaajimowinan, meaning scary stories), examines the things we fear. When you're the one being pushed into the dark, you learn to pick medicine with the things that live there.

We end with chapter 8, titled "Dibaadodamaang Ge-izhibimaadiziyang," which means us talking about how we will be living in the future—through speculative fiction or stories about our future realities. When Bad Indians write our own speculative fiction and fantasy and science fiction—when we create, as Justice calls them, "wonderworks"—we are able to imagine ourselves there, imagine ourselves *having* a future on our own terms, not some space colony DEI project.

• • •

Colonialism and the Enlightenment have given us one story about the world and our place in it. Through dawisijigem, we push everything aside and make room for other ways of telling the stories of the world around us. Dawisijigem invites us into the borderlands by clearing our schedule, clearing our minds of those preconceived ideas of how the world is supposed to work. Even if the centre of influence is one that we have come to respect and admire, the borderlands—or places where the influence of that centre extends and then layers with others—bring us to new ways of thinking and to possibly the creation of new centres.

Dawisijigem brings us to the threshold of a thousand worlds that are struggling to be born. We don't need to know everything about where we are going or how we will get there. Bad Indians make our own roads.

Kwe

The waves rolled on. They had been shallow with little white caps that emerged just before breaking on the shore, but gradually they grew in size and force, reached farther onto the beach where Kwe sat.

Kwe knew from the day before that if she sat there much longer, the waves would eventually reach her. The sand was already starting to dampen, absorbing the seawater being flung at it as the ocean strained toward her. She looked past the waves to the horizon. Yesterday the sky was a deep blue with white clouds scudding across. Today it was dark grey, the sky and water almost merging. She noticed that the waters in the sky didn't move like the waters in the ocean, in which waves formed elongated shapes that lightened from that deep blue-green grey into almost white crests before recombining with the sea below, moving relentlessly toward the shore. The waters above gathered in clouds that become heavier and darker with the weight of it, merging together in deepening shades of grey until they were too burdensome for even the strongest wind to push aside. The sky was a sea straining downward.

Birds flew past her, some landing briefly in the water, others on the shore. Two, white with black-tipped grey wings, squawked at each other, pushing back and forth over some treasure that had washed up or been dropped. Eventually one darted forward and, snatching the prize, flew off amid the angry calls of the other. The second bird looked around for anything missed, and finding nothing, flew after his friend.

She watched one bird, much bigger than the others and brown and black instead of grey with a white head and tail, banking and fanning her wings so that she hovered above the water before diving straight down. The larger bird emerged a few seconds later, wings beating heavily to escape the water. Kitpu, the people here called it. An echo from her childhood surrounded by lakes and forests said miigizhi.

Kwe watched for a few minutes as miigizhi/kitpu flew into the distance, talons firmly grasping the struggling fish, and then returned her attention to the encroaching sea and ponderous sky sinking toward it.

Digging her toes into the sand, she stood up, knowing that even if she moved back from the ocean touching her feet, the sea above would soon be released in great sheets. Toes. Kwe wriggled them in the sand before moving off the beach and toward the shelter of the nearby forest before the skies unleashed their burden, returning the sky waters to the rivers and sea from which they had come. Or had they started in the sky? She didn't know.

Kwe looked at her feet. When she first awoke in that forest hollow, she had hooves. Struggling upright, she found the small, pointed things to be a precarious footing, and she wobbled like the newborn she was. The doe had watched her curiously before backing off and bounding away. She thought for a moment that the doe had known her, had expected a particular response from her, and she realized that the doe was familiar somehow. She knew those eyes and the rasping tongue that had cleaned the slippery coating from her skin. The sensation had been intimate and familiar.

Kwe absentmindedly touched her head now and felt only hair. But that distant morning when she reached for the sticks she thought were tangled there, she had felt antler.

• • •

Over time Kwe learned that the transformation came when she was anxious, and in the beginning, she was often anxious. Kwe had always been able to run fast and easily on two legs, but if something startled her or she felt unsafe, she soon found herself bounding on four legs, small hooves flying across the landscape much faster than she could run on two.

Kwe eventually learned to hold onto the transformation when the anxiety subsided. It could be useful to observe others while holding the shape of a deer. Over time she developed control over the transformation, making only the changes that would help her and becoming as skilled at moving on two hooves as on four. Moving on two hooves was slower but allowed her to walk easily on the hard ground, and she often found herself keeping her hooves rather than returning to feet, unless there was sand or water to wiggle her toes in. Even the antlers, hard and pointed extensions of bone and cartilage, could be useful.

For a long time, Kwe lived among that first herd of deer and remained in the lake-dotted forests of her first people—the ones she had known before the night she fled into the forest. Before she ran, her fear ignoring the warnings the forest itself cast before her: the branches that plucked and the rocks that caused her to stumble. Being near these people worried her. They seemed familiar, but there was so little that she remembered. Eventually she left them behind and ran until she came to a sea she could not run around and then the island with beaches where she could dig in her toes while watching a storm roll in.

Gta'n: that's what they call the island, these people whose words she doesn't understand. She had come with them in a canoe, curious about what lay beyond a sea she could not cross, but she didn't belong with them, so eventually she left the island too and decided to follow the coast. She picked her way along rocky beaches and ran when she found flat expanses of sand. Nothing around her made any sense. Nothing spoke any language she could speak, and she didn't understand much of what they tried to tell her.

So she learned stillness. She sat with the stones, and from them she learned patience and how to read the night sky as well as she read the landscapes around her. She learned that since she had nothing to say that they would understand, she may as well listen to them until she understood.

2

MASHKIKI

What are the conditions we need so that a thirteen-year-old Black kid and their single mom can go look at a dark night sky, away from artificial lights, and know what they are seeing? What health care structures, what food and housing security are needed? What science communication structures? What community structures? What relationship to the land do they need?

—Chanda Prescod-Weinstein,
The Disordered Cosmos

MASHKIKI, AN OJIBWE word, has been translated into English as medicine. Ben, my oldest son, tells me that it means something more like strength from the land. It is related to the word mashkawizi, which means that person has inner strength or is strong, But the ending is like aki, which is the Ojibwe word for land. Mashkiki suggests inner strength belonging to the land rather than a human. "The inner strength of the land" is an interesting way to think about medicine.

We've been talking about mashkiig, which is swamp. And while the words (mashkiki and mashkiig, medicine and swamp) sound similar, they may not actually be related. Homonyms exist in all languages, and unless you know the words are related, it is unwise to assume connection. Nevertheless, swamps are indeed teeming with medicine, with that strength that comes from the land.

So the question before us in this chapter about science and nature writing is, to draw on the questions of theoretical physicist and activist

Chanda Prescod-Weinstein (Black/Jewish): What would it take for our communities to see or recognize that strength? To know, as Bad Indians do, that the world is alive in ways we don't always have to understand and to take that life seriously? To refuse the barriers and boundaries set up to keep us separate and apart from that life? Nature is not something we observe; it is a community we are part of. If the land, as a community of beings, is willing to provide its strength to us, what is our obligation to that relationship? What is our responsibility, as scientists or environmentalists or simply as readers, in a time of climate and ecological crises? How can we divest ourselves of the idea of land as an inert thing—a resource to be controlled and developed, an uninhabited or depopulated place to be depleted and then used as a repository for waste?

If medicine is strength from the land, what kind of medicine do we get from a starving relative?[1] And what stories do we *tell* about that relative?

• • •

Science is one of many ways that we engage with and describe the natural world. It is a way of studying and organizing, of posing ideas and then testing them. But the problem with western science is that it either sees us as outside of the natural world *or* it reduces us to animals. I say "reduces" because for western scientists, animals are something to be studied and controlled; so the stories it tells tend toward a relationship of

---

1 Sarah Taber (settler) is an agriculturalist and has a podcast called *Farm to Taber*. In the episode "Backed Up Like an Alabama Shit Train," Taber talks about the problem of poo. In addition to the problems posed by urban sewage treatment, Taber makes the observation that we pull nutrients from Midwestern soil and then deposit what is left over elsewhere, interrupting the great circle of life. This one-way depletion has forced the reliance on chemical fertilizers with their own environmental consequences. It's a funny and fascinating episode. Ziya Tong goes into great detail on this in her book *The Reality Bubble: How Science Reveals the Hidden Truths That Shape Our World* (Penguin Random House, 2019).

dominance and extraction rather than reciprocity. Like many peoples, the Anishinaabe perspective offers something different—a recognition that along with the rest of the natural world, animals are also persons. They are beings in their own right, with their own relationship to the Creator.

In her book *Remake the World*, documentarian Astra Taylor (Canadian/American) thinks through this idea of rights or personhood in the essay "Who Speaks for the Trees." Citing Steven Wise (unmarked), she writes about the importance of legal personhood as a way to block abuses of power and points out that applying ideas about personhood to animals is not as big a stretch as we might think. Our social media is filled with various animals solving complex puzzles, breaking out of cages, and otherwise demonstrating impressive problem-solving skills.[2] Ziya Tong (Earthling) relates stories in her book *The Reality Bubble* about animals displaying self-awareness, including the Grey African Parrot who inquired about the animal he saw in the mirror. Many animals, from primates to horses to parrots, have been taught to speak or communicate. But what is remarkable about this feat is not just that they have learned a foreign language (we do that too). What is remarkable is that they are learning about the language and demands of a whole other species. Some of the demands might seem absurd to them, but they gamely do it anyway—which makes me wonder what *they* think of *us*. Tong goes on to explore attempts by humans to decode animal speech; it turns out that prairie dogs not only have specific barks for "human," "hawk," "coyote," and "dog," but they have a bark to describe specific humans and new shapes like "circle"

---

2 Astra Taylor, *Remake the World* (Haymarket, 2021), 228–29. Taylor was born in Winnipeg and is now dividing her time between Cherokee and Lenape territories. Miigwech, Astra, for conversations and encouragement. Astra is a founder of a debtors' union you can find at debtcollective.org. Alone, our debts are a burden. Together, they make us powerful.

or "triangle."[3] It's not so odd that a nonperson like a tree or a parrot could be designated a person. Taylor reminds us that in 1772, James Somerset, an enslaved man who had escaped from his owner and was returned as *property*, became a free *person* when the courts ruled in his favour.

I sat on a panel recently with a Muslim woman, Samah, and something she said about Islam sounded very familiar. The panel was part of a series of events intended to build relationships among Black, Indigenous, and Muslim communities. Samah said that of all creation, only humans accepted the offer of free will, so they could decide to worship Allah or not. Mountains and seas and everything within them refused this offer. And so, as she explained it, they exist now as communities with their own distinct relationship to the Creator. This is something Jewish people have also told me. For them, the text I grew up calling the Old Testament is alive with beings—beings who feel deeply, whose physical responses to those feelings can be observed, and who have their own relationship with their Creator that we impede at our peril. As my own understanding of Anishinaabe cosmology grows, this is increasingly familiar to me. And, as Samah spoke, Haudenosaunee friends in the audience nodded along with her.

This is much different from how western science—rooted in centuries of Christian, particularly Protestant, thinking in Europe—sees the natural world. That view has consequences that ripple through decisions made by legislators, industrialists, and environmentalists, all of whom tend to see humans as apart from the natural world rather than a part of it.

Books about science and nature like Prescod-Weinstein's *Disordered Cosmos*, Robin Wall Kimmerer (Potawatami)'s *Braiding Sweetgrass* and *Gathering Moss*, and Kari Norgaard (settler)'s *Salmon and Acorns*

---

3 Tong, *The Reality Bubble*, 90–91. Normally I find designations like Earthling work to erase differences, much like claims of colour blindness do. But as Tong points out, the nations that her parents were from don't exist anymore. For her, being an Earthling is a matter of humility and relationship, a recognition that states and borders don't serve us. Miigwech, Ziya, for responding to my snark with curiosity. I appreciate the work you do and the relations you work to build.

Feed Our People invite us to think about the ways that we enter and build relationship with the land, and then how we receive others. They remind us of the connections between the way that we study the land, the waters, and the skies and social justice issues like incarceration, feminism, and food insecurity. In this chapter, we look at the perspectives on science and nature offered by various marginalized writers and the things that emerged from conversations about those books.

Science—the stories we tell about the structures and behaviours of the world around us—should foreground values like humility. I come to this chapter having just finished Max Liboiron's (Métis) brilliant work *Pollution Is Colonialism*. Liboiron is Professor of Geography at Memorial University in St. John's, Newfoundland and Labrador, where they run the CLEAR (Civic Laboratory for Environmental Action Research) lab and study plastics in fish guts.[4] The lab is described as a "feminist, anti-colonial laboratory foregrounding values of humility, equity, and good land relations."[5] I have adopted some of Liboiron's practices in my writing, and you'll see how the ideas raised by conversations and the books we read aspire to the ideals that this lab articulates.

I hope that you will find ways to think about place, and how land relations impact the work that you do, whatever that work is, just as those in the CLEAR lab do. In their poem "#LANDBACK," Taté Walker (Mniconjou Lakota) writes about the challenges of connecting with the land. "I've been trying to connect / with the land my whole life / but I've never had the language to do so."[6] They describe picking

---

4 Although often referred to as simply Newfoundland, the correct name for the province is Newfoundland and Labrador. The Indigenous population lives primarily in Labrador, so erasing that part of the name effectively erases them. Miigwech, Dr. Liboiron, for reminding me of this.

5 This description is taken from the website for CLEAR, Civiclaboratory.nl, and is accurate as of December 16, 2023.

6 Taté Walker, "#LANDBACK," from *The Trickster Riots* (Abalone Mountain Press, 2022). Reprinted with permission of the author. Miigwech, Taté, for your friendship and generosity.

up trash with their family, collecting "fragments of humanity" in cigarette butts and plastics and then picking up "fragments of language" to describe the medicines that come from the land. They write about gratitude and hope, the painful reality of not knowing each other's language, and singing everything from show tunes to more traditional songs so that the land can know them.

Then Walker concludes with the lines that I have inscribed on my heart and that guide the work that I do. Because how can we imagine a world in which a thirteen-year-old child and her single mom can go look at a dark night sky if we are not in relationship with the land beneath it? How do we even begin to develop relationship if we are not trying to become the kind of people that the land itself wants back?

Walker writes:

> I want the land back, yes
> but even more
> **I want the land to want me back**
> each the other's missing piece
> our jigsaw edges fitting together
> in a long awaited embrace

"#LandBack" means a restoration of relationship rather than the presumption of ownership. It's the way of "doing science" that Liboiron aspires to in their lab, and its themes are present throughout the books we read about science and nature. Katherine McKittrick (Black, feminist, geographer) analyses how academia "does science" because the development of knowledge as it is currently organized enshrines the identities created by empire. It makes them biological, irrefutable. The *incorporation* of identity, she says, into these systems of learning is an *institutionalization* of identity: it cannot bear Black and Indigenous life, or even the ways in which we relate to these things.[7] This is a risk of

---

7 Katherine McKittrick, *Dear Science and Other Stories* (Duke University Press, 2021), 38–39.

inclusion projects, the ways in which our identity is included becomes the institutionalization of that identity; too often that inclusion is one of the Good Ones against which others are found wanting.

McKittrick repeatedly says that "discipline is empire" and in her review of *Dear Science*, Prescod-Weinstein says that Black liberation work is "disruptive to disciplining, to disciplines."[8] Liberation work, for all marginalized people, takes place within science as well as any other social space. It takes place in the development of policies for lab work, in decisions about who to cite, and in our relations to land and each other.

• • •

There are stories that as Ojibwe people we tell only in the winter, specifically when the snow is on the ground. Like many, we view this season as a time of rest, when we're all under our blankets, even the land itself. Bears and squirrels and plants and people are all nestled snugly in our dens and homes.

What does it mean for those of Ojibwe culture, or others who have similar practices, that our conceptions of rest and protocols around storytelling are disrupted by climate change? What happens to the knowledge contained in stories that can only be told when there is snow on the ground if there is no snow? Is there something that should be sleeping beneath the snow so that we can safely tell these stories?

These changes in the climate mean shifts in many communities, human and animal alike, those who hibernate as well as those who migrate. For although western science does not see us as part of the natural world, at least it admits that we have to live within it. And the consequences of a worldview placing our needs above all others are increasingly difficult to ignore.

---

8 Chanda Prescod-Weinstein, review of *Dear Science and Other Stories*, by Katherine McKittrick, *Catalyst Journal*, https://catalystjournal.org/index.php/catalyst/article/view/36952/28911.

When I curated the book list that became a podcast of conversations in which we talked about the books, I tried to organize them so they connected in some way to the month or season in which they would be read. So, in April, we read books about nature, because that's what made the most sense to me and where I lived. Although the equinox is in March, where I live April is when spring is most reliably under way weather-wise. The earliest ephemerals, plants like snowdrops and bloodroot, are already fading, but the larger and more gaudy spring flowers are beginning to show themselves. Early tulips and daffodils. Forsythia bushes explode with colour, and the small animals we haven't seen much of during the winter months are becoming noisy. Birds are starting to come back, and the mashkiig that surrounds my property is alive with spring peepers, those small chorus frogs that emerge from their winter sleep deep in the mud. They call out to each other on warm days to remind us all that they survived another winter. I might be the most indoor Indian you'll ever meet, but I know there is something magical about sitting at a fire in the spring, looking up at the stars, and listening to that chorus.

That way of thinking about time is very local, and making time universal is a problem. For at least one of the panelists that month, spring had arrived on the lower mainland of British Columbia, a place that is home to many Indigenous peoples, some months earlier. Vancouver and Winnipeg are both just past the 49th parallel, but April in Vancouver is tempered by currents in the Pacific Ocean, while Winnipeg, where many of my Cree and Anishinaabe cousins are, can be decidedly ill-tempered. The idea that springtime occurs in April also assumes a northern hemisphere. A.W. Peet (settler) is a physicist who participated helpfully in the chat room when talk turned to physics. Peet lives in Toronto but was born in Aotearoa (New Zealand), where April is not springtime. And of course, while months are a fairly global convention, they also reflect an undoubtedly European way of organizing the year.

Time itself interferes with our rhythms; the twenty-four-hour day, the seven-day week, the randomly dated months all serve a particular purpose, and it isn't ours. Time has a deeply military and industrial history that demands we operate at the same capacity year-round despite our natural affinity for seasonal and even daily cycles. Because of climate change, those cycles are shifting dangerously; plants are budding and blooming out of sync with the insects and animals that rely on them, which impacts what is available all the way up the food chain. Creatures that rely on the sun's position in the sky to time their long-distance migrations are arriving at their destinations hungry and exhausted, with little available to them because a warming planet means the food they needed has already come and gone.[9]

The land is not a single being, although I once thought of it that way. From the smallest microbes to the largest land mammal, tree, or fungus, the land is a community of beings whose health, like that of any community, relies on the interplay between the various members of that community as well as how newcomers (or latecomers) and larger systems interact with the conditions already in place. Water, whether salted or fresh, is also a community, not just a container for one. In her poem, "The First Water Is the Body," Natalie Diaz (Mojave) reminds us of our connection to water, to rivers and to oceans. "We carry the river, its body of water in our body," and later she says, "A river is a body of water. It has a foot, an elbow, a mouth. It runs. It lies in a bed. It can make you good. It has a head. It remembers everything." Diaz concludes her reflection by asking, "Do you think the water will forget what we have done, what we continue to do?"[10]

Ensuring that we listen to the land and the waters—that we remember they too hold memory and emotion—means seeking out those marginalized scientists and writers who pose different questions.

---

9 For more detail on this, please read Tong's *Reality Bubble*, chapter 7: "Time Lords."

10 Natalie Diaz, excerpts from "The First Water Is The Body," from *Postcolonial Love Poems*. Copyright 2020 by Natalie Diaz. Reprinted with permission of The Permission Company on behalf of Graywolf Press, graywolfpress.org.

In the fall of 2024, I heard Leanne Betasamosake Simpson talk about her then upcoming book *A Theory of Water: Nishnaabe Maps to the Times Ahead*. She thought about the work of water and what it had to teach us about how to live together. She talked about nibi as a way of mapping Indigenous nationalisms, the layering and cycling of relationship with many peoples. The way that water moves between scales, from the smallest drop to vast oceans, and what all these overlapping worlds could teach us about fitting in and among and through. Then, during the Q&A time, a Palestinian mother asked Leanne what water could teach us about the trauma that freezes her.

I can't stop thinking about that. Her location as a Palestinian mother was deeply important to her question. This is not the freezing of winter months, that protects shorelines and life beneath the water's surface. This is the freezing of severe frostbite and hailstones the size of golf balls. This is the freezing that happens out of season that destroys new buds and devastates soft fruit crops. And when it eventually, inevitably, thaws, this is the thawing that overwhelms riverbanks and makes travel impossible. This is the thawing of glacial ice and the releasing of microbes a million years old. This is water that remembers what was done, what we continue to do.

• • •

What *would* it take for an urban child to see the night sky? At the end of the conversation in April, I posed that question to the panelists. What do our communities need to see the night sky, to connect with the natural world around us? We need our land back, and for that land to be free. We need a world where a single mother has the means and the time to take their child to a place where the city lights do not drown out the sky. We need a world of mobility, free from physical and financial barriers. We need oceans filled with fish instead of plastic. And we need time for curiosity, a life free from the exhaustion that strangles our desire to see.

When I asked what our communities needed, Neil said we need the curiosity that helps us to notice things in the world around us. So often we go quickly by on our way to whatever is next. Curiosity is a practice that our communities need the opportunity to cultivate. But with time controlling so much of our activity, these opportunities for curiosity become less and less available. Curiosity, and carving out the time it requires, is itself a liberatory practice that means we can look for the mashkiki that shows up rather than just synthesizing whatever we want and then synthesizing something else to manage the consequences.

It isn't just about humans who need access to the night sky. The dung beetle, an insect that pushes its ball of dung backward while looking down at the ground, somehow manages to move in a straight line. Ziya Tong, in *The Reality Bubble*, tells us about scientists who noticed that periodically this little beetle climbs on top of the ball and does what looks like a little dance. Investigating further, they realized that it was looking at the night sky and using the Milky Way to navigate its path! When they compromised its ability to see the night sky, the beetles just rolled in circles.[11] We might not think too much about this little beetle, but the work they do by rolling and then burying poop improves the topsoil our food systems rely on.

I thought about Kwe while I sat on a beach on Prince Edward Island, digging my toes into the reddish sand and watching birds against a storm-darkening sky. I thought about the fear driving her, and I realized that she needed to rest. Before she could connect meaningfully with people, she needed to have a relationship with the land and all it contained. She had to stop running, and it seemed to me that the best ones to teach stillness are stones.

Who we listen to matters. Theoretical physicist Prescod-Weinstein has spoken and written extensively about the ways in which dominant science is enmeshed with white supremacy, which assumes a particular way of being in the world. In *The Disordered Cosmos: A Journey into Dark Matter, Spacetime, and Dreams Deferred*,

---

11 Tong, *The Reality Bubble*, 77.

Prescod-Weinstein reflects on the work of particle physicist, quantum theorist, and feminist theorist Karen Barad (American), who wrote that while quantum mechanics "challenges the idea that the universe can be broken down into separately knowable parts, physicists have yet to allow this lesson to impact their approach to thinking through what we call the most fundamental, basic objects in the universe." Quantum physics, Barad notes, is the purview of primarily western-trained males. As a result, Prescod-Weinstein suggests that what we know will stay incomplete until we are able to think beyond the ways that white men are trained to think.[12] Bad Indians like Hana Burgess, who proposed writing a dissertation without citing any white men, know that without us it *is* incomplete. That despite knowing better, these white male theorists have decided that certain things can be broken down into separately knowable parts *and* that they know them.

In this conversation about science, Ben brought up the work of Lawrence Gross and the quantum nature of the Anishinaabe language, which orients around verbs and process rather than nouns. Prescod-Weinstein reflected that while English is very useful for some things, it may not be the most useful language for everything. What could be known about quantum physics, and the world we inhabit, if scientists had access to language that reflected the processes they study? The language we use to study the world around us shapes what we are able to learn, and it may be that marginalized scientists and the quantum nature of their languages hold a key to that knowing.

• • •

Those who would discover places and the beings that inhabit them could stand to learn stillness. To listen instead of react. Every fall, my social media feed is filled with memes about Columbus getting lost and discovering America. They are lighthearted and meant to poke fun at

---

12 Chanda Prescod-Weinstein, *The Disordered Cosmos: A Journey into Dark Matter, Spacetime, & Dreams Deferred* (Bold Type Books, 2021), 23–26.

the audacity of claiming to have "discovered" two continents filled with millions of people—people who were definitely aware of their own existence.

Let's be curious and shift the centre. Let's look away from the surprised Europeans and toward the Taino and Arawak, the people who were living in what is now the Caribbean and parts of Florida. Let's centre the cod in the waters off the north Atlantic coast, where Beothuk and Norse fishermen had been in relationship for hundreds of years; the salmon that swim inland to spawn; and the eels that once migrated from Caribbean waters, up along the eastern seaboard, down the St. Lawrence River and eventually to Lake Nipissing deep in the heart of northern Ontario. Let's centre the night sky and all the different stories that are told by those who travel beneath it.

If discovery of the world they called "new" meant riches and land for Europeans, particularly European royalty and the institutional church, it meant displacement and dispossession for the Taino and Beothuk, for the Mvskogee and Wampanoag, and for so many others whose collective sense of self disappeared beneath appellations like "Native" and "Indian." It meant displacement of people and animals. Discovery meant damming the rivers and damning the human and other-than-human communities who were flooded or whose migration paths were cut off.

In his books *Raccoon* and *Badger*, Daniel Heath Justice writes beautifully about the history and geography of these animals. He describes their various relationships with humans and other animals, their presence in literature and arts, fashion and housewares, and their impact on our culture, all of which describe in some way the consequences of discovery. Discovery, Justice notes, is dangerous when the only relation that matters is exploitability. If you are valuable, you're in danger. And if you aren't valuable? You're still in danger.[13]

---

13 Daniel Heath Justice, *Ambe: Surrounded by Relatives* podcast conversation.

The dangers of discovery are laid bare in *Undrowned: Black Feminist Lessons from Marine Mammals*, where Alexis Pauline Gumbs (Black) describes a giant sea mammal, *Hydrodamalis gigas*, who was three times the size of a contemporary manatee. Although the peoples of what became known as the Bering Sea surely knew who she was, she was discovered by and named (in the possessive) for the German naturalist who "discovered" her, only to be made extinct twenty-seven years later. She could not sing, they said, but she could hear for miles and miles. What a loss for listening, writes Gumbs, and so to honour her, we can remember. We can be quiet, and listen.[14]

Discovery is dangerous, too, for the night sky, as well as for any place where the "seeing is good," as the Kānaka 'Ōiwi (Native Hawaiians) have learned. In addition to thirteen telescopes already in existence on the Mauna a Wākea, the proposal for another observatory, the Thirty Meter Telescope, provoked an eruption of protests. Bad Indians, in this case the Kānaka 'Ōiwi, occupied their own land in order to stop construction.

The reason Mauna a Wākea already has thirteen telescopes on it is because the people who lived on those islands showed the haole where they could get the best view of the night sky.[15] They shared their knowledge, and as a result of a science rooted in extraction instead of relationship, they lost control—not only over what they knew but over the land and the night sky to which their knowledge was connected.

These are not conflicts between spirituality and science, often framed as primitive versus progressive or uneducated versus educated. Prescod-Weinstein is a theoretical physicist specializing in dark matter. Keolu Fox (Kānaka 'Ōiwi), with whom she coauthored an article about

14 Alexis Pauline Gumbs, *Undrowned: Black Feminist Lessons from Marine Mammals* (AK Press, 2020), 16.

15 Haole means "white foreigner." Haunani-Kay Trask (Native Hawaiian), *From a Native Daughter* (University of Hawaii Press, 1993, 1999), 19.

objections to the enormous telescope, is a geneticist and bioethicist.[16] The Kānaka ʻŌiwi and their supporters are not opposed to science or even to getting a deeper look at the night sky.

Their objection to the building of this new telescope is a refusal of a concept of discovery that wants only to access what is defined as valuable and pour concrete over what is not. This applies to the stories we tell about the night sky as well. The hole in the sky from where Anishinaabe were lowered to earth, and through which we travel to join our relatives, is more commonly known as the Pleiades: the Seven Sisters, transformed by Zeus and chased forever by Orion. Our skies are covered in the concrete of whose stories are classical antiquity and whose are myths and legends.

In the CLEAR lab, the scientists consider the community in which they want to do research an integral part of the peer review process.[17] They hold community meetings to explain what and why they want to study, and they get feedback from the people whose lives are impacted by these things. This process of consulting and community relationship came up during a conversation about food autonomy, when Ziya Tong and Mayam Garris (Black) talked about

---

16 Chandra Prescod-Weinstein and Keolu Fox, "The Fight for Mauna Kea Is a Fight against Colonial Science," *The Nation*, July 24, 2019, https://www.thenation.com/article/archive/mauna-kea-tmt-colonial-science/. In this piece they argue that this Thirty Meter Telescope is excluding Native Hawaiians, disturbing hallowed ground, and dealing in tropes of "confused, angry, dishonest Indigenous" Americans. If we're going to point fingers at people who are living in the past, perhaps we should be pointing at those who persist in colonial behaviour that should have been left in the nineteenth century.

17 For a more detailed discussion about the Community Peer Review Process, you can look at chapter 3 in Max Liboiron, *Pollution Is Colonialism*, particularly pp. 138–45. It means listening to the community and understanding refusal not only as no, which it sometimes is and must be respected, but also as redirection. The right to research is kind of like the right to swing your arms: it ends at the place where I live. Insisting otherwise, even if you have good intentions and some idea of serving a greater good, is to enact colonial relations.

their experiences with communities working on food autonomy. Tong told us about a documentary, *Food for the Rest of Us*, that follows the stories of people who are Hawaiian, Black, Queer, Kosher, and Inuit as they adapt, build, and develop the capacity to feed their communities. Garris talked about moving from North Carolina to Albuquerque, New Mexico, to be part of a farming collective, where they built relationships with the local Pueblos.[18] Rather than following the European pattern of imposing a way of farming that was similar to what they knew in North Carolina, they developed relationship with the land itself, to see what kind of agriculture was best suited to this place. They got involved with seed saving and trading, and over time, the farming collective developed a reciprocal process with the people who have already been farming in that place for hundreds of years.[19]

To go back to the Thirty Meter Telescope on the Mauna: Had that consortium of universities taken the community consultation approach that the CLEAR lab has as a matter of policy or as Garris's collective did in New Mexico, they might have saved themselves a lot of grief. As of late 2024, there has not been any further construction, and the Maunakea Stewardship Oversight Authority, which includes Kānaka ʻŌiwi as well as astronomers, will have full authority over the site until 2028. Lawsuits continue to work their way through the legal system and, for the time being, the project now pays an annual rent for the desired location of one million US dollars with 80% going to stewardship of the

18 In some of the southwest states, the reservations are called Pueblos in recognition of the precolonial ways that the tribal groups there organized themselves.

19 Mayam Garris was part of the *Ambe: Harvest discussion*. At that time, they were part of the Seeding Sovereignty collective, which supports various other collectives "working to radicalize and disrupt colonial spaces through land, body, and food sovereignty work, community building, and cultural preservation." They bring together Indigenous folk with communities of the global majority, which is a strategy that is dear to me. More details at seedingsovereignty.org.

mountain.[20] It hasn't been stopped altogether, but it's been slowed down for rest, and learning.

What conditions do we need to feed our communities? To be undrowned. To know badgers and raccoons. To see the night sky and grip the sand with our toes. What conditions do we need to braid sweetgrass or touch tiny forests of moss? What conditions do our communities need to grow their own food and access what they cannot provide for themselves? What conditions do we need for mashkiki, that strength from the land, to show up, let alone for us to notice it? In our quest for land or land back, are we thinking about whether the land also wants us? Are we considering what the waters might remember?

Or are we content to simply acknowledge the land and the people who came before, a kind of transfer of ownership that recognizes the existence of previous owners while asserting the authority of those who are now in control? While speaking at the Socialism 2022 conference in Chicago, poet Mohamed El Kurd (Palestinian) was asked about his thoughts on land acknowledgements. We had just spent an hour listening to him talking about the violence of Palestinian displacement, fingers snapping in agreement, and I felt increasingly uncomfortable in a room filled with people who did not seem to recognize the displacement that took place so that Chicago could exist, the rooms we sat in bearing the names of the architects of that displacement. A young Black woman stood up and asked him what he thought about land acknowledgements, and he responded, "I imagine that one day, maybe twenty years from now, I will be at a poetry slam in Jerusalem and the

---

20 Ben Gutierrez, "New TMT team changes approach to get community support, but is it too late?," *HawaiiNewsNow*, June 13, 2024, https://www.hawaiinewsnow.com/2024/06/13/new-tmt-team-changes-approach-get-community-support-is-it-too-late-telescope/.

host will take the stage to acknowledge that these are the traditional territories of the Palestinian people."[21]

This does not negate Jewish presence on the land; indeed, Jewish presence goes back millennia, and until relatively recently Christians, Muslims, and Jews all considered themselves Palestinians and lived together in a shared territory. This shifted with the Balfour Declaration and subsequent political maneuvering that imagined "a land without a people for a people without a land," a phrase first proposed by a Scottish theologian in the nineteenth century. The popular slogan, "from the river to the sea Palestine will be free," like #LandBack, imagines that the land itself will be free and that the peoples of that land live together as they had previously done. The Palestinians and Jews organizing in my community and elsewhere have no wish to do anything but live in peace with others at home or in diaspora, recognizing that they all have deep ties to that place. Rabbi Alissa Wise (Jewish American), lead organizer for Rabbis for Ceasefire and co-author of *Solidarity Is the Political Version of Love: Lessons from Anti-Zionist Organizing*, talked with me about finding power in diaspora and the connections between us, much like Aaron Mills describes in his dissertation on Anishinaabe governance. Mills describes a land filled with autonomous centres and borderlands where the influence of these centres layer and share space.[22] A much different world from our contemporary

---

21 After the presentation, I thanked her for speaking up, asking the question. This young Black woman looked around the room and said that somebody had to; somebody had to make them think about where they are and what they are doing even if they think what they are building is more equitable. We don't need a more inclusive settler colonialism.

22 Aaron Mills, *Miinigowiziwin: All That Has Been Given for Living Well Together. One Vision of Anishinaabe Constitutionalism.* https://dspace.library.uvic.ca/server/api/core/bitstreams/fe7103a4-e065-4427-b8bd-042c46e40d07/content. Miigwech, Aaron; you have no idea how often I reference this paper.

world of nations, fixed borders, and an increasing number of stateless people.

• • •

When we think about the conditions that we need in order to grow, see, know, touch, watch, listen, and breathe, we need to think about all the barriers that exist. The lights that drown out the stars, and communities that drown out everything else. Cities aren't inherently bad, but the way that we build them is extractive and disabling. Who has access to green spaces and dark skies is an important question.

How we arrive in a place, and then how we receive others, matters deeply. When I studied social work, a professor once asked us to make a list of the things that somebody would need to do to make a cup of coffee. What steps are involved? We started with the obvious: *boil water*. Then he asked what room we were in. Why did we assume that the person we were writing the instructions for was in the kitchen? So, we backed up. *Go to the kitchen*, we added as an instruction.

Then our professor asked: How are they supposed to do that? What assumptions are we making about the person and where they lived? By the end of the exercise, we had more than two hundred steps involved just to make a cup of coffee. Nobody working in an assisted-living facility or doing homecare work was going to provide a list of over two hundred steps for a client who needed to make a cup of coffee. But it forced us to think about everything we assumed. It forced us to shift the centre.

Shifting the centre helps us mitigate the risks of discovery. What assumptions are we making about the thing being studied? What unintended consequences are we going to have to deal with that could be avoided by slowing down and listening or by thinking about the steps involved and how each of those steps will impact other things? Physicists like Prescod-Weinstein remind us that observation impacts the object of our study. We change things even when we don't mean to.

Consider the problem posed by the consumption of fish from waters that make the fish unsafe to consume. Eating fish from polluted waters seems like a reckless thing to do. If you work for the government or a nongovernmental organization, a reasonable step may be to educate people on the harms of eating the fish and to bring in something else for them to eat. But is that where the task begins?

Bad Indians ask different questions. Why are the fish unsafe in the first place? And what cultural role does eating the fish play in the community? If we replace the fish with another protein, what cultural practices and language that go with them will be lost as a result? What would it take for the people who live in relationship with salmon to be able to eat them safely?

Salmon are a keystone species, which means that their existence helps to define and shape an entire ecosystem. They truly are medicine—the strength from the land and waters—and they show up year after year, for tribes on the West Coast as well as other beings who rely on it.

Dams and construction block their inland routes, and industrial waste accumulates in them and then us. In *Salmon and Acorns Feed Our People*, Kari Norgaard (settler) writes about a report that the Karuk Tribe submitted to the Federal Energy Regulatory Commission in 2004 demonstrating increases in diabetes and other health concerns because of a dam. Eating salmon is more than a dietary choice. The Karuk people know if they don't eat the salmon, then the salmon will think they are not needed and won't come upstream, which has ecological consequences. It isn't just that they want the fish back; the fish want them back too.

The Karuk have been successful in getting four hydroelectric dams decommissioned. And by the fall of 2024, the dam removals had begun. Dam removal is not only acknowledging the sovereignty of tribes or the revitalization of rivers. It is a restoration of the traditions and ways of life that were destroyed when the dams were built. It is a restoration of the ceremonies and stories and the language that goes with them.[23]

---

23 Ann Willis, "The Klamath Dam Removals: A Story of People and Possibility," *American Rivers*, September 9, 2024, https://www.americanrivers.org/2024/09/the-klamath-dam-removals-a-story-of-people-and-possibility/.

Food writer Sarah Calvosa Olsen (Karuk/Calabrese) also touches on the relationship between salmon and the Karuk in her beautifully photographed and narrated cookbook *Chími Nu'am*, but it is her reflections on acorns, which she teaches us how to harvest and process into flour, that I want us to consider. There are many varieties of acorns, with variable taste and nutritional value. In her cookbook, Olsen shares a Karuk story about acorn maidens who were told to weave hats. It's a charming story, meant to be told in winter, so I won't share more, but what Olsen wants us to know is the science and relationship contained in the story. The story teaches people how to identify the different kinds of acorns and to remember that they are relatives, with their own stories and their own feelings, which we should take seriously as we set about gathering them to meet our own needs.

• • •

Thinking about belonging and place leads inevitably to thinking about humans and nonhumans being out of place, invading our places. Raccoons are definitely Bad Indians who refuse to follow the rules laid out for them; they are also a keystone species with a critical role to play in the environment. But unlike salmon, whose empire spans the salt and fresh waters around the world, raccoons are unique to what became the Americas. They are found in other countries now, but they were brought to those places as pets or stowaways. Like my father's family, they are Indigenous, and by Indigenous, I mean that they live in the same tension that we do: existing here for millennia on their own terms, and now living within a system created by latecomers who attempt to control everything about their lives. Like us, raccoons are considered an invasive species even though they were already here.

Plants can also be described as "invasive," mostly because like raccoons and Indigenous people, they interfere with how people want the landscape or gardens to look. How do we recognize which plants are good relatives in new places and which truly are invaders?

In her book *Braiding Sweetgrass*, Robin Wall Kimmerer (Potawatomi) draws our attention to two plants in particular that are not "native" to the Americas: purple loosestrife and broadleaf plantain. While purple loosestrife is pretty, it is also destructive and crowds out native plants like cattails that are edible, provide medicine, and clean the waterways where they live. On the other hand, broadleaf plantain is not particularly pretty, but it is willing to grow almost anywhere with a short taproot for pushing through clay and a dense root system that allows it to live in drought conditions. This plant is also edible and has medicinal uses. Both are prolific, but only one of them crowds out the original inhabitants and takes over the land—like somebody else we've talked about.

Jessica Hernandez (Maya Ch'orti'/Zapotec) and Jennifer Grenz (Nlaka'pamux/mixed) in their books *Fresh Banana Leaves: Healing Indigenous Landscapes through Indigenous Science* and *Medicine Wheel for the Planet: A Journey Toward Personal and Ecological Healing*, both write about their own shift in thinking about so-called invasive plants. They are, Hernandez and Grenz point out, just relatives who are out of place. They deserve a pause before we react to discovering them in our landscape—or perhaps a pause on discovering that *we* have made a home in *theirs*.

Sometimes these plants do need to come out, and Hernandez writes about this in her work, blaming the process of colonialism rather than the plant itself for its relocation to an area entirely unsuited to it, a kind of recentring that shifts our thinking. Without the constraints of climate and soil or natural predation, the relations they grew up with, some plants grow beyond all good sense and crowd out the plants or nutrients that other species rely on. Others carry toxins that may be necessary in their native environment but cause harm in others.

During the conversation about Indigenous foodways, my son Ben talked about his love of urban wild spaces, about following the roots and branches of Bad Indians that stretch across pavement in an abandoned city space, seeking out the life that persists and refusing the boundaries imposed on them. Ben investigates what strength the land is offering, including checking on new arrivals to see how they arrive and build relationship with the land they are on, and how they receive others. His backyard garden is a joyful if chaotic combination of beauty and nutrition, curated to be safely grazed by a supervised toddler.

Therein lies our complicated relationship with raccoons and other boundary-crossing relatives. Their innate curiosity about us, ability to work cooperatively, and connection to the land, water, and sky worlds may be why they figure in the religious iconography of many peoples indigenous to the Americas. It's a far cry from the ways in which they are often depicted in our world—although I also don't want to romanticize them too much. Daniel Heath Justice notes that raccoons weren't universally loved and appreciated before colonization either. Even many who view raccoons affectionately may yet call them "trash pandas." As with the rest of the natural world, how we see them has a significant impact on how we treat them. Are they relatives to be worked with, resources to be extracted from, or invaders who must be repelled? Our beliefs have consequences for how we respond to their presence in our lives.

While we're looking for the medicines that show up for us, we could do worse than modelling ourselves after the curious raccoon, who has everything he needs to see the night sky. As Justice says, it's a raccoon's world. We just live in it.

Kwe

Kwe settled on the log beside her fire, stretching her antlers into the darkening night. She held a small round piece of granite in her hand, marvelling at the depth of time and relationship needed to smooth the stone. The stone had found her on the shores of a great inland sea and had journeyed with her ever since. Although she sometimes travelled far from the vastness of this salted sea, she found herself returning to it after every journey.

The stones in the outcropping not far from where she sat now taught her stillness. It was a valuable teaching. In exchange, she returned often to tell them of other teachings. She told them about the things she had seen, other stones and rocks she had sat with.

When she first came to the beach, she hadn't meant to stay so long. But the stones welcomed her. As she sat with them and listened, she felt herself changing, sinking into the stones. The change was not the quick transformation she had learned to control but a slower change, as if she was absorbing the stones themselves. Soon she stopped moving altogether, and with them she watched and listened.

Aside from the stones, she was alone on that outcropping over the beach for a long time. Birds came and left. Mink ran back and forth. Raccoons peered at her curiously, as if they knew she was different from the other stones.

Like the tides, people came and left, came and left. Centuries of movement in which the people and the landscape shaped each other's rough edges. The whole world moved, circling around her, as if she alone were still. Until the turning world brought the latecomers to her beach. Then everything changed.

• • •

Kwe sat on the long stretch of beach, about midway along the curve toward where Old Woman Rock used to be. Driftwood wasn't her usual choice for a fire; it burned a pretty lavender-blue, but burning it inside gave her a headache. So, for fires inside the curved dome of her shelter, she used wood from the surrounding forest. During the long, warm evenings of the berry moons, she liked to have a fire outside where she could look out at the sea, watching the horizon disappear as the star people began to reveal themselves.

Kwe narrowed her eyes and focused on the shadows growing along that horizon. These large ships have been arriving for years now. She could recognize them from a distance, along with the sounds of their language, which she also recognized but didn't understand despite the presence of villages that have sprouted and spread along the seaboard.

They angered her, these latecomers, coming ashore with plants and beasts as poorly mannered as they, taking root in their settlements and then coursing along the ground. Curling around the Wampanoag villages near where she lived, constricting them before moving into and over what was left behind. Their burrowing roots consumed what remained before tendrils burst outward. Any attempts she had seen to cut these settlements off just created new growth. She watched them build structures to contain the animals that persisted in escaping along with the new plants. Plants, animals, and people were remaking these lands she had become part of. Sickness came too, often ravaging villages before the settlers even found them.

The Wampanoag wondered what they had done to bring this on themselves, and through ceremonies they pleaded with Spirit. But Kwe knew it wasn't anything they did, just as she knew that these strange spirits didn't understand the ceremonies. Plants, animals, people, spirits: all these strangers coming into her home and acting as if it was their own.

Kwe bent to her fire, keeping a watchful eye on the ships as they came closer. She knew they would stop out in the bay, the plants and people and animals coming to the beach in smaller boats, the spirits who came with them clinging to everything. They would see her fire. Kwe considered the attention her fire may draw from the curious people leaving the ships and gave a moment's thought to abandoning the idea. Then she remembered the stories people told about her, hushed voices whispering tales of a woman with horns, a woman who would get you if you were outside unawares.

As with all stories passed down through generations, there were elements of truth mixed in with the fantastical. It amused her to listen to how the stories changed over the years and from one group to another. When she first came around them, the Wampanoag were cautious of her, and if she was seen too close to the village, they burned tobacco and sang songs. She understood the ceremony: They wanted her to keep her distance from them, so she did. Sometimes they left things for her and for the little people, who came to her shelter in colder months, travelling unseen beneath the crusted snow to pass the time with stories that were old before she emerged from beneath the log.

As time went on, the Wampanoag got used to her presence at the edges of their community, and the women joined her for ceremonies and songs. They also got used to her periodic disappearances, and welcomed the medicines she brought back with her to plant alongside their own.

The fire grew. The latecomers in their small boats must have seen her, but they would have been warned by the stories. They had their own word for what they thought she was. Witch.

3

BISKAABIYAANG

Settler narratives use a linear conception of time to distance themselves from the horrific crimes committed against Indigenous peoples and the land. This includes celebrating bogus origin stories like Thanksgiving. But Indigenous notions of time consider the present to be structured entirely by our past and by our ancestors. There is no separation between past and present, meaning that an alternative future is also determined by our understanding of our past. Our history is the future.

—Nick Estes (Lakota/Lower Brule),
Our History is the Future

WHERE YOU BEGIN the story matters. It sets the context. History is generally told in a linear way: first this and second that. But the stories told about marginalized people often begin with what happened second, as Palestinian poet Mourid Barghouti has noted. "It is easy," Barghouti says, "to blur the truth with a single linguistic trick: start your story with 'Secondly.' Start your story with 'Secondly,' and the arrows of the Red Indians are the original criminals and the guns of the white men are entirely the victim," he writes. "It is enough to start with 'Secondly,' for the anger of the black man against the white to be barbarous. . . . It is enough to start the story with 'Secondly,' for my grandmother Umm 'Ata to become the criminal, and Ariel Sharon her victim."[1] If you leave out the first thing—the provocation—our reaction becomes inexplicable.

1 Mourid Barghouti, *I Saw Ramallah* (Anchor Books, 2003), 178.

The search for origin stories can be difficult. The latecomers, the wemitigoozhiwag, invested time and energy in the kinds of documentation from which official narratives about history are built.[2] Bad Indians who are trying to tell different histories find themselves looking for what *isn't* in the latecomer's documentation as much as they look at what *is*. They sift through bills of sale and ledger books, ads for runaway slaves and court proceedings. This has prompted more than one historian to lament that for a long time in Canadian and US history, Black and Indigenous people were only legal persons if they were charged with a crime.

"History is the story we tell ourselves about how the past explains our present, and the ways we tell it are shaped by contemporary needs," writes Aurora Levins Morales (Jewish Puerto Rican) in *Medicine Stories*.[3] History is the stories people tell about us, and it is worth considering the purpose and intentions of those who would invent us.

Many of us eventually decide it is simpler to just give in and accept the stories told about us—to leave the mashkiig to become Good

---

2 Helen Olsen Agger, *Dadibaajim: Returning Home through Narrative* (University of Manitoba Press, 2021), 238. Some Anishinaabeg use wemitigoozhiwag to mean French settlers in particular, but for others, particularly in northwestern Ontario, it refers generally to white people. In *Dadibaajim*, Helen Olsen Agger (Anishinaabe) notes that in her community they refer to European settlers and their descendants as wemitigoozhiwag, the latecomers. The negative connotations of the word come from the way that Anishinaabeg experienced their attitudes and behaviours. I kind of like it because it recognizes that we've been here for so long and the settlers are late. Our creation stories contain knowledge of people from far away, even across oceans, which is why so many tribes were not as surprised by the existence of others as the Europeans were to find us. They already had a place in our cosmology, but we had to be fit into theirs. I don't speak Anishinaabemowin, but I love the stories contained in the words, which is why I scatter them like breadcrumbs. They become a kind of marker to the path we take. Now when you see wemitigoozhiwag, you'll think about latecomers, and French settlers, and lives that pushed us aside even though we were already here.

3 Aurora Levins Morales, *Medicine Stories: Essays for Radicals* (South End Press, 1998), 71.

Indians within a colonial world. Bad Indians stay with the medicine and hold onto our stories, writing them down or recording them so that when others are ready, they can pick up what was lost and return to themselves. As Estes reminds us, our history is our future. And the histories remembered by Bad Indians offer us a future by reminding us that we have a past.

• • •

I was born in the shadow of Nanaboozhoo, in the hospital of a town called Port Arthur, on the north shore of Lake Superior. From this vantage point, a series of tall but otherwise unremarkable mesas look like a giant man lying down. A sleeping giant the Anishinaabe know as Nanaboozhoo.

The formations of rock rising from the earth called the sleeping giant only look that way when seen from the shore west of Thunder Bay. There are, I suspect, many places like this with similar names if not similar stories. For the Anishinaabe, this particular ridge is where Nanaboozhoo laid down and turned to stone.

Nanaboozhoo, whose name is spelled a hundred different ways, is a central figure in Anishinaabe aadizookaan: our traditional stories. He is one of four brothers who were born of a human woman and a manitou, or spirit. Nanaboozhoo and his brothers either are or represent the four cardinal directions. A spirit who participated in creation, he has many powers including the ability to shape-shift, taking on the appearance of humans and animals. And although we often refer to him as male, there are some stories where Nanaboozhoo's gender changes.[4] He gets himself into various troubles, demonstrating for us the consequences of short-sightedness and greed. Like us, he is capable of breathtakingly self-absorbed behaviour as well as great kindness and generosity.

---

4 Nanaboozhoo has the ability to shape-shift and in the stories can take the form of male or female animals and humans.

In this particular story, Nanaboozhoo laid down and turned to stone so that he could slow or even possibly prevent humans' access to silver, hidden deep underground. He had told the Ojibwe about the silver that existed, but it was only for their use; they weren't supposed to tell anyone about it. Discovery is dangerous.

Depending on who is telling the story, it was either a couple of Ojibwe who couldn't help themselves or else a Dakota who tricked them into revealing the secret. Either way, the story about the silver got to Alexander Sibley and the Montreal Mining Company, who ignored the stone giant and opened the vein. For sixteen years, the wound bled silver. Wikipedia says that the Montreal Mining Company "discovered" it in 1868. (I'm sure they did: discovered it right where the Ojibwe or Dakota told them it was.) According to the story, Nanaboozhoo was either so annoyed by the Ojibwe or so concerned about the environmental destruction that follows these kinds of discoveries that he just laid down and turned to stone.

I can appreciate that: emotions overwhelming to the point that I want to turn to stone. Just being so frustrated by things out of my control that, like a recalcitrant child, I sit down and refuse to move. It's a different route to stone than the way Kwe took: sinking into it, turning to stone so that she could share time and space with her teachers.

This story about Nanaboozhoo has a lot to teach us about respect and consent, about the dangers of discovery and the consequences of a world built on greed. The story also calls to mind images of Bad Indians and other protestors blocking railways, highways, and points of entry to call attention to harms or to prevent harms from taking place.

What happens to history, and the telling of it, when Bad Indians sit down and refuse to move?

• • •

We tend to think of colonial history beginning in 1492, when Columbus, on his way to India looking for military reinforcements rather than spices, stumbled into the Caribbean.[5] But for many inland peoples, colonial history started much later. The colonies that became Canada, the United States, and Mexico may have drawn lines on and around the continent, but it took much longer to inscribe those borders on the people themselves. It would take centuries for these states to establish their authority over everyone. And actions like Standing Rock and the blockade at Wet'suet'en suggest this claim of authority remains incomplete.

The interesting thing, for our purpose, is how *recent* this story about Nanaboozhoo is. If it is tied to the "discovery" of this silver deposit, that locates the story near the end of the nineteenth century. This means that for the Anishinaabeg, Nanaboozhoo was walking the earth until fairly recently.

The recent nature of this story also reminds us that for many Indigenous peoples, our elders have stories that predate colonial intrusions. This is why reading history from other perspectives is so crucial. Rather than a single origin story, it turns out these countries have many. Rather than a straight line of progress, history is more like the dense network of rivers and streams that make up the Mississippi river system, or the lakes and rivers that cover Anishinaabe aki (land), where the connection between the waters and the land is that transitional space we are exploring: the mashkiig.

---

5 I attended a conference a few years ago in Toronto, and a graduate student named Zahir Kolia presented a paper about colonialism in which he asserted, based on Columbus's own diaries, that Columbus was influenced by the Crusades, which took place between 1050 and 1300 CE and were nearer to him historically than we are to him, and by a general desire to eradicate Islam. He was attempting to get to India to raise an army that would force the Muslim empire to fight on two fronts. This was mind-blowing to me. It wasn't that Columbus got lost; we were just in the way of what he was trying to do. As we often are. So rather than finding an army, he found what must have looked like limitless wealth—which is important, because then as now, wars are expensive.

The stories the dominant society tells about us begin with "Secondly," with the moment that they noticed us in a particular way. But the stories we tell about ourselves begin much earlier than that. As Levins-Morales and Estes point out, the stories we tell about history serve a present need. Since the needs of marginalized people will be different from that of the society that marginalized them, it is important to listen to the stories *they* tell. Bad Indians know the importance of centring such stories.

The Ojibwe concept biskaabiiyang, which means to return to ourselves, carries the idea of going into the woods. We are a woodland people, and so going into the woods to regain our sense of self and purpose makes sense. But this is also practical, because so much of our history is recorded in the woodlands: petroglyphs and paintings that tell stories about specific places. The past reaches forward to us, casts its shadow over us. As Estes says, "There is no separation between past and present, meaning that an alternative future is also determined by our understanding of our past. Our history is the future."[6]

Nanaboozhoo rests in the stone of Anishinaabe aki, perhaps watching, as Kwe did, anticipating the time when it is necessary or right to emerge from the stone.

Some say that he will awaken again, when the people are ready. They say this will happen when we return to mino-bimaadiziwin, the good life, and live in a more respectful, less foolish way. They say he will return and help us light that eighth fire of peace and brotherhood. Many Anishinaabe believe that we are in the time of the seventh fire—a time of choice between two possible outcomes—and I don't think you need to believe in our prophecies to know that we are at a precipice. With language reclamation, a return to public ceremonies, and the rebuilding of our communities under way, who knows?

---

6 Nick Estes (Lakota), *Our History Is the Future: Standing Rock versus the Dakota Access Pipeline, and the Long Tradition of Indigenous Resistance* (2019), 14.

Perhaps Nanaboozhoo will step out of the rock where he waits and walk the earth again.

Part of returning to a good life means remembering who we are. It means listening to Bad Indians who refused to assimilate their lives or their stories, to hear what they teach us about the past so that we can return to ourselves and know how to live well in the present.

• • •

I arranged the year of Indigenous reading so that the conversation in February would revolve around history. Although Black History Month began in the United States, other countries like Canada, Ireland, and the UK also recognize February in this way. So I decided to stick with the theme that everybody would be thinking about, not to appropriate it but to remind ourselves that Bad Indians come from many places, and that our histories on these lands are entwined through kinship and political struggle. Our struggles and experiences are not only similar; they are connected.

One of the panelists that month, Tiya Miles (Black), has written many books documenting Black and Afro-Cherokee history, two of which were part of our recommended reading. One of them, *The Ties That Bind: The Story of an Afro-Cherokee Family in Slavery and Freedom,* tells the true and complicated story of Shoe Boots, a Cherokee warrior, his spouse Doll, and their children. Doll was also his slave, and in the Cherokee Nation, as well as in the colonial practice of slavery, children inherited the condition of their mother. Elizabeth and her siblings were enslaved within the Cherokee nation, where they were seen as African, not Cherokee. Shoe Boots wanted his children to be free, and so while the Council did agree to emancipate Elizabeth, he was told not to have any more children with Doll; their sons, born after the decision was made, were not freed. The story follows this family through the years of slavery, to the founding of the Cherokee Nation itself, along the Trail of Tears, and then freedom in the years after the Civil War.

Miles also edited a collection of essays that emerged from a gathering of Black and Indigenous academics that become *Crossing Waters, Crossing Worlds: The African Diaspora in Indian Country.* Our struggles are connected, but our relations are complicated. The work to restore ourselves to each other is as hard and messy as it is liberatory and worth it.

Black History Month was originally Black History Week, and emerged in the 1920s and '30s to counter the "Lost Cause" narrative that was being promoted in the South: that enslaved Africans had been treated well by their enslavers and that the Civil War was a "war of northern aggression."[7] In 1969, Black educators and Black United Students at Kent State University[8] proposed Black History Month, holding the first official Black History Month in 1970. Just over fifty years later, I and my friends Seán Carson Kinsella (Nêhiyaw/Anishnaabe/Otipêmisiwak) and Khadija Hammuda (Libyan) joined authors Nick Estes (Lakota) and Tiya Miles (Black) and poet Cheryl Savageau (Abenaki/French Canadian) to talk about history.[9]

I invited Cheryl because her poem "graduate school first semester: so here I am writing about Indians again" captures the erasure of Indigenous people so pervasive in the dominant narratives. Sherman Alexie (Salish) does this in his poem "How to Write the Great

---

7 I had a history teacher who insisted that the war was not about slavery but about states' rights. States' rights to do *what,* Mr. Hudak? States' rights to do *what.* Even in the early 1980s, my classmates and I knew enough to argue with him.

8 Yes. That Kent State. The May 4 massacre at Kent State also took place in 1970, when members of the Ohio National Guard opened fire on unarmed college students during a rally that opposed expanding the Vietnam War into Cambodia. Four students were killed and nine wounded. Neil Young, John Denver, Grace Slick, Steve Miller, Bruce Springsteen, the Beach Boys, and Jon Anderson of Yes, among many others, wrote songs about this violence. Young's "Ohio" may be the most familiar and is actually how I first learned about the shooting.

9 Unless otherwise noted, all podcast citations in this chapter are from *Ambe: Our History Is the Future.*

American Indian Novel," which has a great line in it imagining a future in which "all of the white people will be Indians and all of the Indians will be ghosts." Alexie's fall from grace prompted me to seek out other poetry that conveyed a similar idea.[10] Alexie is wrong about this happening in some imagined future anyway, as shown by the paintings, poetry, and literature Savageau studied. White people already hold a central place of belonging to a land they didn't even know existed until Columbus stumbled on it, and we are already ghosts.

The poem offers snapshots of Savageau being scolded by her increasingly frustrated professor for bringing up what isn't in the text and for making people feel guilty.

> stop writing about Indians
> she told me again
> only louder as if
> I was hard of hearing
> you have to allow authors
> their subjects, she said
> stop writing about what isn't in the text
> which is just our entire history[11]

At one point her teacher tells her that "there's only/one story about Indians/and we all know what it is." Savageau's next lines are cheeky: "so I asked her if there are an/infinite number of stories about/white people."

---

10 And that's all I'm going to say about that.

11 Cheryl Savageau, excerpt from "graduate school first semester: so here I am writing about Indians again" from *Mother/Land*. Copyright 2006 by Cheryl Savageau. Originally published by Salt Publishing. Reprinted with permission of the author.

Predictably, her professor accuses her of being racist, prompting her decision to cut class the following week rather than write another paper about the Indians she knew were there.[12]

This is a familiar experience for Bad Indians in academic spaces, as my friend Seán Carson Kinsella pointed out from his time as a student and now working in a college. Trying to write about your own people is often not the history that professors are looking for, nor is it the perspective welcomed in committees (unless it is the DEI committee, although sometimes not even then).

The problem is that whitestream history *does* contain an infinite number of stories about white people. An infinite number of stories means that white people get seen as individuals, or perhaps as part of smaller groups who are collectively seen as white. Even as we use the word *white*, we know that we are talking about people who are English but also people who are Canadian and American, Irish, or German.

White is also malleable and shifting. Until recently, the US census counted Arab and Middle Eastern as white. The promise of whiteness, contained in Canadian and US versions of history that proclaim these countries "nations of immigrants," is a paper towel absorbing the people spilled across the lands they have claimed. Some to be faithful followers and others to be swept aside. And absorbed or not, once we're no longer useful, we are all disposable.

There are also an infinite number of stories about marginalized people, but so often the stories are written by or for white people, and

---

12 "Racism, specifically, is the state-sanctioned or extralegal production and exploitation of group-differentiated vulnerability to premature death." Ruth Wilson Gilmore, *Golden Gulag: Prisons, Surplus, Crisis, and Opposition in Globalizing California* (University of California Press, 2007), 28. Too often we make racism about discrimination or hurt feelings, and while it can certainly be those things, at its core racism is about the state's power to directly or indirectly shape or exploit entire social groups toward premature death. I love this definition because it makes very clear what is at stake and the importance of considering who has social and political power on a broad scale.

they wind up conforming to the single story allotted to them by whiteness.[13] This is why I chose multiple books for each genre for our conversations. Multiple stories from Bad Indians can be put into conversations with each other and prevent, or hopefully minimize, the ways we misunderstand or misread the stories being told.

We do have infinite stories, thousands of worlds; people just need to dig beyond those made famous by the systems that benefit from our erasure.[14] Savageau's poem continues:

> the famous historian
> said only that there may have been
> Indians in the area,
> while she wrote
> at length about
> white men dressing up
> as Indians
> to protest against the rich
> stealing their lands

The "famous historian" that Savageau refers to is Laurel Thatcher Ulrich, whose book *A Midwife's Tale: The Life of Martha Ballard Based*

---

13 Chimamanda Ngozi Adichie (Nigerian) has written and spoken eloquently about the dangers of the single story. We think that we know people, but all we really know is a reductive stereotype about that group of people. This is the writing that Deborah A. Miranda cautions us about when she says we must know who is telling the story so we understand the stake they have in inventing us.

14 Don't let this be the only book you read about Indigenous or marginalized literatures! In my workshops I cite other writers, and people keep track of the books or podcasts I mention as a resource for participants. In one workshop a woman was ordering books as we went along, and by the end of the weekend she had spent $400 on books. I don't want to bankrupt you, but I do hope that these footnotes, the appendix, and bibliography lead you to other authors and resources, to those thousand worlds and infinite stories that are out there.

on Her Diary is, as the title notes, about the diary of a midwife named Martha Ballard who lived in Maine while the eighteenth century was becoming the nineteenth. The diary mentions a "young squaw" who came and visited her over a 3-week period, along with passing references to local natives and Black people. But the details and expanded research Ulrich does centre on white people, including white people who pretend to be Indians.

The diary describes incidents in Malta, Maine, that took place between 1806 and 1809, when groups of men dressed up as Indians to resist the expansion of the town's authority into unincorporated land, just as those who participated in the Boston Tea Party a few decades earlier had done. The Indians themselves are ephemeral, ghosts whose existence serves only as a backdrop against which history takes place. This is ironic given that Ulrich laments the erasure of women's voices by strategies that are very similar to her own erasure of the original people. In one poignant sentence she notes, "With white men fighting over the land they had once possessed, Kennebec's few remaining Indians slipped into anonymity."[15] The Abenaki and others did not "slip into anonymity." Those who weren't killed or relocated were simply erased.[16]

During this conversation, Tiya Miles commented on Savageau's poem because Ulrich's book about Martha Ballard had been important during her own graduate studies. At one time Miles had planned on writing a book about the untold history contained in these pages. Miles drew our attention to the diary's description of an African American

15 Laurel Thatcher Ulrich, *A Midwife's Tale: The Life of Martha Ballard Based on Her Diary, 1785–1812* (Vintage Books, 1990), 322.

16 In a personal communication, Savageau told me that she had read *Grad School* at a reading at Harvard, and unknown to her, Ulrich was in the audience. After the reading she introduced herself to Savageau and said she was right, that she had been blind to Native people in the same way that men had been blind to women. I share the story with Savageau's permission because the things we write often represent who we used to be, and as Savageau noted, I don't know if her scholarship has changed, but I do respect her admission.

slave woman who had brought some plants. As with the reference to the "young squaw," there is little to no discussion of who these women were, what their lives were like. It was all about the white midwife—who was undoubtedly, as Miles said, a fascinating person. But unlike the white members of this community, the Black and Indigenous people slip in and out of the narrative, their moccasined feet leaving barely any trace.

• • •

It was this conversation with Tiya Miles that prompted me to think deliberately and intentionally, radically even, about gaps, because she brought up the gaps that we have in our own stories about the past. Estes had observed that while settlers came to Canada and the United States as individuals, people with infinite stories, Black, Latine, and Indigenous people come to these countries burdened by the single story associated with each group to explain why they were included in some ways and excluded in others.[17] This creates gaps.

Although we (Black/Indigenous/Latine) were already here, our presence predating the existence of Canada and the United States by hundreds if not thousands of years, we did "come to these countries" in a very real sense. Citizenship in colonial nations was reserved initially for white landowning men and not extended to those of us who existed here before there were borders. Even though we lived within these borders and were subject to its laws, the Fourteenth Amendment (1868), which states that anyone born in the United States is automatically a citizen, did not apply to tribal members. Despite being contained and controlled by the United States, our lands surrounded by its borders, we were somehow not in it.

---

17 Latine is a gender-neutral form of Latino and Latina. Latinx is also gender neutral but is falling out of favour as Latine is both easier to pronounce and consistent with the Spanish language itself, which already uses "e" as a gender-neutral ending.

It would be another sixty years before legislation brought citizenship to Indigenous people within US borders. You can say that as sovereign nations, we were citizens of our own tribes, but in a modern state, citizenship confers rights that don't belong to anyone else, and this was one way to deny us access to basic rights like the ability to buy and sell property, hire a lawyer, or be represented in the government that made decisions about us.

In Canada, we did not become citizens until 1947; the Inuit and other circumpolar people living in the far north had to be included retroactively through an amendment in 1956, explicit control over them and their land becoming important only with the rise of the Cold War. Before 1947, Indigenous people in Canada could be enfranchised individually, brought into citizenship, through military service, post-secondary education, or just arbitrary meanness on the part of a band manager. Enfranchisement before 1947 also meant loss of Indian status, which included the ability to live on reserve, among other things.

An early pathway to citizenship for Indigenous people in the United States was through the transformation of collectively held tribal lands into private property through the allotment process of the late nineteenth century. In his discussion about allotment and how it impacted his own family, Estes reminds us of the importance of oral history, and the gaps that exist because of our reliance on the written word, ledger books and birth records: the documentary detritus of government bureaucracy. Estes is Lower Brule Sioux and a trained historian who, in addition to writing his own book, *Our History Is the Future*, contributed an essay to the book, edited by Daniel Heath Justice and Jean M. O'Brien (White Earth Ojibwe), *Allotment Stories: Indigenous Land Relations under Settler Siege* that relied on oral histories as well as what was documented officially.

We often associate the allotment process—the late-nineteenth-century breakup of reservations—with the tribes living in Oklahoma. *Killers of the Flower Moon*, written by journalist David Grann (unmarked) and made into a film directed and produced by Martin Scorsese (unmarked), is a true crime story of a series of murders that devastated an Osage community in Osage County, Oklahoma, during the 1920s. I was familiar with *Killers of the Flower Moon*, but friends told me about *Mean Spirit*, a fictional account of this same time period by Linda Hogan (Chickasaw), who tells the story from within the communities impacted by the violence of American avarice. Bad Indians centre marginalized writing, and we know that fiction contains truths as well as any other story, so I found and read the book. More than a true crime novel, it tells a broader story of an Osage community, the devastation of their culture and the persistence with which they maintained it in the face of a mean spirit that entered their lands wearing a white face and bloodied, oily hands.

After promises that the land would remain theirs for as long as the grass grows and the rivers flow, the relocated tribes and those who were already living there were now required to set aside their collective ways and live as nuclear families on the same parcels of land as the Americans who wanted to settle there. Land was divided up and allotted, with the best farmland going to white farmers who could use it "correctly." When oil was found on the useless land given to useless Indians, Americans found ways to get that too. Native people documented as "full bloods" needed white guardians to help them manage their oil money, and white saviours descended in short order; bankers, lawyers, managers, husbands. Over sixty wealthy Osage were killed, or reported as killed, as white people gained control over their holdings. Most of the guilty were never charged, and their financial crimes were backed up by American laws. The jurisdictional nightmare of allotted land, a crazy quilt of land under state and federal jurisdiction depending on who owned it, made prosecuting crimes almost impossible.[18]

---

18 Rebecca Nagle's (Cherokee) podcast *This Land* tells the story of *Sharp v. Murphy*, a death penalty case that went to the US Supreme Court over who had

Hogan writes about women who were married as a business investment by white men greedy for their oil money, about competency courts that ruled full bloods were incompetent and that those who were mixed had reduced blood, which meant reduced payments. The Lakota FBI agent who investigates the murders reflects on similar deaths in the Badlands of the Dakotas, the deaths of Indians nothing more than a ship's wake as white settlers flooded Indian Country. The Osage hold onto their culture and their ceremony, and one by one Hogan's characters return to their old ways. They are Bad Indians who refuse to be assimilated, appealing to their own ways of relating to the world around them rather than seeking justice in a world organized to deny it to them.

Reading Hogan's book, I was struck by how very recent all this is. The book takes place in the 1920s, and many of the tribal people in the plains were still living close to their old ways. Hogan describes a community of Hill People who lived outside of town and rejected modern ways, her story following one particular woman and her daughters who had left that community to live in town. By the end of the novel, many of the Osage living in town had returned to this hill community, if not to stay then at least for ceremony and wisdom about how to live a good life.

The novel *Waterlily*, written by Ella Cara Deloria in the early 1940s, tells the stories of two generations of Sioux women and teaches us about the importance and structure of kinship relations in Lakota society. Deloria interviewed Sioux women who remembered these ways of living. Along with others, these books remind us that our ways are

---

jurisdiction to prosecute the murder. The defense argued that as the murder took place on Muscogee Nation land, Oklahoma did not have jurisdiction. Oklahoma argued that because of allotment the reservation no longer existed. However, the case was eventually decided in favour of the Muscogee Nation and resulted in the largest restoration of tribal land, 19 million acres, in US history to date. You can listen to it wherever you get your podcasts. *Sharp v. Murphy* is explored in season 1 of *This Land*, a podcast series by Crooked Media, 2019, https://crooked.com/podcast/this-land-episode-1-the-case/.

neither remote nor inaccessible. They are right there amidst the grasses that grow and waters that flow, waiting to be picked up by any Bad Indians willing to listen to them.

Estes's Lakota family was deeply affected by the allotment process. Their land allotment is actually under water, the result of a dam. While interviewing one of his grandfathers, he learned about family relations and the ways in which people's relationship to each other was tied to their relationship with the land being allocated. Surveyors and bureaucrats reduced a curvilinear world of land and waters and the people connected through them to the flat, Euclidean geometries of governmental documentation. They drew lines and angles on places and people so that they fit into the columns ascribed to them. This world of paper, his grandfather said, replaced the world of Indigenous relations in the way that it took land-based relations and carved them up the way they carved up the land.

• • •

How dangerous it is to try to tell the history of an individual or a people. This is what Khadija Hammuda (Libyan) said, in our conversations about gaps and missing stories. How easy it is to lose track of our place in, as Astra Taylor puts it, that "complex web of relations that transcend our current moment."[19] That complex web includes so much more than ancestors and descendants, relatives, and neighbours. That web includes the systems around us, the stories we tell about their legitimacy to make decisions about our lives, and the crimes that are backed up by the laws and rules of those with authority.

Hammuda and I had met while working in child welfare, and like me, she spent a lot of time reviewing and assessing people's histories. Ahead of the discussion about history, she had read *All Our Relations* by Tanya Talaga (Anishinaabe), which tells the story of Canada from an Anishinaabe perspective, our own Anishinaabe history of course

---

19 Astra Taylor, *Remake the World* (Haymarket, 2021), 244.

going much further back. Hammuda is an immigrant, somebody whose family found safety and stability in Canada, so this book and conversation had a profound impact on how she understood her place in the story she had been told about Canada and what her relationship is to the state and the various ways it benefits from the displacement of others.

Many have written about this realization. It is a hard thing to come to a place seeking safety only to realize that you benefit from the same kind of policies used to displace you.[20] Rabbi Danya Ruttenberg (Jewish American) and the authors of *Safety through Solidarity: A Radical Guide to Fighting Antisemitism*, both Jewish Americans, reflect on a history in which every generation is filled with those who are willing to find a place for themselves within narratives of conquest, as well as others who find their belonging in the layered relationships of diaspora. This is true for all of us pushed violently into the mashkiig. There are Good Indians who find safety in assimilation, turning their backs on those they leave behind, assuring the powerful that these are "not my skinfolk, not my kinfolk."[21] And there are Bad Indians who refuse it, who refuse to confront myths of conquest by creating our own and instead find belonging in the connections between us.

It comes down to how you enter the land, form relationships, and then how you welcome others.

Hammuda took what she learned from Talaga's book and applied it to her family, her community, and her profession. "You don't realize how deeply rooted you are in the colonial narrative until you're faced with the facts," she said. The only way we get to that realization, to those facts, is by reading the histories told by those writing from within the gaps and margins left to us and then allowing those histories to help us

---

20 Rabbi Danya Ruttenberg, "Jews and Colonialism," Life Is a Sacred Text, September 16, 2024, https://www.lifeisasacredtext.com/colonialism/. In her essay, she also cites Diaz's words on how we enter the land.

21 Hurston, *Dust Tracks on a Road*, 237.

think about our own relationships to and within the systems around us. Because we are not atoms alone in the universe; we are stories told from the connections between us.

• • •

The shadow of Nanaboozhoo reaches from the mashkiig north and west of Lake Superior where I was born, across these gaps, and into the margins. His long shadow brings the past into the present, the way the stories we tell about history are meant to do.

I don't know what the Ojibwe of that area made of the rock formation that became known as the sleeping giant—before the silver, before Nanaboozhoo laid down and inhabited the rocks left by ancient glaciers. But like the stories *Mean Spirit* and *Waterlily*, the story of Nanaboozhoo and the silver mine reminds us how recent our life before colonialism truly is. It means that for my relatives, he walked this earth until recently.

This is something that keeps surprising me. Raised as I was with my mother's family in the colonial centre, I absorbed that single story told about Anishinaabe history—my own history—that placed us so far in the past. But Nanaboozhoo, the spirit-man who shaped so much of Anishinaabe life and identity, walked the earth until just over 150 years ago. My paternal great-grandfather Isaiah McCauley (Irish) was born in 1876, just a few years after Nanaboozhoo encased himself in stone. My father told me stories about Isaiah playing the pipes on the shores of one of the lakes that dot the lands around Sioux Lookout. As a young man working for the Hudson's Bay Company in outposts all around Lakes Superior and Nipigon, many of his Cree and Ojibwe customers would have been part of the world in which Nanaboozhoo walked.

Canada became a nation just over 150 years ago. In the graphic anthology *This Place: 150 Years Retold*, illustrated histories told by a variety of Indigenous authors pull our history into the present. It was published to coincide with Canada's 150th year since confederation, which took place the year before Nanaboozhoo laid down, immersing himself in the rocks of the land he loved and knew so well. In it, Indigenous peoples across Canada tell the stories that bridge the gap between our lives as independent peoples and our lives as people living under occupation, navigating life in the systems meant to dispossess us.

It was in that book that I learned of the Fiddler brothers, two Cree men from northern Ontario who faced execution by the RCMP in 1907, one generation after Nanaboozhoo laid down. They were charged in the death of a woman believed to be possessed by a harmful spirit.[22] Reading this, I realized these stories were not just fables or cautionary tales but real to the people inhabiting the world in which my great-grandparents lived. Just as real as the spirits invoked by Christians, but not taken seriously. If the existence of spirits was ever taken seriously, they were perceived to be demonic, the only source of spiritual power available outside the church in the cosmology of Protestant Christians.[23] That realization forced me to rewrite a chapter of *Becoming Kin*, which is what good learning should do. I had used the harmful spirit as a metaphor for greed and avarice, but understanding that it was in some sense real forced me to think differently. Forced me to consider that the colonial greed and avarice I described was not the result of a spirit from these lands but an infection brought from overseas. Like Hammuda and Ulrich, we need to be open to the changes provoked by other stories and the relationships they open up for us.

---

22 The story of the Fiddler brothers is told in more detail in the book *Killing the Shamen* by Chief Thomas Fiddler and James R. Stevens. It is a fascinating book, noting how distant the Canadian government was for Ojibwe and Cree people living in that area. Although I did not follow the protocol against naming, and thereby calling in, the harmful spirit while writing *Becoming Kin*, I do now. New teachings, new me.

23 If you want to do a deep and interesting dive into how the Reformation arguably severed Christians from the world as a spiritually infused place and the resulting violence, check out the books *Witchcraft: A History in Thirteen Trials* by Marion Gibson (British) and *Sacred Violence in Early America* by Susan Juster (unmarked).

As we return to the shadow cast by Nanaboozhoo over my life and the stories we tell of Anishinaabe people and history, we will consider that the history of Anishinaabe aki itself is varied. There is no single story of how we came to exist there. Our creation story identifies a specific place: Manitou Ahbee, north and west of where Nanaboozhoo waits encased in stone, is where the first man was lowered to earth by zhemnido.[24] Our stories describe his exploration of this land, learning how to fish, meeting other people. They tell about the often chaotic, sometimes helpful presence of Nanaboozhoo.

In her book *Dammed*, Brittany Luby (Anishinaabe) opens her examination of the impacts of hydroelectric development in the lands of the Winnipeg River watershed by looking at the various stories told about how Anishinaabe presence came to be on the land where we emerged as people.[25] People occupied this area as far back as 8,500 BCE, but who those people understood themselves to be is unknown. Cree and Anishinaabe languages contain references to glaciers, which suggests knowledge not only of glaciers receding but also that they had not always been there.[26] There are accounts that suggest we migrated there from the east coast, leaving scattered communities across the northern shores of what became Lake Ontario before separating into

---

24 We do not worship the "great spirit." That is a mistaken interpretation by missionaries and anthropologists. All of creation has spirit; there is no hierarchy. What there is, is a mystery. A great something that connects us all and takes action. That invests itself in us and around us. Remember, we are process oriented rather than concerned with discrete objects. Zhemnido is not separate from us, not separate from anything.

25 Brittany Luby, *Dammed: The Politics of Loss and Survival in Anishinaabe Territory* (University of Manitoba Press, 2020), 3–5.

26 Josh Manitowabi told me that giiwedin, which means north, contains the idea of going home and that elders have said it refers to the glaciers going north. So our language not only knew that the glaciers had been there, but that they had not always been there.

two groups travelling along the northern and southern shores of Lakes Michigan, Huron, and Superior either following prophetic voices or having been pushed out of the lower part of what became Ontario by the Haudenosaunee Confederacy and in turn displacing Lakota and Cree peoples.

This seems to be a precarious foundation on which to build the story of a people. But nobody really has a single story. We may be forgiven for thinking that we do, when all too often the only story visible to us is the river that flows past.

But history is not a single river; it is the dense network of rivers and streams that make up the Mississippi River system or the lakes and rivers that cover Anishinaabe aki. Like the waters that surround us, history is not a single, linear story. It is rivers flowing in and out of each other, separating and converging. The things that happen in one river inevitably impact the life of another.

Does it matter if there is a single correct story about Anishinaabe aki? Is it possible that each of these stories carries the history of some of the people who collectively became known as the Anishinaabe?

Stories have a way of resurfacing, of insisting on being heard. Perhaps the truly precarious foundation is the one that relies on a single narrative about the history behind us.

Kwe

Kwe turned her head toward town, from which came a sound, something like screaming. She was familiar with the sound of the children's laughter, the sound of villagers singing in their meeting house. It was different from the singing of her own people, but she had come to recognize the melodies and some of the words. Many of the songs were about gratitude to a creator they call God and Lord. She appreciated their gratitude if not their behaviour.

The midwife, Maude, was training her daughters, so they often joined their mother on early morning or late-night walks through the woods along with the dark-skinned woman who lived with them, Amima. A few years earlier Maude and her daughters were gathering plants in the forest and they strayed into the area where the Wampanoag women also gathered. Kwe's habit was to skip the first patch of anything that she found and then take no more than half of the next. She had noticed Maude doing the same thing, looking carefully at the leaves and then patting them before moving on to another patch she would pick from. Kwe recognized one of their songs about gratitude in the low hum of Maude's voice as she worked.

Maude's behaviour was different from many of the townspeople, who just took whatever they wanted, often ripping out good medicinal plants and casting them aside to put in gardens or allowing their pigs to graze on them. The animals caused almost as much destruction as the humans who tended them, so Kwe's curiosity about this woman got the better of her. She found herself taking note of Maude's patterns, then being in the same place, so they inevitably began to spend time together, silently harvesting the things that they needed.

Over time they learned enough of each other's languages, and they began to share stories about plants. The Wampanoag women shared how they worked together with songs to bring healing, and Amima shared her own stories from the islands that had been her home. Maude and her daughters listened. The little people hissed, and retreated further into dark places. They didn't trust these latecomers.

This time she was sure it was screaming. Kwe stood up and looked toward town, smelling smoke. This was not a cooking fire; something was wrong. Then with sudden clarity she heard Amima's voice, and others from her own community. Pleading.

Before there was conscious thought, Kwe felt the antlers emerge, bone and cartilage extending several feet above her head and becoming pointed and sharp. She began to run, dropping to all fours as feet became hooves to race across the grass and fields that separated her home from the town.

• • •

The first one to fall was the man bearing a lit torch. Her pointed antlers lifted him off the ground and threw him aside, his torch landing on a patch of dry grass. The fire caught and ran up the side of a building. Kwe ran toward Amima and the two Wampanoag women, tied to stakes, but she couldn't get near them. The flames gripped her friends tightly, squeezing the women into blackened shapes, empty mouths stretched wide. No longer able to scream, their silence became a living thing amid the sound of the fire, leaping now from one building to another and the chaos caused by her attack.

Rage filled her and she turned on the men, knowing only that they did this. She didn't know which of them burned her friends, but she knew that they were all guilty. No one of them could have done this without the agreement of the others. They tried to run, but she was faster and she charged at them, lifting them with her antlers and casting them aside, trampling those who fell.

Eventually she stopped before a cluster of women, huddled together and crying. They were terrified of her. Kwe looked at her hooves, stained a deep crimson. Blood dripped to the ground from her antlers, she felt it on her face like tears. Tears for her friends and the community that had become her home. Tears for Amima. Tears for Maude and her daughters now looking at her in fear and, was that anger? As she turned away, she understood the hissing of little people. This is what they feared would come of sharing stories.

Time to go.

• • •

At first Kwe kept to the ocean as she ran, following the water until she didn't understand the language anymore. Where the land spread low and flat and the rivers widened into marshes, she found more villages. She learned to recognize them, the dangerous ones. They called her people savages, but it was they who acted the part.

So, she acted a part too—tempting the dangerous ones into dark places and either dispatching them herself or leaving them for the little people and others whose names she knew better than to speak. Keeping to the lowlands, Kwe moved cautiously through forests. Something howled overhead, small furred creatures with long arms that swung from branch to branch. Cautiously, she picked her way back to the ocean, where breezes cooled the air, which was often heavy and humid.

For a time, she lived among small deer, and learned to make herself small like them. The ocean was beautiful, shades of blue and turquoise that she had only seen in birds and flowers. The people were unfamiliar, with dark skin and flashing eyes. Their language was different, and their clothing was not like the latecomers. She didn't see the signs of danger she has learned to recognize, so she relaxed a little and built a shelter like the ones that they lived in.

And one night, after swimming in the turquoise ocean beneath a full moon, she allowed one of them to come inside.

4

NIINWI

"I never understood how foreigners could come and tell us where to die and where to live. Where to be buried and how to breed."

—Tanya Tagaq,
Split Tooth

IN ANISHINAABEMOWIN, we have two ways to say *us*. Niinwi is exclusive: *us but not you*. It's like telling your friend about a vacation that your family is taking. Or: We are going to dinner, but you aren't coming with us. Giinwi means *us including you:* We are all going to dinner. These words, niinwi and giinwi, aren't good or bad; how they are used is what matters.

So what, exactly, do we mean by "we"?

Mother's Day is in May, and while I wasn't particularly invested in conventional dates as I planned our year of Indigenous reading, it also felt wrong to ignore it and act like we weren't thinking about mothers while surrounded by Hallmark moments, brunches, and lines at the places that don't take reservations.

I started to think about what mothering is, what kinds of caregiving get valued. Who does the work, for whom, and to what end? This led me to thinking about gender itself, and the ways that we are all constrained by the way that western societies think about gender and gender roles, which goes back a very long time. In the book *Jewish and Christian Women in the Ancient Mediterranean*, coauthors Sara Parks (New Brunswick/settler-descendant), Shayna Sheinfeld (Jewish), and Meredith J. C. Warren (Métis/Irish/British) describe the Greco-Roman society's strategies for controlling gender in ways that sound very familiar. They write that in the ancient world, the ideal gender was, of course, male. It was not only ideal, it was the only real gender; the rest of us were just "various degrees of failure to measure up."[1] If you doubt this, think about how many ways *man* is used as the term for everyone, and how hard people still fight against changing that language. Herein was the challenge for me to describe this month's panel. "Everybody except cisgender heterosexual men" isn't a very appealing title. Nether was "resisting the patriarchy," which still centres patriarchy in a way that I didn't like. It sounded as if it was something we just had to live with, but it isn't. Patriarchy is not inevitable. We can choose to go a different way. We can refuse. We can turn our backs on it and build something else: an us that excludes patriarchy.

The title I chose for that month's conversation was "refusing the patriarchy." Because while we do have to deal with the consequences of this marginalizing world that we live in, we can locate the centre where we are. We can build a way of thinking and living that doesn't beg for inclusion within the very systems that pushed us aside. Sandy Grande (Quechua) writes about refusal in the introduction to her masterwork *Red Pedagogy*. Basically, refusal is the decision to deny the things that deny us. Bad Indians are experts at refusal. We know that more inclusion and more participation aren't going to fix the harms of colonialism and the white feminism that supports it. So we look to the stories of those we share space with—others in the mashkiig—and we build our communities there.[2]

---

1 Sara Parks, Shayna Sheinfeld, and Meredith J.C. Warren, *Jewish and Christian Women in the Ancient Mediterranean* (Routledge, 2022), 10.

2 Sandy Grande, *Red Pedagogy: Native American Social and Political Thought* (Rowman & Littlefield, 2004, 2015), 6–7. Grande is one of many Indigenous scholars writing about refusal: Audra Simpson (Mohawk), Glen Coulthard (Yellowknives Dene), and Jodi Byrd (Chickasaw), to name a few others.

Grande also discusses the problems of white feminism and rejects the term *feminist* for herself, preferring a theory of *indigenísta* to a theory of feminism. Indigenísta, like kwe, is a more expansive understanding of gender that is located in our relations as Indigenous peoples rather than in notions of some common sisterhood that isn't actually at all common.[3] Like Grande, I have long struggled with the idea that patriarchy was the overarching *ism* that imposes control; because men who are racialized negatively simply don't have the same power that white men do. It was through Grande and her discussion of indigenísta that I started to think something else must be at play.

Parks, Sheinfeld, and Warren introduced me to the term *kyriarchy*. Kyriarchy is the social system that keeps all the various oppressive systems (racism, sexism, ableism—it goes on and on) in place.[4] It is, if you will, the paddle controlling the marionette's strings. That is how the foreigners tell us where to live and die, where to be buried, and how to breed. Our ability to reproduce, through childbearing or teaching, is controlled with racism, gender, ability, and other social categories being used to decide who is "out of place" and why.

This moves our discussion about power and gender into a more nuanced space, because kyriarchy looks at all the ways that systems of power work together to privilege a very specific few. White feminism is able to find inclusion within that system, because race is not a barrier. White women have long been part of that owning class. I remember being amazed by the agency of women in the slave-owning south when I read *They Were Her Property: White Women as Slave Owners in the American South* by Stephanie Jones-Rogers. It a fascinating look at the

---

3 Grande, *Red Pedagogy*, 183.

4 The writers of everyday feminism offer a detailed description of the kyriarchy and why this term matters on their blog at https://everydayfeminism.com/2014/04/kyriarchy-101/.

wealth these women had and their active participation in buying, selling, and breeding human capital.[5]

Tagaq's (Inuk) words about foreigners telling us where to live and die, how to be buried and breed: These are not metaphorical in the least.

• • •

White feminism is an example of a destructive *us but not you*, those foreigners who tell us where to live and how to breed. White feminism leaves people behind. They get to enter the workforce; Black and Indigenous women stay behind to care for the homes and families that white women want to be free from. Residential schools claimed to train Indigenous girls for domestic work, and beginning in 1955, the Canadian "domestic worker program" imported Black women from Caribbean countries for that same kind of labour.[6] For decades, these women could be dismissed or deported if they got pregnant, and most of them were not permitted to bring their own children. White women's liberation from housework and family responsibilities has often required the labour of Black, Brown, and Indigenous women.

My friend Angela J. Gray (Jamaican Canadian) participated in this discussion about refusing patriarchy. Her mother was an undocumented domestic worker from Jamaica and, after being born prematurely,

---

5 The transatlantic slave trade was abolished around the same time as the land in Virginia was exhausted for agriculture, so the plantations literally became breeding grounds. In *Loaded: A Disarming History of the Second Amendment*, Roxanne Dunbar-Ortiz (American) notes that Thomas Jefferson bragged to George Washington that the birth of Black children increased Virginia's capital stock by 4 percent every year (65).

6 Media is filled with reports about human trafficking and generally focuses on sex workers or children. Globally, domestic workers providing childcare or housekeeping labour make up a large segment of trafficked workers, whose precarious status leaves them vulnerable to sexual predation by their employers. Even with the meager legal standing provided by migrant worker programs, all migrant workers are vulnerable because their presence in the country is tied to a single employer and as soon as their labour is no longer needed, they are deported.

Angela along with her twin were taken into foster care right from the hospital. They were told that their mother "voluntarily" gave them up and returned to Jamaica in the months after Angela was born—something that turned out to be as false as the birthdate the government made up for her and her twin. In truth, Angela's mother did not consent. The bureaucracy of child welfare, through the same language of safety and well-being that pervaded justifications for residential schools, ensured that Angela was raised in a white Canadian family. The taking of Indigenous children, in what became broadly known as the Sixties Scoop, was just one part of the larger movement to "rescue" racially marginalized children by placing them with white families.

One of the key differences between the feminisms of white women and those of Black and Indigenous women is that the family is not something we need to be freed from in order to accomplish things. It is the place where we are free—perhaps the *only* place where we are free—and as such, it becomes the basis for the liberation of our communities. Queer and nonconforming folk create their own families, chosen families that are also a place of liberation and safety. Christian families often see themselves doing this as well, their families being a place of refuge where they nurture and replicate the values of a dominant and dominating society, while ours tend to challenge it. That is why so many systems work against our families, putting children like Angela in white foster homes and deporting or incarcerating their parents.

Within the so-called pink-collar professions, it is largely racially marginalized women who are at the lowest rungs of this labour market, doing the work that makes the advancement or liberation of others possible. The liberation is for you but not us.

So the question before us that month was: How does the writing of marginalized people help us think about *us* in a way that includes everyone without erasing ourselves? This is a challenge for those of us who live in the mashkiig. Rather than simply defining ourselves by what we are not, or by what others need, we must think about who we are, give value to who we are and what we need. The books we read that month were a mix of fiction, memoir, and nonfiction that moved us from the sexual violence of the early colonial period up through contemporary experiences of health care and queer life.

We were almost all "civilians" in the conversation that month; our only conventionally published author was activist and journalist Taté Walker (Mniconjou Lakota), who contributed an essay to the *FIERCE* anthology, although Seán Carson (Nêhiyaw/Anishinaabe/Otipêmisiwak), who also joined us, has published their smutty poetry in various zines.[7]

One of the panel participants, Nick Thixton (white/Jewish), organizes and works around abortion access, specifically for transgender people, and participates in abortion storytelling.[8] Because of that work, they recommended a book about reproductive justice in Native communities. Barbara Gurr, the author of *Reproductive Justice: The Politics of Health Care for Native American Women*, identifies herself as a settler, clarifying her relationships within the Pine Ridge community and careful not to speak for or on top of them. Not only does she detail important barriers to women's health care on US reservations, but the thoughtful way she described her land relations in the introduction and throughout the book modelled the kind of relations that we hope to see. Too many academics come to our communities to study us and then leave, our only real value being the data our lives and bodies produce.

Our bodies produce joy and connection as well. In one of Carson's poems, "in cree," about a couple's most intimate moments, the

---

7 Zines are works of original or copied text and images, often artfully presented with little regard for conventional permissions. They are published independently, usually by photocopier, and either distributed for free or sold to raise money. The name is shortened from "magazines," and they are a popular way for marginalized communities and the organizers who come from them to publish. Although zines are relatively recent, this kind of communicating has been around longer than the printing press.

8 Abortion storytelling is simply the practice of telling one's story about abortion in an organized way. It confronts anti-abortion rhetoric, breaking down stigmas and creating community. Words have power and storytelling is a powerful form of education and liberation. Find out more at reclaimproject.org.

response of her body to his use of the Cree language evokes the larger reclamation of stolen language present in our words and our bodies. The things we say call forth physical reactions, which makes the things we say so important—particularly in this month where we tried to recentre ourselves while discussing books about queer and Two Spirit people and reproductive justice, books about sexual violence and the feminisms that emerge in marginalized communities.[9]

> so it began,
> during, before, and after.
> she learning
> cree,
> him learning
> the way her body speaks.[10]

• • •

Sometimes *us but not you* can be necessary and constructive. Unlike a destructive *us but not you* that builds a world out of assimilation and compliance, a constructive *us but not you* works toward a world in which many worlds can coexist. It works toward an us that *can* include you rather than be threatened by it.

I tell the story of the deer abandoning the Anishinaabe in *Becoming Kin*. It is so rich, and I find myself coming back to it again and again. In the story, the Anishinaabe had been behaving selfishly—the very embodiment of a destructive *us but not you*. And so, the deer left. Eventually we put things back together, but first we had time apart. Those who have caused harm needed time to come to terms with the harms done, even if they were not intentional, and to make the

---

9 Two Spirit, given that it is a spiritual identity within many Indigenous communities, is not interchangeable with queerness.

10 Seán Carson Kinsella, "in cree," *Hart House Review*, 2014. Used by permission of the author.

necessary changes. Those who have been harmed must take the time they need to rebuild. Without taking that time apart, those who have experienced harm are likely to accept meaningless apologies and reconcile with what feels like an inevitable but perhaps survivable status quo.

In her short story "In Parallel," adrienne maree brown (mixed-race Black/queer) tells a similar story about a world in which aliens calling themselves the Garacz have separated "the dominants" from everyone else into a parallel world. The Garacz's intergalactic role is to "support traumatized species to heal the wounds." Part of that work means separating those who see themselves as superior until they sort themselves out; then, one by one, they can be restored. The Garacz remove people not simply along racial lines but according to what brown describes as an "internal alignment with the dominant worldview."[11]

Sometimes *us but not you* is necessary for healing and resurgence. That time apart is what allows us to find a way to describe ourselves according to who we are, rather than who we are not. In the dominating centres, we are constantly reminded of what we are not—of our failure to measure up. By working together in the mashkiig, our solidarities with each other help us define who we are.

There is a freedom in this kind of *us but not you* that I came to appreciate in my years of podcasting with Kerry. Our conversations rarely took white feelings into consideration, as we and our guests talked about the things that mattered to us. Until then I hadn't realized how much I had self-censored and performed. Until then I hadn't known what a Good and Careful Indian I had often been.

In these conversations with Kerry, and then during that year of Indigenous reading, we learned each other's vocabulary of race and marginalization. We rehearsed having hard conversations and learning

---

11 Published in *Fables and Spells: Collected and New Short Stories* (AK Press, 2022), 204–20.

from our missteps in real time. We practiced standing together, a real *us* in the midst of a world that often said *but not you.*

• • •

People often say that violence is never the answer, forgetting that their capacity for peace relies on the often invisible-to-them violence of policing and border maintenance. In the FX series *Reservation Dogs*, which I mentioned earlier, the character of Deer Lady is played by Kaniehtiio Horn (Kanien:keha'ka) and it follows her from childhood, where she is taken to an Indian boarding school, through her transformation into Deer Lady after a doe offers help, and then her years meting out vengeance and punishment. Deer Lady's later violence, killing the now elderly boarding school guard, is only incomprehensible if we forget about, or find ways to justify, the violence done to Native children throughout the Indian boarding school system shown in the episode directed by filmmaker Danis Goulet (Cree-Métis).[12] The series shows a number of interactions between Deer Lady and the character Big from when he was a child and into adulthood, with Deer Lady often protecting him during his youth. At one point she tells him, "You're going to want to give up, but imagine your grandma is with you every single step of the way. Be good, fight evil, and you'll never have to see me again."[13]

Be good. Fight evil. A protective us but not you could mean defending those boundaries. In the story of the deer abandoning the Anishinaabe, we don't know what they might have done if the Anishinaabe had pushed their way into wherever the deer had withdrawn into. That may not have gone well. And in her story about the Garacz, adrienne maree brown doesn't leave that kind of boundary-crossing possible. Their removal of those with an internal alignment with the dominant worldview could itself be seen as violence. Klee

12 *Reservation Dogs*, Season 3, Episode 3, "Life among Wolves."

13 *Reservation Dogs*, Season 1, Episode 5, "Come and Get Your Love."

Benally (Diné) explores this in his book *No Spiritual Surrender: Indigenous Anarchy in Defense of the Sacred*, pushing back against the idea of "safe spaces." So often our focus on safe spaces—on inclusivity and acceptance—creates an *us including you* that actually puts the most vulnerable among us at risk of harm. Instead, Benally describes spaces that create internal safety by being hostile to viewpoints that lead to oppression: hostile to anti-trans perspectives, for example, or anti-Blackness.

Ptesáŋwiŋ, White Buffalo Calf Woman, creates hostile spaces. Unlike Waawaashkeshi'Kwe who was created in this world, Ptesáŋwiŋ is a spirit being—a deity who came to this world and brought the Lakota their ceremonies and sacred items. According to the story, there was a disturbance, unexpected thunder, and a warrior was sent out to find out what happened. He saw a naked woman and intended (or tried) to take what wasn't offered. So she vapourized him.[14]

This is not, of course, where the story ends. Ptesáŋwiŋ's purpose in coming to the Lakota was not to vapourize wrongdoers; it was to bring gifts and teachings to the Lakota, including the pipe and ceremonies associated with transitions like grief or stages of life. Ptesáŋwiŋ's uncompromising demand for respect shows us that her gifts and ceremonies are meant to exist in a space where we are respected as our authentic selves, protected by our hostility toward those who make us unsafe. Too often we are asked to compromise this by those with social or political power and call it peace.

Walker captures how powerful ceremony spaces like this can be in their poem "From Ptesáŋwiŋ, with love." Sitting in a sweat lodge at seventeen years old, this is *the first time* they heard one man tell other men not to rape a woman. Before the pipes and ceremonies and teachings, the importance of respecting the autonomy of others is Ptesáŋwiŋ's first gift. Sit with this poem for a moment and think about when you first learned that you were worthy of that kind of respect.

---

14 Taté Walker, "Origins" from *FIERCE: Essays by and About Dauntless Women* (Nauset Press, 2018), 48–60.

Ptesáŋwiŋ tells us how to relate to one another
don't hurt women, the medicine man says
and he is speaking directly to the men at sweat
that is not our way
and it is not what Ptesáŋwiŋ taught us
don't beat on your women
don't rape them
don't kill them

though he is retelling Ptesáŋwiŋ's
Rules for Being a Good Relative [tm]
this is the first time I'm hearing a man
tell another man
not to rape a woman
~ Taté Walker, "From Ptesáŋwiŋ, with love"[15]

So how do we get from niinwi to giinwi? From *us but not you* to *us including you*? What do we learn from stories from the mashkiig that allows us to show up as our authentic selves?

• • •

Two of the books we read that month in particular highlight the power of marginalized people writing about living within a power structure created and sustained by those who would tell us where to die and where to live, where to be buried and how to breed.

In their submission for the *FIERCE* anthology, Walker chose to write about Ptesáŋwiŋ as a woman they would claim as a hero. The editors pushed back. Ptesáŋwiŋ wasn't "real," they said, in any sense that white audiences would understand. They were looking for somebody better documented who would embody a kind of feminism they understood. The editors wanted Good Indians: those who would offer an

15 Walker, cited with permission of the author.

Indigenous way to access existing power structures (the kyriarchy) rather than confronting them.[16]

But we aren't going to fix a flawed system with more inclusion and more participation. We have to confront it. Besides, as Walker points out, Ptesáŋwiŋ *is* real. The Lakota have the pipes and gifts she gave them. Walker's life had shown them how powerless and "inferior" women could be, and the teachings from Ptesáŋwiŋ offered another way to think. There is, they write, a fundamental connection between ceremony and femininity in Očéti Šakówiŋ beliefs that refuses the hierarchy offered by western systems.[17]

Maria Campbell's (Métis) story in *Half Breed* about growing up in Saskatchewan contains another example of that kind of control. It was written as a memoir rather than a history, because that was the kind of writing that publishers wanted from Indigenous people in the 1970s. Memoir, as we will see next chapter, is a necessary approach to writing about history, but it is not seen as authoritative. Worse, Campbell's recounting of her sexual assault by an RCMP officer was removed from the original publication altogether. When the anniversary edition was being prepared for publication in 2019, Campbell noticed the omission and insisted that it be restored.

The consequences of refusal land hard on our queer and Two Spirit relatives, consequences that are becoming increasingly dangerous as legislation that targets them for exclusion spreads. In our conversation that month, Carson reminded us of the need to care for our Two Spirit elders, and brought up the memoir *A Two Spirit Journey: The Autobiography of a Lesbian Ojibwa-Cree Elder.* Ma-Nee Chacaby (Anishinaabe) writes that being Two Spirit is going to be a hard life because it doesn't

---

16 There are many marginalized feminists who are following the path forged by white feminists into capitalism and the drive to own. I won't be citing any of them.

17 Očéti Šakówiŋ refers to the Seven Council Fires that includes the Lakota, Nakota, and Dakota peoples.

fit neatly into the categories of a world that wants people to be this or that so they can be controlled; and so an *us that includes you* must also be an *us but not you,* in our hostility to and refusal to tolerate queer- and transphobias.[18] Chacaby also writes about being tired of hiding, the need to speak up about injustice, and leading Thunder Bay's first Pride parade in 2013. Despite decades of hardships, they are a language teacher and elder, a spiritual person and a bit of a joker.

As a Two Spirit youth who didn't yet have the language to think of themselves as Two Spirit, Walker was sent to a camp where they were, in their words, taught to hate themselves. Carson is constantly thinking about how they can show up in a space. We all know the stress of getting ready for an event or a meeting and how quickly we start to hate everything in our wardrobe; but Carson's remarks about how they show up hit differently. Can I wear a skirt? Will I be taken seriously if I wear lipstick? If they find out I write smutty poetry? Will I be safe?

Will I be safe.

• • •

In 2004, Amnesty International released a report called "No More Stolen Sisters: A Human Rights Response to Discrimination and Violence against Indigenous Women in Canada." It begins with the story of Helen Betty Osborne, a Cree teenager from Norway House First Nation in northern Manitoba who was murdered in 1971. She was

---

18 The main objection to this kind of exclusion or intolerance is that queer- and transphobic people need to be educated, and education takes time, so we have to be patient and not push too hard. I disagree. I don't mind educating and talking, but we have to be careful that our emphasis on education and patience does not come at the expense of the most vulnerable. We need to be very careful about whose needs are being prioritized and how this strategy makes vulnerable people unsafe. If you are going to have a faith or community group that "goes slowly," then your faith or community group is not safe for queer and trans people. I allowed this argument to silence me once. Never again.

killed while living in The Pas, where she had gone to attend secondary school after two years at the Guy Hill Residential School.

I remember watching a made-for-TV movie about her rape and murder by a group of young men, and the subsequent cover-up, and realizing that simply being visibly Indigenous put me in danger. Made me unsafe. At risk.

At risk: It's the kind of passive voice that ignores responsibility, putting the emphasis on the person at risk of harm rather than the reasons for why they are at risk. The passive voice has consequences for how we understand social issues, where we look for solutions. In the fall of 2023, I was part of a panel discussing Palestine, and *Toronto Star* columnist Shree Paradkar (Bangalorean) showed us multiple examples of how the media uses language, including active and passive voice, to preserve Israeli innocence and dehumanize Palestinians.[19] Bombs drop, buildings explode, children starve. All of it seemingly takes place spontaneously. The same passive language is used to talk about the harms done to Indigenous women and girls and Two Spirit people. We are at risk.

We are both at risk and asterisk peoples, as Eve Tuck (Unangax̂) would say. Tuck coauthored a paper titled "Decolonization Is Not a Metaphor," in which she and her coauthor write about the ways that white people absolve themselves of responsibility for the group-differentiated vulnerabilities to premature death faced by Black and Indigenous peoples. One of those ways people do this is to describe us as *at risk* because we are perpetually on the verge of extinction, and *asterisk* because we don't really matter. Asterisk people are not statistically significant; we're that small sample size that isn't worth being specific about. People might say trans* or LGBTQ*. As if including

19 Paradkar is from a region in India called Bangalore, marking her as Bangalorean rather than "Indo-Canadian" or "Indian." Marking her as Bangalorean recognizes the complexity of the people who live within India and avoids flattening them into a single homogenous group.

nonbinary or IAA2S were just too many letters. In their reporting on the 2020 election in the United States, CNN took a lot of mocking for an election-night graphic breaking down racial voting categories. In order of size, the voting groups were White, Latino, Black, Something Else, and Asian. For a while I, along with many users of Native Twitter, put "something else" in their bio. Asterisk.

Where you locate the problem becomes the place you locate the solution. "At risk" is the difference between talking about the percentage of women who experience sexual violence and the percentage of men who perpetrate it. There are reasons why Indigenous women and girls and Two Spirit people are at-risk and asterisk people in this settler colonial world. There are clear patterns. The Amnesty report determined in 2004 that Indigenous women and girls were in danger and called on all layers of government to do something. It said that "Canadian officials have a clear and inescapable obligation to ensure the safety of Indigenous women, to bring those responsible for attacks against them to justice, and to address the deeper problems of marginalization, dispossession, and impoverishment that have placed so many Indigenous women in harm's way."[20] In the following year, 2005, the Native Women's Association of Canada established the Sisters in Spirit initiative, which began holding annual vigils on October 4. Their primary role was to do research on these high rates of violence and to initiate policy changes and education; the vigils were just one part of that.

More reports came out. Grassroots organizers started crowdsourcing maps in Canada and the United States to document the missing and murdered, doing the work that local and national police services refused to do. Because we knew that the problem was not located in us. There

---

20 "Stolen Sisters: A Human Rights Response to Discrimination and Violence against Indigenous Women in Canada," October 2004, https://www.amnesty.ca/sites/amnesty/files/amr200032004enstolensisters.pdf, 35.

is nothing wrong with us that puts us at risk, that makes us asterisks.

In one of the books we read that month, *The Beginning and End of Rape,* legal scholar Sarah Deer (Mvskoke) goes back to the founding of the original colonies and describes the long pattern of dispossession and relocation (aka trafficking) of Indigenous women and girls often under the guise of safety and always with the consequence of sexual violence. Sexual violence is a strategy of war, a way to demoralize the people and literally interrupt the reproduction of their society. I would argue that it is also a strategy of colonization and nation building. Rather than the traumatic but time-limited experience of war, colonization and the subsequent nation building grind on for centuries. The sexual violence that was part of the foundation described by Deer is also part of the ongoing maintenance. This is why, I believe, we see so much reluctance by governments and white feminists alike on both sides of the border to deal meaningfully with this violence as it targets marginalized people.[21]

All this labour and organizing eventually forced the Canadian government to hold a national inquiry. Although plagued with internal problems and rules that constrained the questions they could ask—like preventing them from looking at the role of policing—the inquiry went forward. The group released a report, along with many calls to justice, in June 2019.

One of our panelists for the conversation in May, Robyn Bourgeois (Nêhiyaw iskwew), testified before that inquiry. She is an activist scholar in the Centre for Women's and Gender Studies at Brock University whose doctoral research focused on the violence against Indigenous women and girls, particularly the participation of Indigenous

---

21 Another form of sexual violence that is rarely talked about is white women accusing racially marginalized men of sexual assault as a way to exert control over them. You may be familiar with the story of Emmett Till, but these accusations continue and have devastating consequences for those who are accused.

women in state-sponsored anti-violence work like that done by the Native Women's Association of Canada and Sisters in Spirit. She has also spoken openly about her own experiences on Vancouver's Downtown East Side as a trafficked adolescent. In her work, Bourgeois confronts the ways that we are put at risk, made vulnerable and invisible, so that predators like serial killer Robert Pickton can spend years taking victims from that neighbourhood, some of whom Bourgeois knew, without interference.[22]

Refusing to take our place within the kyriarchy, that collective of political categories that allow some groups to make demands of those in other groups, is hard, and it comes with consequences. Bourgeois also talked about experiencing targeted harassment for her refusals, expressed through published writing and speaking engagements. Her insistence on being heard and seen resulted in being heard and seen by white men who challenged her expertise and, unsurprisingly, portrayed themselves as the real victims of a feminism that refuses to take its assigned place.

Gurr's book *Reproductive Justice: The Politics of Health Care for Native American Women* describes how being asterisks puts people at risk in the health care system. She writes from within the Pine Ridge Reservation in South Dakota and shares personal stories to demonstrate the impact of national policies that restrict and control the reproductive health care that is available to Native women. She writes that "Native women's bodies have historically been viewed as threats to the production of a unified national identity, therefore becoming sites of

---

22 Pickton was a serial killer operating in the lower Mainland of British Columbia and is believed to be responsible for the murders of at least twenty-six and up to forty-nine women, many of whom were sex workers on Vancouver's Downtown East Side. He was convicted in 2007 and died in prison in 2024. A subsequent inquiry found that police failed multiple times to connect the killings or to take seriously the reports of women going missing. Opal, the commissioner of that inquiry, commented that "The women didn't go missing. They aren't just absent; they didn't go away. They were taken." Passive vs. active voice. It matters.

both active and passive regulation by the state."[23] It's a more academic way of saying what Tagaq said: Our brown bodies, and their ability to make more brown bodies, are threats to a white nation. So they use laws and funding to control how we live and die, how we are buried and breed.

After the fall of *Roe v. Wade*, some people suggested that US reservations enact their sovereignty by offering abortions. As Gurr notes in her book, that simply isn't how health care on reservations works. Over 85 percent of Indian Health Service facilities, where most American Indians and Alaska Natives get their health care, don't offer abortion services, nor do they refer to abortion providers because the 1977 Hyde Amendment banned the use of federal funds for abortions except in very specific cases. The IHS relies on federal funds. This, Gurr speculates, combined with a lack of access to birth control, may be what leads a disproportionate number of Native women to choose sterility, a permanent solution to a temporary problem. Lack of resources means lack of real choice.

This was an interesting finding for her, and one that she struggled to understand given the long history of imposed sterilization done to marginalized women around the world. Sterilization is a kind of sexual violence used to control when and how we breed, whose children we raise. And forced sterilization does not belong in the distant past. It is ongoing, women still report having their tubes tied without their consent after having a C-section, and the lack of real choices in reproductive health can make choosing such a thing the result of no choices at all.

The traditional birthing in *Split Tooth*, a novel written by Inuk singer and activist Tanya Tagaq, is a contrast to the strictures described by Gurr. The birth is infused with the spiritual and the supernatural as the northern lights themselves seem to take part. People can, and

---

23 Barbara Gurr, *Reproductive Justice: The Politics of Health Care for Native American Women* (Rutgers University Press, 2014), 29.

do, develop their own birth plans that include traditional practices. But it shouldn't be so hard, it shouldn't be such a fight. Reproductive health care should be funded to centre the needs of the people receiving it, not the sentiments of politicians who have never cared about us. Amid the crushing trauma in *Split Tooth*, Tagaq tells a story of what is possible when we centre ourselves within a community that cares. We need these stories to help us imagine these things in our own lives.

The problem is not in us. The problem is in a patriarchy, a kyriarchy, that must be refused, and in the white feminisms that protect it through an *us* that excludes so many. That is the problem with white feminism. It is able to find a place within the kyriarchy because race is not a hindrance to it. And like too many who achieve something with relative ease, it is too easy for too many white women to believe that the inability of others to measure up must be their own problem. We live in a world where there are consequences for showing up as our authentic selves, where inclusion has come to mean an *us* at the expense of at-risk/asterisk people.

The perspectives brought by marginalized writers—those who are relegated to the outskirts and mashkiig of the nations built on top of us, who are on the losing end of every nationalist hierarchy—are critical if we are going to make effective change. These are the writers who have no investment in the status quo. These are not Good Indians or model minorities or any other such thing. We are not interested in rescuing our current society and building a kinder, more inclusive nationalist project. We are Bad Indians, experts at refusal, and determined to locate the problem outside of our bodies to create an *us including you*, where our authentic selves do not diminish yours.

Kwe

She had that dream again. It was so vivid that even after she was awake, she could still smell the pine resin in the air, clouds of smoke from burning sage, and the lingering notes of a song calling the grandmothers. Biindigen, nokomisag. For a moment in the darkened dome of her shelter, she thought she was in a sweat lodge near the great inland sea of her childhood, the air hot and heavy with the steam of water poured on rocks taken from the fire. But as she accustomed herself to her surroundings, she remembered that she was a long way from home. The tug of this dream was getting stronger and persisted longer into wakefulness. It felt like being called to a ceremony she had forgotten about.

Kwe looked at the back of the man beside her. He had found her just as she was taking her human form again and had nothing to cover herself with. He took off his own shirt, the soft sleeveless cotton common for the people of this area, and offered it to her. Their relationship and the community she became part of kept her balanced between who she had been and what she might have become in those early rage-filled years.

It was not her nature to stay in one place, and she often disappeared for periods of time. As he aged and she did not, these disappearances became more frequent. Their children—they had several adults with children of their own—were used to caring for him in her absence. He understood what their children did not, and he knew that one day she would not come back.

Time to go.

• • •

For years after she left, Kwe followed the clues in her dream, the smell of pine and sage, that led her on a meandering route to stay just outside the reach of the latecomers who were now spreading far from their coastal colonies. That was getting more and more difficult, as their reach extended deeper into the land. And it wasn't just their reach; their violence and selfishness changed the original people, as if a sickness had come with the latecomers from across the ocean.

At first, she thought the clues in her dream were leading her northward, home, but she quickly realized the clues were leading her to communities who needed her. And she gave the original people gifts to strengthen what they had against the mean spirit brought by the latecomers.

She taught them the ceremonies she had learned from stones and water, and they taught her the things they remembered, which led to more remembering, and gradually the people returned to themselves. She eliminated those whose violence would interfere with the growth of those who were being restored, and the stories that resulted kept the people safe long after she left. Inevitably the tug of her dream, the welcoming song, and the smell of pine and sage would lead her onward.

Her path eventually led her north toward the pine-covered hills and land dotted with lakes connected by rivers and swamps that lived in her memory. As the years passed and she travelled toward home, it became impossible to avoid the latecomers. They had scarred the land, first with great wagons that carved paths in the prairies and through mountain passes. Then they had built trains and laid tracks so the latecomers could travel faster. And eventually they built roads and highways, where they travelled alone.

It was a relief when she finally arrived in the land of her birth. It wasn't untouched, but it wasn't yet important to the latecomers either. And the swamps were hard to build over anyway.

Kwe closed her eyes and breathed deeply, the scent of pine all around her now. She reached for the smell of sage and, finding it, turned down a faint path, to where she saw a domed structure covered in blankets and tarps.

A young man worked outside chopping wood, long braids under a baseball cap worn backward and emblazoned with a "Caucasians" logo. He wore a plaid jacket, and when he turned around, she saw a black T-shirt with an image of Sabe, Big Foot, walking away. "Live, laugh, lurk," it said; she smiled, feeling like that described her life. Live, laugh, lurk. Discovery is dangerous.

He added two pieces of wood to the fire, which burned over large rocks and sang quietly to himself, the same song she now heard coming from inside the lodge, punctuated by drumbeats. "Biindigen, Nokomis-sag, way oh way ha, oh way oh way ha, oh-oh, Biindigen Nokomis-sag, way oh way ha, oh way oh way ha."

He looked up at her. Kwe was about to speak when he said, "Aniin! Animiiki Benesaikwe has been waiting for you. She's inside," and he lifted the flap. Puzzled that he seemed to know who she was, but curious about who had been singing this song that she has been following, Kwe crawled into the darkness.

• • •

"Did you realize that you've been speaking entirely in the third person?" the young woman asks, her tone more casual than the observation seems to merit.

Kwe's eyes flew open in surprise. "I have?"

"Yes, it's as if everything you told me happened to somebody else." The young woman scattered some more medicines on the rocks, cedar and lavender along with sage and something Kwe couldn't quite place. They sparked and burned out before the young woman doused the glowing rocks with water, the sweat lodge filling with moist heat. A sharp snap as one of the rocks cracked open.

Kwe could barely breathe, but whether from the humidity or the young woman's words she couldn't be sure, so she held tightly to the round stone she has carried for many years, closed her eyes, and began her story again.

"I was born in the woodlands near the great inland sea. It was early in the morning just before sunrise, so my father called me Morningstar."

5

N'DADIBAAJIM

What you get right now is me, and I pray that as I grow, you hold that space with me, and that as you grow, I hold that space with you. May we look back on our long-ago selves with kindness and know that there were always things we should have done better.

—Kaitlin B. Curtice,
Native: Identity, Belonging, and Rediscovering God

THE ANISHINAABE HAVE a collection of teachings called the Seven Grandfathers, although I have sometimes heard them referred to as the Seven Grand*mothers*. Sabe, featured on the young man's T-shirt, is also known as Sasquatch, or Bigfoot. And while we may laugh along with the world's hide-and-seek champion for his "live, laugh, lurk" motto, there is a deeper truth here. For the Anishinaabe at least, Sabe represents honesty, which is more than truth telling.

James Vukelich Kaagegaabaw (Ojibwe Anishinaabe), a language and cultural teacher, wrote a small book called *The Seven Generations and the Seven Grandfather Teachings*, in which he talks about each of these teachings from the perspective of the Anishinaabe word, rather than the English translation. What is translated as *honesty* is the Anishinaabe word gwayakwaadiziwin, and it has to do with living in a way that our words align with our actions. Broken down into its components, it says: "Observe how I live and the truth will come out of it."[1]

---

1 James Vukelich Kaagegaabaw, *The Seven Generations and the Seven Grandfather Teachings* (James Vukelich, 2023), 71.

Bad Indians might tell our own stories on our own terms, but we also aspire to this kind of honesty. Perhaps this is what makes us dangerous: When you challenge all the stories and demand better, the life that results from these truths is unsettling to those who have investment in settlement.

Although Kwe's story is fiction, it is also revealed now to be a kind of memoir. Anyone who has participated in a sweat knows that in a darkness lit briefly by the glow of heated stones, we go around the circle and share the truths of our lives. This is where Kwe tells her story to Animiiki BenesaiKwe, whose song reached back in time and called her forward.[2] We can't call the grandmothers and be surprised when one shows up!

Thus called, Kwe—a grandmother now, carrying the teaching of gwayakwaadiziwin—sits in the darkened sweat lodge. And as any of us would in that space, she unburdens the truth of her life. This is memoir: the unburdening of the truths of our life and the hope that the things we say align with it. As we use memoir to peer into the lives of marginalized writers, to see how they have lived and discern the truth that comes out of their words, Kaitlin Curtice (Potawatomi) reminds us that memoir allows us to see a part of the writer that they may no longer be. It is a snapshot of time from which they have, possibly, grown. We should approach these offerings with kindness, knowing that there were always things we, too, should have done better.

• • •

When I first set up this series of conversations about books, I placed memoir right after history. History is where we tell broad stories about communities and nations. Memoir is when we tell our own history, which should be easy but it isn't. What's easy is what Kwe was doing:

---

2 Miigwech to Nicole Joy Fraser for permission to use her welcome song, and her name, in this work! Such an honour to have you here with me. And Miigwech to Johnnie Jae, the burnt ball of fury, for permission to reference one of your T-shirt designs. You can find more at https://johnniejae.com/.

talking about traumatic things as if they happened to somebody else, distancing ourselves with academic language and statistics. It is harder to shift from third person to first. To talk about what happened to me and the feelings left in the wake. That is what memoir is. N'dadibaajim is "me telling my own story" in the context of everything else.

At the time that this panel took place, I hadn't read many memoirs. Although I have since then, it was a gap on my shelf that shifted the conversation somewhat. That month we had Ernestine Hayes (Tlingit) who wrote *The Tao of Raven* and Curtice (Potawatomi) who wrote *Native*. Demita Frazier (African American) is working on a memoir that includes her years with the Combahee River Collective and talked with us about *How We Get Free*, which was written by Keeanga-Yamahtta Taylor (Black) about the collective. Jenessa Galenkamp (Métis), a photographer, and Joy Henderson (Afro-Lakota), working on her own memoir about growing up in Toronto, rounded out our panel.

Rather than discussing the memoirs we had read, we wound up discussing the memoirs we had written, or were in the process of writing. So in large part the question before us was *why*. Why write these memoirs? What was it about our lives that needed to be documented and shared with others, and who were we writing for?

Dadibaajim are oral narratives connected to land and relations. In Helen Olsen Agger's (Namegosibiing Anishinaabe) book *Dadibaajim: Returning Home through Narrative*, she documents the oral narratives told by family members that describe each person's relationship to the land and each other, which is essentially what memoir is.[3] There are many books like this, collecting the stories of what makes a place home and how we fit into that place. *How We Go Home: Voices from Indigenous North America* and *Beginning Again: Stories of Movement and Migration in Appalachia* are anthologies with a range of stories that help us understand that relationship between place and people.

---

3 The prefix "n'" on dadibaajim indicates me. I am the one telling the story.

How We Go Home gives us twelve stories from Indigenous people writing about how the past impacts the present, from relocation to boarding schools, substance misuse, and more. Their trauma becomes a place of transformation into activism and advocacy, which isn't to say that trauma made them who they are. Quite the opposite. Their refusal to accept trauma as an inevitable part of life shaped the changes they work toward. *Beginning Again* was a surprising book for me. I chose it from a monthly subscription I get through Haymarket Books, because I know so little about Appalachia, and reading this book revealed just how little I knew.[4] It contains stories about migrants and refugees alongside Black, Indigenous, and white Appalachians and their various experiences in that area. Both books unintentionally echo Diaz's words about entering the land and building relations, and then how they welcome others.

How We Get Free: Black Feminism and the Combahee River Collective, which is one of the books we read that month, is another collection of interviews documenting the story of a community, in this case a radical group of queer Black women who changed the world, including sisters Barbara and Beverly Smith, and Demita Frazier, who cofounded the collective, as well as Barbara Ransby and Alicia Garza. The collective began the way much activism begins, as a reading and consciousness-raising group, and their impact continues to shape the way we talk about the convergence of identity and politics. They are very Bad Indians indeed, and I appreciate them and their work deeply.

4 There are many publishers with monthly subscription programs, which allow you to choose one or more books each month from their publication list. It's a great way to read intentionally and radically, because it exposes you to topics and authors you may otherwise not come across. Independent bookstores owned by marginalized people are another great place to buy books and attend talks. The timing of this particular book was interesting. I had ordered it weeks before Trump announced his running mate, and *Beginning Again* introduced me to a much different Appalachia than the one J. D. Vance has written and talked about.

Because of the disruption of colonial and nationalist projects, many of us have little more than names and dates to go along with the pictures in our photo albums, the genealogy of our connection to a community. But it is dadibaajim that tells us who we are through the stories of elders and other members of our communities. This is the work that Joy Henderson is doing in documenting her story of growing up in Regent Park, a neighbourhood in Toronto that was disrupted by renovations that became gentrification. She is collecting and recalling the stories of elders, aunties, and grandmothers, so that their history is not lost and the rich tapestry of that community is not rewritten as broadcloth.

We listen to these writers, follow their stories through the mashkiig, and the lost pieces of ourselves begin to fit together. This doesn't have to be because they are our stories as well; our lives may have taken completely different paths. But we may yet see something of ourselves in the people contained in these stories, and that helps us understand ourselves a little better. There is nothing like reading memoirs, or anthologies like these, about marginalized people to understand my own relationship to them a little better.

• • •

Finding my father changed everything. It was not because I suddenly found out I was Ojibwe, or even because it suddenly became real. It had always been real—real enough that teachers, classmates, and others tried to sort me according to categories laid out by Hollywood. Was I a Good Indian or a Bad Indian? Was I going to go along with the dominant narrative about my ancestors and all that descended from that narrative? Or was I dangerous, bent on challenging and confronting a comfortable status quo? (Comfortable for *whom* is always the question.) And the fact is that for too many years I was a Good Indian. The stories around me didn't offer any alternative.

What finding my father changed was my perspective.

I've told you that I was born northwest of Lake Superior. I was about two years old when my parents' marriage ended and my mother moved us south to be with her family. I knew that he had come down once and said goodbye to me while I was asleep, but nothing more. During the decades in which I had no contact with my father, I assumed he was two thousand kilometers away in northwestern Ontario. I was wrong.

One of my mother's former students, from the same community as my father and his family, contacted her to thank her for being an influential teacher, for believing in him and helping him complete his high school diploma.[5] When I needed help getting information to apply for my status card, it was this former student's contact information that she gave me. He knew the answers I needed about my paternal family to complete the form, and just as the conversation was drawing to a close, I asked him if he knew where my father was. He did. Roy was driving a cab in a city less than six hours from where I sat. A city that was within thirty minutes of a family cottage I frequented for most of those silent decades.

I started calling cab companies, asking if Roy worked there. Eventually one said yes, so I left my name and phone number. Unsure if he would remember me, I added that I was Vicki's daughter. He called me back. And the letters and phone calls began to fly back and forth. This was long before email and social media. No FaceTime, no Zoom, but he was real. And finding him clicked so many pieces of myself into place.

In his interview for the book *Beginning Again: Stories of Movement and Migration in Appalachia*, Rufus Elliot (Monacan) talks about the complexity of Indigenous identity, those who are raised in their communities and those who are not but have genealogical ties to it. His community only gained federal recognition in 2018, despite long and demonstrable ties to that area, and that lack of a land base or

---

5 Part of what she did was help him come south so that he *could* get his high school diploma. Something that wasn't available to him in Umfreville.

recognition contributed to the dispersal and relocation of his community.[6] Elliot was fortunate to have been raised in a town that was largely Monacan people, and he believes that it is the responsibility of those who stayed, like his own family, to make those of us who were raised outside feel welcome and comfortable.

Growing up, I had no relationship with the Indigenous community despite there being a Friendship Centre in my city and two reserves within a two-hour drive. Indigenous people are made so invisible that I didn't even know they were there.

When I found my father, I set out to find other Indigenous people, reasoning that if he could be unexpectedly nearby, so could they. In Canada, Friendship Centres and Native Women's Resource Centres are one way in which those who stayed, those who grew up within the native community, show welcome and care to those who have genealogy but no relationship. These organizations, like Urban Indian Centers in the United States, are hubs for Indigenous people living in cities, and they provide services and social activities that bring us together. I lived just outside Toronto at that time, so I quickly found these centres downtown and began spending time with them.

Powwows were another easy and obvious first step, and during one visit to my father's home in North Bay, he took me to the powwow at a nearby reserve.

---

6 This lack of a land base is a strategy of colonization and modern nation building. One of the key features of the modern nation-state is that only one group of people can lay claim to a specific geography, which means all others no longer belong. At best they can be thought of as minorities within the larger nation; at worst they are expelled and become stateless migrants who don't belong anywhere. This is the long history of Jewish people and the context within which the violence of Nazi Germany unfolded. Politicians talk about Israel being a place for Jewish people to belong and be safe, but they never talk about why Jews have been unsafe in Europe and elsewhere for thousands of years. And if they are the only ones who belong in Palestine, what of all the others who also live there? The *creation* of diasporic populations is also political strategy.

It was an extraordinary day, full of dancing, drumming, and fry bread. At one point the emcee directed our gaze upward, where an eagle soared in circles above us. In southern Ontario where eagle populations have been devastated by the machinery of "civilized life," their presence is met with excitement bordering on prophetic. But in the north, where my cousins live, the relationship is much more casual.

Like us, eagles have been pushed aside, their natural habitats filled in and paved over to provide a foundation for "civilized life." And like us, they are returning to the places where they had been whispered memories. The society around us thinks we've vanished, along with the eagles, a sad and tragic past to be lamented for a minute or perhaps on a designated day. And then the world continues pouring pavement and concrete on top of what it does not understand.

On the day of that first powwow, my father and I had gone early for sunrise ceremony. Although I have been to many since then, the sunrise ceremonies at Nipissing remain precious. It was at one of these ceremonies that the elder greeted me with "n'daanis," which means *daughter*. In that moment, it felt like he was identifying something very specific about me. I've kept it as a name, and in some ways, it feels more like me than any other name I have. Perhaps because in the early years of building a relationship with my father, he sent me cassette tapes, one of which included the song "Nitanish," by Innu folk-rock band Kashtin. I have always been my mother's daughter; with this name, I know I am my father's daughter as well.

Unlike other types of storytelling, where we can distance ourselves through an academic or narrative voice, in memoir we are expected to speak for ourselves, to tell our own stories. In fact, many of the books that we read that year used memoir to shape their writing. Prescod-Weinstein's *Disordered Cosmos* talked about her experiences as a Black Jewish woman in a STEM field. Estes's *Our History Is the Future* told the history of the Standing Rock movement against the broader history of the United States, along with personal narratives about his life and his family. Our discussion about gender and refusing patriarchy included several memoirs.

We talk about ourselves because we cannot disconnect ourselves from the world around us. This poem by Diane DiPrima (unmarked) describes the crisis of the kyriarchy, that overarching system of oppressions, as a war against the imagination. It is a war against the ways in which we imagine ourselves to exist in the world around us and the stories we tell. Sit with this fragment, and remember to look it up so you can read the whole extraordinary piece.

> history is a living weapon in yr hand
> & you have imagined it, it is thus that you
> "find out for yourself"
> history is the dream of what it can be, it is
> the relation between things in a continuum
>
> of imagination
> what you find out for yourself is what you select
> out of an infinite sea of possibility
> no one can inhabit yr world
>
> Diane Di Prima, "Rant"[7]

These stories we tell are not things that happened to other people; they are the things that happened to us, the things that we did. Dadibaajim are the oral narratives that elders use to teach children so that knowledge goes from one generation to the next. We clear space through

---

7 Diane Di Prima, excerpt from "Rant" from *Pieces of a Song: Selected Poems*. Copyright 2014 by Diane Di Prima. Reprinted with the permission of The Permissions Company on behalf of City Lights Books, citylights.com. I encountered this poem in an essay written by Kelly Hayes, a Menominee writer and activist living in Chicago. She described reading it aloud on her way to an action and the power these words had to centre her as she anticipated challenge. Miigwech, Kelly; I learn so much from you.

dawisijigem, by burning out the underbrush to make room for new life, so we can tell our own stories about history, the land and the waters, as well as belonging. How will our children know who they are if we don't tell them who *we* are? This encourages us to live in a way that our words align with our actions, because we know that children watch and listen. Memoir ties all these things together. No one can inhabit your world, so you must tell the story yourself.

Reading memoirs is a powerful way to listen to the voices of those who are violently pushed to the margins and find both community and medicine in that mashkiig. Reading and listening to memoirs can help us consider how our struggles are not only similar but connected and to find inspiration for our own tentative steps forward. It helps us understand and recognize how various oppressions intersect in our own lives.

The apathy or helplessness that we often feel in the face of injustice is by design; it keeps us from acting. But the stories contained in the memoirs of marginalized people give us purpose and direction in the midst of that injustice. Memoir is where we lift history in our hands. It's where we find out for ourselves, and in our own words, how the people living through these moments are changed. It's where we may see pieces of ourselves in the relation between their stories and our own experiences.

• • •

When reading memoir, it is important to remember that the authors are telling their own story within the constraints of the publishing industry and the world around us. We saw in the last chapter how Campbell's work was edited to remove a pivotal story about her sexual assault by an RCMP officer, how the editors of the *FIERCE* anthology struggled with Walker's essay about Ptesáŋwiŋ. We self-censor as well, thinking about the dominating audience and what it may, or may not, be willing to accept about us. Learning how to resist that internally and externally takes a community that supports us.

Friends suggested that I write an article about finding my father, so I did, and it became the first piece I ever published. The powwows I attended formed the narrative backbone of the article. The piece, a memoir in 1,365 words, was published in the May 1995 issue of *Canadian Living*.

Along with my story, the magazine features a photograph of me with my oldest son, who was six years old at the time. It's a nice enough picture. But the sweater I'm wearing belongs to the photographer. And my son is shirtless, with a feathered medallion on a leather strap hanging around his neck.

There isn't anything real about this picture. The photographer staged it, and it represents her idea of how we should look rather than who I actually was. When the photographer arrived, I had been wearing a purple dress with a full skirt that I liked because of the way that it moved when I danced at the powwows I attended.[8] I was excited about publishing my first article and having a professional photographer come to the apartment to take my picture. Wearing that dress for this photograph felt important to me, because the piece ends with a reflection on that first powwow at the Nipissing reserve and some words about how the powwow is the trail that would guide others like me home.

You can imagine my confusion when the photographer's first words were to ask where my traditional clothes were. She wanted the whitestream vision of Pocahontas—braids and buckskin—not a young mother with bobbed hair and a purple dress.[9] I was not yet confident enough to push back, so I accepted my place as a Good Indian.

---

8 Typically, powwows allow anyone to dance whether or not they have regalia, dance a particular style, or are native. Exhibition dances are set aside for specific styles, but most songs are for everybody.

9 Matoaka was a member of the Powhatan people, born in 1596. Pocahontas is her childhood nickname, and while she may have saved the life of the English colonist John Smith, she did not marry him. Years later she was abducted and held for ransom, which her father did not pay. She was eventually baptized as Rebecca, married tobacco planter John Rolfe, went with him to England where she was celebrated as an example of a "civilized savage," and died at 20 or 21. She was buried at St. George's Church in Gravesend, England.

I put on her orange sweater and let her stage the photograph to suit the story she wanted to tell. The feathered piece that Ben is wearing is a barrette; it isn't a necklace. I don't even remember where the leather strap came from.

My friend Jenessa Galenkamp (Métis) related her own experience of this kind of erasure during our discussion about memoir during our year of Indigenous reading. She had read Tuscarora author Alicia Elliot's book *A Mind Spread Out on the Ground*, which is a memoir in the form of a collection of essays reflecting on her life as a Tuscarora woman living with trauma and mental illness. The title comes from the Mohawk word used to describe depression, Wake' nikonhra 'kwenhtará: 'on, which captures both the individual experience of depression and the collective experience of colonial trauma. It describes a mind that has fallen, stretched or sprawled on the ground; it's all over the place and a little bit messy. So often our writing, those of us who write from the margins, appears to be this way: all over the place and a little bit messy, like the often-fragmented communities we belong to.

That's because we're picking up pieces of ourselves and examining them, trying to reorder them in a way that makes sense to us. In an interview for California Book Club, Deborah A. Miranda reflects on her own book as well as comments made by Gloria Anzaldúa. She commented on the fragmented nature of storytelling that happens when you are writing around the fragments of what is available to you. Our stories are rarely straightforward narratives, she says; they are mosaics, and our writing often reflects that.[10]

In one essay, Elliot writes about photography, particularly the way that photographers like Edward G. Curtis (unmarked) preserve Indigenous people as images stuck in time rather than actual people. Having studied photography, Galenkamp found herself connecting with this. She was familiar with many of the photographers that Elliot

10 California Book Club: Deborah A. Miranda, 28:45, https://www.youtube.com/watch?v=DflbCJL8PsY&t=449s.

mentions—photographers who, according to Galenkamp's teachers, had done a "great job" of capturing the American West and the dying frontier, including one whose photo series on Black and Indigenous people was titled "Before They Pass Away."

In one assignment, Galenkamp was to create a series of self-portraits that captured aspects of herself she considered important, and for one of the images she decided to showcase her Métis relations, braiding her hair and wearing feathered earrings. "I can really see the Indian," her teacher said. "You look like Pocahontas."

Confusion turned to anger at the teacher, for a comment rooted in stereotypes, and then at herself, questioning if she had invited this by the way she had staged her own photograph. Her experience and reaction were familiar to me and every person on that panel.

After the photographer hired by the magazine left my apartment, I logged onto the electronic rez, our nickname for the Native Net bulletin board service popular in the 1990s. Foreshadowing Galenkamp's reaction almost three decades later, I was confused by what happened, then angry at the photographer for putting me in that position, and finally at myself for going along with it.

After I'd poured this out on the message board, a Lakota friend responded, assuring me that jeans and a white T-shirt were his traditional clothes. James was Oglala Lakota and lived on the Pine Ridge Reservation in South Dakota—which, because of Hollywood as well as the connection the Oglala Lakota have with the American Indian Movement, made him something of a rock star to me at that time.[11] He was the realest of real Indians, a Bad Indian, one might say. The photographer had left me feeling disconnected and artificial, James drew me back in.

---

11 Was? Is? I don't even know his last name, so I have no way of knowing if he is still with us, but over the years I have shared this story with a few other Lakota from Pine Ridge on the off chance that they recognize something in it. James, if you're out there! Miigwech.

When we tell the stories of others, through writing or photography, we exert a kind of control over them. We make choices about how to dress or describe, what to emphasize, and what to leave out.

For both Galenkamp and I, these experiences were an outrage against how the dominating world sees us but also a reminder about the way that we see others in our writing and photography. What are we framing, capturing, and then interpreting for the world? Memoir allows us to make our own choices about this framing, capturing, and interpreting. And, as Curtice notes in the epigraph, this framing and interpreting changes over time. As we pick up more pieces of ourselves, gain access to more fragments, we may see them differently. We grow and hold space for each other, hopefully viewing our long-ago selves with kindness even while we reorder the things that no longer make sense.

• • •

One of our panelists for this conversation about memoir, Demita Frazier (African American) was interviewed by Keeanga-Yamahtta Taylor for *How We Get Free: Black Feminism and the Combahee River Collective*, a collection of transcribed interviews forming a kind of collective memoir. As Frazier talked about the important work of the Combahee River Collective in developing and offering a vocabulary of collective resistance, she reflected on gaps caused by the ways that Black women are typically vanished from the historic record and the importance of memoir in bringing light to these gaps. Black women's role in organizing and community building is often disregarded or relegated to the supporting role offered to mothers whose caretaking makes it possible for men to do the Real Work, just as early feminism erased the labour of Black women in the liberation of white women.

The women of Combahee wrestled with expressing personal power while working together to achieve collective goals: individual autonomy alongside the needs of the many. This is consistent with the way that many Anishinaabe stories teach us how to govern ourselves: communities rooted in both collective good and a deep respect for individual autonomy. Frazier said "the quest for freedom was never about individual freedom. It was really about the collective freedom from the oppressions that we suffered as Black women and as Black people."[12]

In late 2023, the hand drum group I belonged to was looking for ways to support the Muslim and Palestinian women in our community. At that time, it was almost impossible to get aid into Gaza. But rather than thinking about what we could not do, we thought about what we could. We invited them to join us for an evening of drumming and talking together. Understanding that our freedom is bound up together, we offered them hospitality and care, a gesture that grew into multiple events, across multiple communities.

This collective care, as opposed to individualistic and commodified "self-care," is reflected in the memoirs of many marginalized writers. That "we" in the title of the book about the Combahee River Collective is an *us that includes you*. We are not free unless we are all free.[13]

Reaching into the gaps for the stories of those often left behind reminds us to look for the gaps in our own spaces. It reminds us to consider who is missing and why; through these stories the people being excluded offer us reasons for their absence, explanations for who has access to certain spaces and under what conditions. These stories may be uncomfortable, but they can also be transformative if they help us to apply that awareness to our own spaces—to not only notice the gaps and the barriers but respond to them as well.

---

12 *Ambe: Memoir.* https://www.thousandworlds.ca/ambe-memoir/.

13 This adage is heard frequently in twentieth-century Black writers. Audre Lorde: "I am not free while any woman is unfree"; Maya Angelou: "The truth is, no one of us can be free until everybody is free"; Fannie Lou Hamer: "Nobody's free until everybody's free"; and Martin Luther King: "No one is free until we are all free." In the late 1800s, Jewish poet Emma Lazarus said, "Until we are all free, none of us are free."

We all belong somewhere, and reading these stories of collective care can help us to mobilize in ways that overcome gaps and barriers. In that sense, reading these memoirs can be a kind of prerequisite—a 101 course that helps us to enter new spaces with an openness to hearing about other experiences.

• • •

The *us that includes you* can also mean the land. In her memoir, *From a Native Daughter: Colonialism and Sovereignty in Hawai'i*, Haunani-Kay Trask (Native Hawaiian) refers often to Native Hawaiians' genealogical relationship to land, something Keolu Fox (Kānaka 'ōiwi) also says and that he, a geneticist, identifies as a scientific rather than mythic statement.[14] Creation stories around the world typically describe the people emerging from the land in some way, connecting us to our homes through genealogy, not conquest.[15] Trask and Fox emphasize that relationship to remind us that we-including-you includes the land and all that comes from it. This is the heart of the Land Back movement: not a shift in possession but a shift in relationship.

Black memoir often seeks that rootedness, with writers feeling the displacement of being uprooted and forcibly relocated again and again, as the people of the diaspora look for a place to be at home. In her memoir, *I Am Woman*, Lee Maracle (Sto: lo) offers belonging to the Black diaspora, saying that they have found their place here in a way that settlers, whose actions imposed another way of life on top of Indigenous peoples, have not. She does not deny the hardships faced by some white

---

14 Trask and Fox are both from the islands of Hawai'i; the difference in marking reflects how they have identified themselves. Trask used the term as political strategy to remind those who settled on the islands that they are not native to that place.

15 This is the crux of the problem with having a global creation story in which everybody's genealogy traces back to a garden in what is called the Middle East. If that's our true birthplace, then nobody really belongs anywhere, and conquest is all we've got for asserting belonging or authority.

settlers who were exploited and harmed, but she notes that they found belonging not through relationship with the land and the people of that land but through oppression: by aligning themselves with power against Black and Indigenous peoples. They enacted the very harms they experienced on us. In contrast, she says, the Black diaspora formed relationship with the land and the people of that land.[16] History and memoir are filled with the stories and experiences of solidarity dating back to the original arrivants.

Edwidge Danticat (Haitian American) writes about the impacts of migration and exile throughout *Create Dangerously: The Immigrant Artist at Work*, but it is her discussion of the Creole word *dyaspora* that caught my attention. More than a simple dispersal of people to foreign lands, in Creole it refers specifically to hundreds of thousands of Haitians scattered around the world. Like Indigenous, dyaspora is a political category that describes their relationship to not only the states where they reside but their home community as well. Being a dyaspora, writes Danticat, is a title like Mr. or Miss that describes her distance from the landscapes of home. Many of us write from the edges of our own communities as well, with feet in both worlds.[17]

This yearning of diasporic people to go home is something that Rinaldo Walcott (Black/Caribbean/Canadian) explores in his essay "Diaspora against the Nation-State." He observes that historically, state-sponsored returns of African Americans to places in Africa failed everybody. The returnees come back with suitcases filled with the authority of the state who sent them home to save the savages left behind, and homecoming looks suspiciously like conquest.[18] We do this too,

---

16 Lee Maracle, *I Am Woman: A Native Perspective on Sociology and Feminism* (Pressgang Publishers, 1996), 120.

17 Edwidge Danticat, *Create Dangerously: The Immigrant Artist at Work* (Vintage Books, 2010, 2011), 50.

18 Rinaldo Walcott, "Diaspora against the Nation-State," *Briarpatch Magazine*, April 8, 2024.

educated natives going back to reserves, confident in their knowledge of how things should be done. But it is not about blood and never has been; it is about how we enter the land and form relationships.

Reflecting on trips to Dakar and then Palestine, Ta-Nehisi Coates writes about this desire to go home. The creation of very specific places where we are said to belong creates people who belong nowhere, and we all want to belong somewhere, to have a place that is home. But for diasporic peoples, home is too often a place that exists only in our imagination. He writes about the Door of No Return on the island of Gorée in Senegal and the city of David in Jerusalem, their significance in the stories told about them, not in the historical record.[19] It is not what it once was. The land and the people went on without us, and if we are not careful in how we go home, we will see only our own reflections and not the people who are there.

But as Rabbi Alissa Wise noted in chapter 2, there is both belonging and disruptive potential in diaspora itself, in the border-crossing relationships that form between us when people enter land in a good way and then welcome others, when we bend toward a common purpose and refuse to create our own myths of conquest. To return to Walcott, diaspora challenges the nation-state because it changes our perspective on what it means to belong: We belong to each other not to the state. Diaspora reminds us that we are not atoms in the universe; we are not discrete groups with bordered homelands. We are stories, a thousand worlds held together by the connections between us.

In *The Cooking Gene*, James Beard Award–winning author, chef, and historic interpreter Michael W. Twitty (Black/Jewish) recounts what he called the Southern Discomfort Tour, in which he travelled through the southeastern United States, looking through archives for family records, meeting with cooks and people working on projects promoting food autonomy in the Black diaspora, and working on plantations as an

---

19 Coates, 2024. Gorée as imagined origin on page 52. The mythologizing of the City of David on pages 201–2.

interpreter, doing the cooking labour his ancestors would have done and interpreting that work for guests. Like Sara Calvosa Olsen (Karuk) in the cookbook *Chimi Nu'am*, Twitty weaves together his family and spiritual history through food, describing it as memory, a mnemonic device through which we tell and retell stories of ancestors, preparing dishes and repeating phrases that connect us to those who have gone before.[20] Twitty is a convert to Judaism, and I have learned somebody raised Jewish will often welcome converts by saying "you were with us at Sinai." This is beautiful, and adds a layer of meaning to Twitty's description of food in this way while he talks about Passover. Food as a mnemonic device connects him to Sinai and everything in between just as it connects him to enslaved ancestors and Africa. Like Olsen, he looks broadly for the people and the food, from ingredients to meals, to create intricate layers of relationship and belonging that stretch across oceans.

Living in a way that our words align with our actions extends not only to the stories we tell about the food and the way it connects us through time to ancestors but also the way it connects us to each other. When I visited with Olsen during a trip to Santa Cruz, California, she took me to the Pie Ranch, a collective whose vision of regenerative farming and food system education led them to form relationships with the Indigenous peoples around them to create a program of antiracist education alongside food system justice. Not only is the property shaped like a wedge of pie, but, in addition to everything else they do, they sell delicious handmade pies. While in their shop I picked up a copy of *Feed the Resistance*, a cookbook and "handbook for feeding your political activism." Standing on the West Coast, I thought about my middle son on an island off the eastern coast of Canada, up to his elbows in fifty pounds of ground beef, making hamburgers to raise money for local communities.

---

20 Michael W. Twitty, *The Cooking Gene: A Journey through African American Culinary History in the Old South* (Amistad, 2017, 2018), 72.

Indigenous presence is threaded throughout Twitty's memoir, both modelling and exploring the kind of solidarities I am constantly seeking in the literary and social margins. Like many in the Black diaspora, Twitty has stories of distant Native ancestors that may or may not be true. While I am reluctant to hear this from white people, it is typically a way to ignore their settler heritage and find a kind of innocence by identifying with the oppressed, I am aware enough of our own anti-Blackness to know that for many generations, a Black Creek child who may have become Twitty's ancestor might not have found belonging in her Creek community.[21]

That family story prompted him to find relationship rather than identity—to look for the ways that land and food helped his ancestors form connections with Southern tribes. Food and cultivation are some of the many ways that our communities overlapped and shared knowledge with each other. Twitty situates the roots of Southern hospitality in the domestic labour of Africans from Senegal, Gambia, and other ethnic groups who valued teranga: peaceful living through the hospitable treatment of others. The generosity of our ancestors flows back and forth between us.

The story of Thanksgiving is also a story of Indigenous generosity, an ethic of peaceful living through the hospitable treatment of others that is also echoed in the traditional stories that shape our lives. Unfortunately, it is not a story of reciprocal generosity flowing back and forth between communities. On Thanksgiving Day in 1970, 350 years after the Mayflower arrived, some members of the American Indian Movement participated in a protest organized by local Wampanoag—Everett "Tall Oak" Weeden, Frank James, James Frasier, and perhaps others—who wanted to confront historic wrongs, particularly regarding those in Wampanoag country that are rarely publicized. Earlier, the town of Plymouth had asked Frank James to give a speech at the 350th anniversary of the landing of the Mayflower, a speech they censored for

21 You will recall the story of Shoe Boots and Doll from chapter 3.

telling the truth about that history. Rather than be silenced, the Wampanoag staged a protest that included covering the famous rock in sand and taking over the *Mayflower II*, a replica of the original built in England and sailed over in 1957. Russell Means (Oglala Lakota) gave a speech in which he praised the Wampanoag for their generosity, without which the Pilgrims likely would have starved, and then castigated the settlers for exploiting that generosity.

Early in 2024, I went to see that rock. I had given a lecture in a small university about thirty minutes from Plymouth and decided to make a stop before going home. It was underwhelming, particularly when I learned that it wasn't the actual rock that the *Mayflower* passengers stepped on as they came ashore. That rock might not even exist, and the one that is celebrated and protected was brought from farther inland. The whole story, from feast to rock, is more myth than history, one that erases the violence of colonial settlement.[22]

A friend told me about Plimoth Patuxet, a nearby museum where you walk through a Wampanoag homesite as well as a Pilgrim village as they would have existed in 1627. It opened the year after the protest in Plymouth and for a while it was a promising collaboration between settlers and the Wampanoag, in which history was made tangible. I've been to such villages before, costumed performers playing the role assigned to them, in this case Pilgrims recently arrived from England. This kind of performance can be powerful and interesting, but in this case, I found it sad and troubling. After forty years of good work, the

22 On August 19, 2024, the *Cape Cod Times* reported that the town of Plymouth will no longer be including official land acknowledgements in board or committee meetings because they "could have future binding implications." I have very mixed feelings about land acknowledgements, but in this I am somewhat intrigued by the concession that they could actually be an admission of responsibility although disheartened by the response. Rather than agree that some reparations are in order, they decided to pretend that it has always been theirs.

museum has taken a downward turn, and the Wampanoag have not only withdrawn their participation but are actively boycotting it.

On the day that I went, the Pilgrim village was staffed with costumed performers offering historic performance in the first person, talking with me as if it was 1627 and I was a visitor from another village. In the Wampanoag homesite I found only contemporary interpreters telling me what the Indians were like at the time. It had the jarring effect of making the Puritans feel accessible and interesting while making the Wampanoag remote and invisible. Barely ghosts in their own village, a handful of Wampanoag and Native staff do remain, hanging onto the remnants of a once flourishing exhibit site. However, they work alongside white docents, and no one receives proper training in the history, interpretation, or seventeenth-century skills, and neither site is well maintained.

I went to this village with Twitty's memoir on my mind and a blog post he wrote about working as an interpreter in Southern plantation museums. In the blog post he confronts a two-star review left by somebody who had toured a plantation, expressing dismay about the tour guide's "radical" lecture about slavery. He refuses the title of reenactor and describes his role of interpreter as somebody who is charged with educating people about the past. In response to white dismay over a radical lecture of slavery that made her feel uncomfortable about something she says she didn't do, he says something interesting about that role: "I take my job seriously, because frankly you're not the one I'm centring on," Twitty wrote. "I'm performing an act of devotion to my Ancestors. This is not about your comfort or anyone else's, it's about honoring their story on its own terms, in context."[23]

It is easy, when performing as an interpreter or a drum group or a writer, to forget who we do this for. To shift and adapt ourselves for

---

23 Michael W. Twitty, "Dear Disgruntled White Plantation Visitors, Sit Down," *Afroculinaria*, August 9, 2019, https://afroculinaria.com/2019/08/09/dear-disgruntled-white-plantation-visitors-sit-down/.

the audience, and too often that audience is white. The numbers, both demographically and financially, take on outsized importance. When my Wampanoag friend was involved with the Plimoth Patuxet museum, she felt as Twitty does, that the work the Wampanoag were doing was not only about educating (mostly) white tourists but about honouring the story of her ancestors and telling their stories on their own terms and in context. She told me that the first-person style of interpretation used in the Pilgrim village didn't work on the Wampanoag homesite. There, interpreters used a third-person style of interpretation, speaking about the past while enacting seventeenth-century Wampanoag life throughout the exhibit site. This allowed interpreters to present much more accurately about the past, educate the visitors, and answer questions; to express history from their own perspective and in that way, perform an act of devotion to their ancestors.

People can, and do, accuse us of letting people put us on display. And there is a risk when we dress up in beads and buckskin, braid our hair and put on feathered earrings, when we don ribbon skirts to sing on the stages of those whose policies and practices harm our communities, or allow photographers to remake us in the image that exists in their imagination. There is a risk when we allow ourselves to centre the audience who doesn't care about Indigenous rights or land or anything beyond our existence as what novelist John le Carré (unmarked) calls "decorative beasts." There is a risk when we allow their concerns and feelings to shape our actions and our stories.

Decorative beasts. Le Carré writes in *The Looking Glass War,* "The marble fireplace was supported by blackamoors of ebony; the light of the gas fireplace played over the gilded rose-chains which linked their thick ankles. The fireplace came from an age, it might have been the seventeenth century, it might have been the nineteenth, when blackamoors had briefly replaced Borzois as the decorative beasts of society."[24]

---

24 John Le Carré, *The Looking Glass War* (Penguin Group, 1965), 122.

Ruth Wilson Gilmore (African American) uses le Carré's description, which illustrates the way that western society diminishes the people it racialized as being beneath them, rendering them as objects that are decorative and functional, when she writes about places of learning, and refusing the role that racially marginalized people have been allocated.[25] In the academy, as well as in organizations and in politics, too often we are decorative beasts: Good Indians and diversity hires meant to do nothing but adorn mastheads and perhaps stand off to the side and slightly behind, lending credibility to white institutions. Haunani-Kay Trask's memoir, *From a Native Daughter: Colonialism and Sovereignty in Hawai'i*, describes the conflicts that resulted from her refusal to play this role at the University of Hawai'i—what happened when she chose instead, as Bad Indians do, to centre Native Hawaiian knowledge and priorities.

In various ways, each of the memoirs we read for this conversation addresses the opportunities and consequences of such refusal in whatever sphere the author is writing from. This makes the question of our audience, who we write, photograph, perform, or interpret for, critically important.

Part of our conversation about memoir addressed that question, because it is important as a writer and a reader. Writers always think about their audience, who are we writing for, but readers need to think about this as well. Who is the memoirist writing for? What is *my* relationship to that audience? The panel included two published memoirists (Curtice and Hayes), two in the midst of writing memoirs (Henderson and Frazier), a photographer (Galenkamp), and myself deep in the midst of writing and revising *Becoming Kin*. It was a question that Kerry and I talked about as well throughout our podcast, *Medicine for the Resistance*. Who was our audience? The answer to that question shapes both what and how we write, how photographs and stories are framed and captured for interpretation.

25 Ruth Wilson Gilmore, *Abolition Geography* (Verso, 2022), 51.

Becoming Kin was written for the various communities I am part of, but primarily it was intended for the white Christians I grew up with and those I often find myself talking or organizing with who retain the politics but reject the justifications offered by theology. *The Tao of Raven* by Hayes and *Native* by Curtice were also primarily for white people—as responses to the persistent questions and "I never knew" that so many marginalized people have to deal with.[26]

The Tao of Raven weaves together the Tlingit story of Raven stealing the sun and bringing light to the world with Hayes's own life. The Tao is an ancient belief arising from the people Indigenous to what is now the Henan province of China about the natural order of the universe that underlies everything, a pathway, as Machado says in his poem "There Is No Road," that we make by walking. In the Tlingit story of Raven he takes a very long path: becoming a pine needle to impregnate a young woman who gives birth to a child that eventually tricks his grandfather into opening the boxes that contain the sun, moon, and stars brightening the world while leaving the house itself in darkness. Against this backdrop Hayes tells her own story, as well as that of US nation building and subsequent displacement of Alaska natives. Taking our cues from Raven, we too must be moved by compassion, and willing to take a long path in order to bring light into a dark world.

Curtice's *Native* also uses memoir to confront the generational impacts of colonization and US nation building on her and her family. She addresses it from within the Christian faith and writes bluntly about the way that the church has provided theological cover to these colonial projects and the nations they built.[27] It is too easy to blame it on "bad Christians" or people who were not "real Christians" or some

26 If you find yourself thinking "I never knew" when you learn about an injustice, or deceptive way that history is taught, that provides you an opportunity for action. Why didn't you know, who benefits from people like you not knowing? Then do something about that.

27 Theological cover is the beliefs that make it okay to do the bad thing.

version of these excuses, but the truth is that theology hasn't changed much from those years. Churches rely on the same commentaries, sing the same hymns, and preach the same sermons about Christian exceptionalism.[28] Her memoir ends on a hopeful note: Her sons are being raised with greater connection to their ancestors and the land that remembers them.

I remain intrigued by Twitty's remark that even while he knew that working as a historic interpreter, his audience would be primarily the white tourists who flock to these living museums and through their entrance fees, pay his wages, he refuses them as his central focus. His work is an act of devotion for his ancestors.

I hear echoes of Twitty's response to white indignation in the desire of marginalized writers to write for themselves, something voiced by Ernestine Hayes and endorsed by the rest of us. Hayes talked about her first two books being for a largely white audience—the people who keep being surprised that Alaska Natives still exist. She said that she wanted her next book to be for her. Curtice said something similar, the necessity and exhaustion of writing books as a way of answering the same questions she is asked again and again. We want to emulate Toni Morrison, who said that she had decided early in her career that she would write for her neighbours, consciously writing for a Black American audience.[29]

It always amazed me that so many of the people who took the time to tell Kerry or me how much they loved our podcast identified themselves as white or settlers, because they were not our intended audience.

---

28 If you do go to church, and your church has a hymnal, look at the years that the hymns you sing were written, and think about what was going on at that time socially and politically. Think about how marginalized people might have heard those words or experienced the beliefs that flowed from them.

29 Myles Burke, "In History: Toni Morrison on Why 'Writing for Black People Is Tough," BBC, February 12, 2024, https://www.bbc.com/culture/article/20240209-in-history-toni-morrison-on-why-writing-for-black-people-is-tough.

The title of the podcast itself, *Medicine for the Resistance*, told you who it was for: We wanted to offer medicine to those who resist dominant narratives, and in our minds that was people like us: Black and Indigenous. We cleared space and told our own stories in a way that was bold and frank, inviting scientists, historians, writers, and poets, all of us at-risk and asterisk people. We created a space that was hostile to those who meant us harm while welcoming to those violently pushed to the margins. Together we refused to be the Good Ones, to be decorative beasts. We did not filter our conversation to accommodate white feelings.

Decorative beasts are an alibi, Gilmore tells us—living symbols who illustrate the ideological triumphs of western thought over all others. She also notes that this provides opportunity. I like to imagine a time when these decorative beasts break free of the concrete encasing them, just as Nanaboozhoo will one day step out of the stone in which he waits. We are living in a moment of opportunity, with access to platforms and resources, books and equipment. Do not mistake decorative beasts for Good Indians—although some may be, I don't know. There are many others waiting for the time to be right, surviving until the inevitable crisis sets us free.

How incredibly refreshing those conversations were for Kerry and for me. I told her that I had not realized how exhausting that filtering was until I was able to stop doing it. These conversations I convened about books, in which we were reading at the edges of a thousand worlds, were similar, in that the white people we included knew what they were getting into. These were discussions from the mashkiig, drawing on the wisdom and medicines there, with no intention of saving or reforming a society that had pushed us aside. We sought to tell stories that showed the truths of our lives. We sought to make an act of devotion for our ancestors, whose footsteps marked a path we could follow, those whose stories we could lift in our hands as living weapons against further displacement.

Kwe

The diner is briefly, blissfully, almost empty. It's that lull between the breakfast and lunch crowds, when you can stop and drink your own coffee before it gets cold, so you do. You keep an eye on the tables where stragglers finish their plates and cups and chat with friends before looking around to gesture for the cheque or a refill or something you forgot to bring them.

You breathe deeply. The diner doesn't smell like cigarette smoke anymore, not like it used to, anyway. The smell still comes inside, clinging to flannel jackets and backpacks, but it's been at least a decade since you had to empty out ashtrays while clearing tables, and for that you are grateful. It's not because you mind the smokers, as you smudge your own lungs regularly; but what a mess the ashtrays made in the dish bin.

"Miss? Hello?" The man sitting alone at a window booth snaps his fingers at you like he's sitting in a fancy café instead of an anonymous diner in Thunder Bay.

Sighing, you put down your coffee. So close to having an entire cup while it's hot. You smile brightly as you walk over, feeling your long black braid bouncing against your back, and ask, "yes, what can I get for you?" He holds up a credit card, so you pull his bill out of your apron and remind him that you can take him at the cash register. He acts like it's an inconvenience to gather his things and follow you to the counter, but he does, the waft of his expensive cologne trailing behind both of you. You run his card through the machine and notice the scant tip he left you.

Hours later your shift ends during the lull between lunch and dinner. You cash out your tips, say your goodbyes, and head out the door.

It's warm for late fall, so you decide to walk along the waterfront and watch the big ships before it gets dark. You've never been farther south than Thunder Bay, and the ships laden with Prairie wheat and containers that rode trains all the way from Vancouver are still exciting. You know it's not what the containers say, but you smile every time you see the ones you once misread as "Happy Lloyd." For a moment you're jealous of their travels. But you grew up on a northern rez, and Thunder Bay is enough city for you.

It starts to get chilly when the sun sinks below the sleeping form of Nanaboozhoo, so you tug on your sweater and stand up to go home. Misho will assume you've stopped to watch the ships and the sunset, but if you're late, he worries. Too many relatives disappearing like fallen feathers into that inky water and the ships that travel on it. It's just you and him now.

Your own parents disappeared into bigger cities on different ends of the country, trying to get as far away from each other as they could, leaving you with your Misho and Kookum. You left Cat Lake for high school and got stuck in Thunder Bay. When he couldn't live alone anymore, your uncle dropped him here and continued on to Winnipeg. It's okay, though. He knows a lot of the old stories, and you like to listen to them, especially in the winter, when he tells the stories he can't tell until there is snow on the ground.

As you turn away from the water and begin the walk home to Bay Street, you hear footsteps that wouldn't be alarming except you smell that cologne you noticed in the restaurant and feel a shiver of real fear. You hurry down another block, but the footsteps keep pace, and right in that lull between streetlights, in the cover of dark he grabs your shoulder and pushes you face first against the wall, holding you there with his forearm.

Before he can do anything else, however, the pressure is gone. You turn yourself around carefully. There's a woman with a fistful of that cashmere coat he's wearing in her hand and is lifting him right off the ground. Holay she's tall! Must be Cree, you think, maybe Lakota. They're tall, aren't they?

"You need to get out of here," she says. Nodding, you run down the final block toward home, turning back just before you round the corner. And what?

You stop and blink. The shadows must be playing tricks, because it looks like that Cree or maybe Lakota woman has antlers. And now that you think about it, her feet looked strange too. Like her shoes were small and rounded to look like hooves. Misho told you that story, but you thought it was like all his other stories. Or maybe his other stories are like this one.

• • •

The next morning you go to work like you always do. The diner is full of gossip and chatter.

A dead body was found in the water last night. It was the body of a businessman from Toronto. The newspaper says that his neck was broken, and the gossips say that he was trampled. They tell each other about hoofprints nearby, and about the round bruises. But they have never heard of anyone being trampled by deer anywhere, let alone in the city. The white gossips laugh at the ridiculous story, but the darker faces speak quietly in Anishinaabemowin.

You notice an old woman in a floral headscarf reading the paper and smiling into her coffee. She's bent over, but you can see that she's tall. Like a Cree or Lakota, maybe.

You walk over with the coffeepot and then slide into the booth across from her. It's the only tobacco you've got, so you slide your pack of smokes over and look into her older but very familiar eyes.

She smiles, and reaching out, she covers your hand along with the pack of smokes, saying, "Miigwech, my girl."

6

ANISHAA DIBAAJIMOWINAN

We talk about honoring our ancestors, our elders, but I want to promise you, Anishinaabeg of the future, that we do the work we do because we honor you as well—you are our "desirable future"—not through the amazing, badass work that you are going to undoubtedly do, but because you are Anishinaabeg—you are our wildest dreams come to life. Because you will be proof that no matter how hard it tries, settler colonialism will never extinguish our presence, our lifeways, our relationships with land and environment, and our hopes and dreams. I hope that we can do work to make you proud of us, because we are already proud of you.

—Niiyokamigaabaw Deondre Smiles (Black Ojibwe),
To the Anishinaabeg of the Future

BEFORE THERE WERE stories, somewhere in West Africa there was Ananzi. He travelled the countryside and saw how hard the people worked. He watched them rest at the end of long days, and their quietness troubled him. Maybe they sang songs and danced to the drum, but the movements were directionless and the songs had no words. It was as if they were alone despite being together.

Ananzi knew what he would do. He spun a web that took him into the sky and presented himself to Nyame, the sky god who held all the stories of the world. After some back and forth, Nyame agreed to give Ananzi the stories if Ananzi would complete a series of tasks. The tasks seemed impossible. Ananzi is a spider, after all, but he is also clever. And we know he succeeded, because we have stories.[1]

Anishaa dibaajimowinan: "stories we just thought up." What are these thought-up stories if not letters to the future? Proof that no matter how hard it tries, settler colonialism, and the nations it created, will never extinguish our presence and all that goes with it. Dadibaajim is an act of devotion to our ancestors, but it is also an act of devotion to those yet to come: those we believe will exist despite attempts to extinguish us. And telling stories we just thought up is also an act of devotion to each other, this telling of stories, this shaping of ourselves as people.

Bad Indians know that the universe is, as Muriel Rukeyser says, made up of stories and not atoms. It is made up of these connections between us. These connections will, with care and attention, become living entities in their own right. Bad Indians, even with our deadly sense of humour, take that life seriously.

Anishinaabe stories are often bawdy and at times might be considered vulgar. We have a story about a woman who married a giant penis—a story I love to tell, because I get to say that he was a real dick. On the face of it, it is a ridiculous story, but it is also a story about a woman who acted with agency in an abusive relationship. There is no condemnation of her, no judgement. He was abusive; she dealt with it. (She didn't kill him, but she did reduce his capacity for harm.) One of my teachers, Stephanie Stephens (Anishinaabe), says that the bawdier the story, the more we should pay attention to the details, because they contain important information. It's easy to focus on the ridiculous nature of the story, important to pay attention to her ability to take action and the long-term consequences. Imagine living in a world where

---

1 A much longer and more detailed version of this story is told by Kesha Christie (Afro-Caribbean) of Talkin Tales on the *Ambe* podcast episode "The Stories We Tell." https://www.thousandworlds.ca/the-stories-we-tell/. Miigwech Kesha for your generosity and laughter. You bring joy even to my memories.

women experiencing violence were taken seriously, where their consent was valued, and their autonomy respected.

Stories have been with us for a very long time. Pictographs like those at Agawa Bay in Lake Superior and visible throughout Anishinaabe aki are images telling ancient stories that people still know. Images, like our stories, that are alive and worth honouring with tobacco or other offerings.

Toni Morrison, in her essay "Rootedness: The Ancestor as Foundation," attributes the popularity of the contemporary novel to the rising middle class and its isolation from extended family and community, where the stories we just thought up have traditionally been held. Morrison explains that in the absence of multigenerational families and stable communities, we needed some way to teach each other how to be human.[2] We needed to teach others how we express our humanity, to learn to live together in communities that are constantly coalescing and remaking themselves. Novels become a kind of permanence in an impermanent world.

Novels don't solve our troubles, but they do offer us other ways to look at the things that trouble us. For Richard Wagamese-ba, writing, from his journalism to his fiction and memoir, was a constant search for belonging and connection, exploring the things that troubled him about his personal history and our collective history as people within a nation built on our displacement.

One June evening I sat amidst the pines at Bruce National Park, near the tip of a peninsula separating Georgian Bay from Lake Huron, and talked by video with a group of Indigenous people about his writings. Wagamese had passed away a few years earlier, and the group included a close friend of his and a handful of others who had read some of his books.

---

2 Toni Morrison, "Rootedness: The Ancestor as Foundation," *Black Women Writers (1950–1980): A Critical Evaluation*, ed. Mari Evans (Anchor Doubleday, 1984), 340.

In many ways my life has travelled a similar path to that of Wagamese, the shadow of Nanaboozhoo stretching over both of our lives. Our Ojibwe relatives are from northwestern Ontario, his from Kenora and mine from Sioux Lookout. We were both raised in St. Catharines, Ontario, by white families; his were adoptive parents and mine were my maternal family. We both felt the dislocation from the land and our families, spending much of our lives with an empty feeling inside that wouldn't go away no matter what we did. Daniel Delgado (Quechua, Jewish), who participated in that discussion, told us he felt himself connecting deeply with the way that Wagamese articulated the longing. As a person living between two diasporas, he felt that longing too.

One of the beautiful things about Wagamese's fiction and nonfiction is the importance of land. I don't mean only the spellbinding description of Frank Starlight running with elk beneath the moon in his posthumously published novel *Starlight*. I mean, too, the urban landscapes of *Ragged Company*, where unhoused Indigenous relatives find community and belonging through the storytelling of a movie house, because we belong in urban spaces too. The concrete and asphalt covering everything are repurposed and recombined, but they are still relatives who come from the land even if we don't recognize them. Mined and moved, concrete and asphalt are just as displaced as we are. That sense of belonging is in the relationships between us, and as Ojibwe Anishinaabe, Wagamese knew that the land is part of those relationships.

In her book *We Measure the Earth with Our Bodies*, Tsering Yangzom Lama (Tibetan) writes about a family's flight from Tibet, their decades in a refugee camp, and then their move to Toronto. Beginning in the 1950s, it follows two sisters who journey across the Himalayas and into the exile of the Tibetan diaspora. There is an ancient statue, the Nameless Saint, that is said to vanish and reappear in times of need which Dolma, the daughter of one sister, finds in an art collector's vault. The artifacts of colonized people frequently wind up in art collections and museums—one more thing about us that requires restoration.

The title refers to the act of prayer in which the petitioner moves along the ground, stretching out their body again and again to stay in contact with the earth. The Chinese occupation of their land restricts their movement through the use of travel permits. Tibetans can no longer move freely in their own country, and as migrants, they cannot move freely elsewhere either. If measuring the earth with your body is a spiritual practice, and I would say that it is, then in addition to being a physical and social violence, this restriction of movement is also spiritual violence.

Anishinaabe do this too, not by prostrating ourselves but by walking. Our earliest stories are about Nanaboozhoo walking the earth and then walking it again with a wolf. Walking it again with a wolf meant seeing it again, seeing it the way that his companion saw it, experiencing it differently. We measure the earth by travelling along it, by placing our feet and our bodies in contact with the land that knows us. In that way, we petition our mother to care for us, to remember us, to take pity on us.

Monica Byrnes' (Irish American) novel *The Actual Star* contains three layered stories told in the past, present, and future, all converging at the Actun Tunichil Muknal (ATM) cave in Belize. The cave is a Mayan archaeological site, believed by ancient and some contemporary Mayans to be one of many entry points to the Mayan underworld of Xibalba. The novel centres on Mayan cosmology, particularly the nature of Xibalba and, by extension, the nature of the world that we live in. The protagonists of each story are the same people, reincarnating again and again. The past tells the story of twin rulers and their younger sister in the twilight of the Mayan empire of 1012; the present focuses on a white Belizean girl from Minnesota and twin brothers who work as ATM tour guides in 2012; and the future is a world that emerged from catastrophic climate change and war, a restructured world without borders, permanent settlements, or family connections.

Niloux, the protagonist in the 3012 storyline, develops a practice of asking the gods of each place if they know her, a practice that reminded me of my own experience of being remembered and an interesting way to think about belonging. Rather than the idea that a particular piece of land *belongs to* the Anishinaabe, it suggests that the land (and the gods of that place) *know* the Anishinaabe. This is consistent with the way that many of my teachers have talked about our relationship to Anishinaabe aki. The land (and the gods of that place) may know others as well. I had not asked the gods of Lac Seul if they knew me, not in so many words, but they reached back anyway.

Three years after that discussion about Wagamese, I'm back at Bruce National Park, and this time I offer tobacco to the waters and a cedar, asking if I am known or possibly remembered. I hear this petition in the writings of Wagamese and Louise Erdrich. Erdrich, like Wagamese, reaches deeply into urban and rural places to tell the stories of Ojibwe people and the lands that know them. They both write about our complicated belonging to place and each other, asking constantly if and how they are known.

I hear this petition, too, in the writing of Tommy Orange, who wrote the beautiful and heartbreaking novel *There There* as well as the prequel and follow-up *Wandering Stars*. Both novels tell the connected and overlapping stories of a group of urban Native American families, who measure the earth with their bodies and stories, asking the land and each other if they are known.

I hear this petition in the writings of other marginalized people, like Tsering Yangzom Lama and Omar El Akkad (Egyptian), who seek belonging and connection in lands far from home. I hear it in Toni Morrison's *Beloved* and Kai Thomas's (Afro-Canadian) *In the Upper Country*, as enslaved people and their descendants measure an unfamiliar land with their bodies and ask if they are known. I hear it in the writings of peoples displaced across oceans or mountain ranges, one way or another separated from the land that knows them.

These fictions tell the stories of how we measure the earth with our bodies, our feet, asking again and again if the gods of this place know us.

• • •

I first connected with Omar El Akkad after reading his novel *American War*. It is set in a not-too-distant future in which the United States has descended into another civil war, and it asks important questions about relationship and belonging in the context of refugee camps and a reconfigured state. It's an excellent book.

I read *American War* right after I heard Justice talk about looking for us in the future. Do Indigenous people show up in a writer's vision of the future? So I tweeted out that *American War* was just about the saddest book I'd read, and that I wondered, as I read it, where the Indigenous people had gone. Did I miss them in the book? Maybe I missed them, I said.

El Akkad responded to my tweet with the generosity and openness I have learned to associate with him, calling it a valid and important criticism. Three years later, his subsequent book, *What Strange Paradise*, set on a fictional island in the Mediterranean, was released. I had not expected to find people who were Indigenous here, on this island over there. And yet there we were.

The opening scene conjures that horrific image of Alan Kurdi, the three-year-old Kurdish Syrian boy whose drowned body washed ashore in 2015 following the wreckage of a migrant ship, but in El Akkad's book the little boy gets up. This is what we all so desperately wanted that September in 2015: for little Alan Kurdi to open his eyes and be okay.

The book is about a migrant ship that capsizes in the Mediterranean and the callousness of people to the crisis of migrants, at various points contrasting the lives of those categorized as migrants with those who are tourists. When the bodies of migrants wash up on the beach of a luxury hotel, the beach is closed for cleanup and retrieval. A sign is posted, and management apologizes for the inconvenience.[3]

The novel has two epigraphs that capture this callousness and set up the context for this magical, tragic story. Ambrose Bierce (unmarked) was a journalist and Civil War veteran who wrote, "It does not appear to be the duty of these two men to know what was occurring at the center of the bridge; they merely blockaded the two ends of the foot planking that traversed it." Then there is Peter's response to Wendy asking if he ever felt love, in English author J. M. Barrie's *Peter Pan*; Peter says, "I taught you to fight and to fly. What more could there be?"[4] These combine to provide the challenge that El Akkad lays before the reader. Wendy is asking about love and Peter dismisses her, just as those whose duty it is to block the ends dismiss what is happening at the centre. If whatever happens in the centre does come to our attention or asks us to care, management apologizes for the inconvenience.

El Akkad repurposes the story of Peter Pan, the boy who never grew up, to tell the story of Amir, the child who got up after washing ashore. Barrie's novel has a shipwreck, an island, a one-legged pirate, and in one part of the story Peter is dressed up like an Indian. El Akkad's novel includes a wrecked migrant ship, an island, and a one-legged colonel searching the island for one small survivor. There is a brief scene in *What Strange Paradise* in which Vänna, the young girl, looking for something dry that Amir can wear, gives him a Cleveland Indians T-shirt she took from a tourist's hotel room. I'm not suggesting El Akkad did this because of my tweet; it's right there in Barrie's book. But my tweet, and his response, did provide another reason for me to reach out

---

3 Omar El Akkad, *What Strange Paradise* (McClelland & Stewart, 2021), 188. In this scene, caution tape had closed access to the beach while morgue workers cleared the bodies that had washed ashore. Afterwards, hotel workers put the lounge chairs back along with a sign apologizing for the inconvenience.

4 El Akkad, epigraph.

to him, and so I did. We had a conversation about his book that confronts so many of the ways that western liberals talk about migrants.[5]

In that conversation, El Akkad talked about the frequent moves he experienced as a child and then an adult, the lack of belonging to any one place that has shaped him and his writing. Like Ziya Tong (earthling) in chapter 2, El Akkad doesn't have a simple answer to the question "where are you from?" That question often implies (if not outright states) that there is a place where we belong, and *this* place is not it. He talked about moving around and being a guest on somebody else's land since he was five years old. Like Amir, El Akkad is rooted in the relationships between people rather than place. These novels—stories we just thought up—become a kind of rootedness, stability in an unstable world.

This is why we often gravitate toward sequels or revisit the novels we have read so often. There is a familiarity, a connection with particular stories or the worlds they create that we long to return to. As a child, I often felt untethered. By the time I was nine, my mother and I had lived in at least four different cities with four different family configurations (five of each, if you include the months we lived with her sister and brother-in-law). I found stability in books—Nancy Drew books, in particular. There was something comforting about the world created by the people who wrote as Carolyn Keene.[6] A stable circle of friends, crimes that got solved, and a defense attorney father who ensured that any sympathetic criminals got a fair shake. It didn't seem to matter that I didn't see myself in those books, as it wasn't myself that I wanted to be at that time anyway.

---

5 The essay I wrote about *What Strange Paradise* does contain spoilers, but if you are interested, you can find it here: https://www.thousandworlds.ca/what-strange-paradise/. Miigwech for your generosity, Omar. I find myself returning to your books and our conversation again and again.

6 Sorry if you didn't know that Carolyn Keene wasn't a single author. I remember being very upset when I learned that.

Last year my husband and I stayed at a hotel in Nipigon, Ontario. There was a bookshelf on the main floor that was filled with Nancy Drew and Hardy Boys books, and our room had a copy of *The Phantom of Pine Hill* (1964), featuring Nancy's boyfriend, Ned, dressed up like an Indian on the cover. Ned and his college classmates were dressed up like Indians for a water pageant—a kind of parade that tells the history of the community but on the river—and Nancy had him help her chase somebody down while he was still in costume. My husband and I laughed about the chances of a book with that cover being in our room. But it really isn't that unusual. High schools and colleges still feature students dressed up like Indians to tell a particular story about their community. How we are seen matters as much as whether or not we are seen; it matters how they invent us, with what intentions, and for what purpose.

• • •

If stories are the connections between us, something we can root ourselves in, I have to return to *The Actual Star* by Monica Byrne and the recurring trio of characters in the past, present, and future stories.[7]

In Mayan cosmology, as in many traditional stories of the so-called Americas and elsewhere, twins are a significant part of beginnings. As a story, twins may offer a way of dealing with duality and tension. In *The Actual Star*, we learn that these three siblings have experienced many more lives than the ones we are following and that they had originally been a pair of twins. Over the millennia of rebirth, the intensity of their care for each other was such that the connection between them became its own person. That seemed deeply profound to me, and I had to put the book down and think about that.

The relationship between two people was such that it became its own entity: What if that's what we're doing when we root our stories in

---

7 Miigwech, Monica! For your writing, for your friendship. For your advice when I planned my own trip to Belize as a result of this book. Next time I'll stay in Cayo.

the relationships between us? What if connection between us becomes something substantive, a being in its own right? What if our relationship to the land of our birth is more than geographical? If the land and the gods of that place know us, then that knowing—not our ownership or historic presence or any such thing—is what creates our belonging. That emphasizes the importance of what Diaz writes in this book's epigraph, how we arrive and build relationship, and then how we welcome others. Perhaps our roots do lie in the connections between us, that "us" including the land that knows us.

To return for a moment to Ananzi and his gift to the people, a story Kesha Christie (Afro-Caribbean) told us during a podcast conversation about storytelling: The way I understand it, without the stories, the people had nothing to bind them together. They had nothing to connect them to the past, nothing to carry them into the future. By giving them stories, his gift to the people was connection.

Louise Erdrich explores stories as beings in *Books & Islands in Ojibwe Country*, in which the living stories of Ojibwe pictographs are painted across the granite islands of Lake of the Woods at the Minnesota–Ontario border. Stories are, Erdrich says, alive in their own right and honoured with gifts by those who visit them. Stories told on granite and birchbark are kept alive and remembered by Anishinaabe over millennia (Anishinaabe presence goes back to at least 2000 BCE, according to archaeologists).[8]

Erdrich asserts that the stories left behind make sense to modern Ojibwe because these stories weren't left behind by ancient peoples who would one day become the Ojibwe. We left them there, us. And our stories prove our presence through time—stories like the one about the giant beaver.

The giant beaver was the largest rodent to live in what would become North America. Bigger than a human, *Castroides ohioensis* was

---

8 Louise Erdrich, *Books & Islands in Ojibwe Country* (Harper Perennial, 2003, 2014), chapter 3.

more linebacker than contemporary beaver. He lived during the last ice age and was one of the large animals that covered this continent during the Paleolithic period. He was discovered in the nineteenth century, and paleontologists don't know if he built dams—because those were built in water with wood, not exactly a recipe for longevity. Paleontologists don't know, but Anishinaabe do.[9]

We have a story about Nanaboozhoo and the giant beaver; it is a traditional story told in a contemporary way by Leanne Betasamosake Simpson in *A Short History of the Blockade.* It makes sense to consider the political strategy of the blockade through the lens of this story about Nanaboozhoo and the giant beaver; because what is a beaver dam if not a blockade? After the giant beaver builds a dam that floods the place where Nanaboozhoo and his grandmother are living, they come up with a plan to catch him and make things right. In the end, rather than simply eliminating the giant beaver or letting him swim away and have his giant dams become somebody else's problem, Nanaboozhoo engages in some diplomacy. And the giant beaver becomes the much smaller amik we know and love. In our stories we rarely destroy other beings, even when they threaten us; we engage with them. This is not a weakness. This is survival. You might be able to defend your hoard nine out of ten times, but eventually you will lose. Better to make them allies if you can.[10]

During the conversation about oral storytelling when we heard about Ananzi, we also heard from Sonia Sulaiman (Palestinian), who told us a tale about a fox who got his tail back. It's a charming story of a little fox who drinks all the milk, the woman who refuses to give back

---

9 In her book *The Indigenous Paleolithic of the Western Hemisphere*, Cree-Metis paleontologist Paulette Steeves writes about beginning her fieldwork by listening to the traditional stories of the people from that place. These stories consistently contain information about that long-past world. Lewis Borck (American) of the Black Trowel Collective has a similar practice.

10 This is something that archaeologist and survival instructor Chris Begley discusses in his book *The Next Apocalypse: The Art and Science of Survival.* It's also a persistent theme of the comic and TV series *The Walking Dead.*

his tail until he replaces the milk, and all the relationships he builds on his way to doing that. Sulaiman commented that traditionally the men in her community told stories that were "true," like histories and biographies, and women told stories that were "all lies, from beginning to end." This made me think about the ways that we talk about fiction, or "the stories we just thought up." Novels aren't "true" in the way that histories and biographies might be true, but that doesn't make them unimportant or even untrue in their own way.

Many of these stories Sulaiman describes—the ones that are true and those that are "lies, from beginning to end"—have been disrupted by a hundred years of colonial violence in Palestine and preserved much the way Anishinaabe stories have been preserved—which is to say, preserved by people who had oddly romanticized ideas about us, along with grievous misunderstandings about our cosmology. Sulaiman has had to sift through these ideas and misunderstandings and dust them off to get a clearer picture of her own folklore.

Similarly, the poetry and traditional stories written down by Bamewawagezhikaquay, aka Jane Johnston Schoolcraft (Ojibwe), were heavily edited and altered by her husband, geographer and political figure Henry Rowe Schoolcraft (American). Bamewawagezhikaquay was one of the earliest known Ojibwe writers and lived most of her life in northern Michigan. A more recent volume of her stories and poetry, edited by Robert Dale Parker (unmarked), seeks to restore her voice, noting that "Just as Henry worked with the Jackson Democrats to support the 'removal' of Indian people from their land, so he sometimes seems to try to remove Indian people from their own stories."[11]

• • •

Marginalized peoples, like Palestinians, are recovering their stories from the mess that European anthropologists and historians have made of

---

11 R.D. Parker, *The Sound the Stars Make Rushing through the Sky: The Writings of Jane Johnson Schoolcraft* (University of Pennsylvania Press, 2007), 61.

them. We tell or retell them ourselves, on our own terms, and often in ways that reflect how our stories connect with those of other communities. We build homes together in the mashkiig.

In her novel *Beloved*, Morrison (Black) tells the story of an enslaved woman finding freedom and remembers the relationships that escaping slaves had with Cherokee and others who offered them shelter. Paul D is one of the men enslaved on the Sweet Home plantation with Sethe, around whom the story of *Beloved* revolves. After an escape attempt, he is sent to a prison camp in Georgia, from which he escapes along with some fellow prisoners. They go to a Cherokee encampment where they are fed and have their leg irons removed. Although the Cherokee were a slaveholding tribe, they also assisted those who fled. Seeing these connections between our communities, and the lands that know us both, in works of fiction helps us to imagine them in our lives too.

Thomas (Afro-Canadian) also draws Indigenous peoples into his novel *In the Upper Country,* about a community of free Black people near the Canada–US border just before the outbreak of the Civil War. David, the first Native person we meet in Thomas's book, is working with a slave catcher, an interesting choice in a book where stories exchanged between two women reveal the web of relationships between Black and Indigenous people at that time. Thomas explained to me that he didn't want to romanticize that relationship, as it was, then as now, complicated and often mediated by whiteness. We never find out what Cash, the older woman being sought by the slavecatcher, said to David, but he abandoned his "partner," took his horse, and left.

Many of those who are retelling traditional stories are publishing them in the original language as well as English. Storytellers like Isaac Murdoch (Anishinaabe) and Patricia Ningewance (Ojibwe Anishinaabe) are publishing books of traditional Anishinaabe stories in both English and Anishinaabemowin (the Anishinaabe language), a boon for language learners but also an important way to preserve the story itself. Retaining the language is a way of retaining aspects of the stories themselves. My son's partner, Angela (Anishinaabe), who speaks and reads the language, says that the English and Anishinaabemowin versions of the stories in these books aren't exactly different, but there are choices made in the translation from Anishinaabemowin into English that are interesting and sometimes unexpected.

Waubgeshig Rice (Anishinaabe) is the author of two books we are going to come back to in chapter 8, which centre on stories we tell about the future: *Moon of the Crusted Snow* and *Moon of the Turning Leaves*. Both of these books contain some Anishinaabemowin that is not translated into English. Rice made a conscious choice not to translate the snippets of Anishinaabemowin in his books, so unless you speak the language, at times you don't know what the characters are saying.

Entire passages or poems in Gloria Anzaldúa's (Chicana) *Borderlands/La Frontera: The New Mestiza* are written in Chicano Spanish and only intermittently explained. The kriol spoken by Javier and Xander, the brothers in the 2012 storyline from *The Actual Star*, is not translated either. Kriol is an English-based language spoken in Belize, Belize being the only mainland country in Central America colonized by the British, which makes it easier to figure out through context and growing familiarity. But this is not always the case, and I accept that the detail of whatever they are saying isn't for me. The feeling of exclusion that results might be the point that the author is making. Stories can serve to remind us of our disconnections as well, refuse to give us a place in which to root ourselves.

Just as El Akkad repurposed *Peter Pan* to tell us the story of a migrant child lost at sea, in his short story "Heartbeat," Rice retells the very British legend of King Arthur for a tale about a young boy named Art, and about restoring a community's voice and culture.[12] Rice has talked about the end of the world happening when the forestry

12 This short story is published in the anthology *Sword Stone Table: Old Legends, New Voices*, edited by Swapna Krishna and Jenn Northington (Penguin Random House, 2021). Miigwech, Waubgeshig, for not translating the language, for letting it be there on its own.

industry and missionaries came to his own community, displacing the people and their stories. Throughout Canada and the United States, ceremonies, gatherings, and the language itself were all forbidden and confiscated, and in his own community their drums went missing. Missing, and maybe protected. Hidden away like the language and ceremonies that are now reasserting themselves. Rice isn't sure. When he was invited to retell a story of King Arthur, Rice thought about those drums and wondered what might happen if a boy found drums instead of a sword in a stone.

Given how connected drumming is with songs and stories, the loss of those drums, through colonization and missionizing, was both deliberate and devastating. It is no accident that drum circles are one of the first things that form in communities that are regaining their sense of self. That is where Rice locates his story. Rather than pulling a sword from a stone and revealing himself as the true king, Art finds the drums and reveals them to his community. And like the stories about Ananzi and the little fox, Art goes through some things to find these drums and brings stories back to his people.

Broadly speaking, fiction allows writers to use a kind of shorthand, so that if you are familiar with the reference, a single sentence can do the work of an entire book. Repurposing old stories is one way to do it, referencing cultural events or pop culture. We bump up against it in books with unexplained language or references that we don't understand.

My short story threaded throughout this book contains a lot of shorthand, references that a reader unfamiliar with Anishinaabe or other Native practices may not catch easily. The unnamed waitress smudges her lungs, she had to move for high school, and she makes an offering with what tobacco she has. Just before she encounters Kwe in the darkness of Thunder Bay, the waitress refers to people who go missing as "fallen feathers." This gestures toward the book *Seven Fallen Feathers* by journalist Tanya Talaga (Anishinaabe), who wrote in 2017 about systemic racism and the failure of policing through the stories surrounding the lives and deaths of seven teenagers—young people who, as hundreds of others have done, had come to Thunder Bay for high school from their northern communities.

It is a constant tension for marginalized fiction writers: How much do we explain so that our stories make sense to people outside our communities? If you aren't familiar with our worlds, our writing becomes opaque. Calling the relatives "fallen feathers" hints at tragedy, but unless you are familiar with Talaga's work, you don't get the full horror of what that phrase points to. The missing didn't just die or disappear; they were murdered, and their stories were dismissed by those whose slogan "to serve and protect" clearly refers to only part of the population.[13] The waitress is right to think it unfair that this violence limits her world, but her grandfather, Misho, is also right to worry. Without Kwe's intervention, the waitress may have been the one found in the water.

We understand each other best when we know each other's stories and allow our interpretations of those stories to be guided by the people from the community where they were written rather than our own beliefs about that community. As marginalized people, we know that the stories being told about us are incomplete and unreliable. But we often forget that this is true for others as well: The stories being told about them are no more accurate than the ones we chafe against.

As Diaz says in the book's epigraph, what matters is how we arrive and build a relationship. Once we are there, it becomes about how we receive others. We may arrive to marginalized writing through

---

13 Over the last decade, much has been written and produced about systemic racism within the Thunder Bay police service, and as of May 2024, their own website acknowledges the need to look at policies and practices. If you want to know more, the podcast *Thunder Bay* hosted by Ryan McMahon is illuminating.

fiction or nonfiction, through poetry or memoir. Who and how we read plays a role in the way in which we understand that writing. When I come up against an unfamiliar community, I often pause by reading and thinking before rushing headlong into questions and discussions, my impulsive curiosity masking what is actually a demand for labour. In that way, reading becomes a kind of 101 before we venture out into relationship—the downside of which is, of course, our surprise when we realize that the people we meet are not exactly like the ones we read about. Reading widely helps us avoid that and resists the notion of a single story.

The stories that are true, as Sulaiman would describe them, tell us about each other, important learning to be sure. But it is with Ananzi's help, the stories we just thought up—those lies, from beginning to end—shower down on us from Nyame's court, are pulled from the places we hid them. Our stories reveal our connections to each other through journeys like that of Art or the little fox, and those connections become living beings in their own right. They are letters to a future we believe will exist. Fiction puts flesh and blood on the bones of nonfiction writing.

We measure the earth with hands and feet, bodies touching the ground and asking if we are known. In our own hands, our stories, those letters we write to the future, become that living weapon Diane Di Prima envisioned in her poem "Rant": a weapon carried by Bad Indians in the war against the imagination being waged against us.

And so, with weapons in hand, we turn toward horror.

Kwe

The ornamental grasses in the park danced as if a breeze passed through them. But the night air was still and thick, the humidity of a late summer night weighing heavily on everything. I watched the movement of the grasses and corrected myself. They weren't dancing, and there was no breeze. It's more like a hand moved roughly through them, leaving some broken and the larger patch untouched.

Pensive, I ran a finger along one broken stalk. There didn't seem to be anyone nearby, but it was dark and the park was full of shadowed corners. I liked coming to this park on the night of the new moon, because I could see the stars clearly even though it means I couldn't see people. Small towns don't generally offer much in the way of danger or light pollution, and in this park, I could lie down on the picnic table without anyone bothering me. A satellite chain was making its way across the sky; another Starlink launch to distort the stories told by the stars, as if they weren't already distorted and hidden by the Greek myths written on top of them.

Did something touch me?

What was that?

I sat up quickly, hand to my cheek. I felt the pressure in my skull as antlers readied to emerge. But there wasn't anything there—just the lingering sensation of somebody having stroked my cheek, and a smell I couldn't quite make out. Wool, maybe, but musty and old.

A few minutes passed, and, satisfied that I was in fact alone in the park, I laid down again on the table. The satellite chain had moved to other skies, and I could pick out the familiar stories from the stars above. Yet even they seem unsettled. For a few minutes, curtains of red I normally associate with the far north skittered across the sky before disappearing.

The next morning, I made my way to a diner for coffee. The breakfast crowd was talking excitedly about the unexpected view of the northern lights. So I had seen them; it wasn't just my imagination. We were far enough south that sightings are rare, and they were causing a stir.

I moved a newspaper somebody left behind out of my way, and was about to discard it when I noticed the headline. The body of a young woman had been found near the water, her neck broken.

How did this happen while I was here? There hadn't been any of the usual signs. I know I can't save every woman, but it's unusual for me to be so close to a threat and not feel the disturbance of some violent intention. I can normally follow ripples of energy to the source before harm is done.

I picked up the paper and read the article. The woman's name was familiar. She was part of a group agitating for the removal of a statue from the park where I had been the night before. I hadn't given the statue much thought, and I didn't understand the wemiti-goozhiwag fixation on creating them anyway.

Suddenly I knew. Broken neck and broken grasses. The smell of old musty wool: It was like the woolen coats worn by soldiers commemorated in statues across the country, woolen coats in red, blue, or grey depending on the war and whose side they were on.

I remembered that smell. The gunpowder and violence I associated with it crowded my memories, a trail of smoke leading to an old story. A warning about creating bodies without spirit that attract spirits looking for a body.

The latecomers were trying to assert their own power, foolishly opening doors without any awareness of what might come through them.

• • •

A few days later I returned to the park and joined the crowd no longer willing to wait for politicians dithering over who should be appeased. People were singing and drumming for the two groups on either side of the statue, who were pulling rhythmically on chains looped over the statue's head and shoulders. Back and forth the statue rocked on its platform. A large poster-board photograph of the young woman who had started this campaign leaned up against the stairs.

An older woman who looked vaguely familiar stood off to the side, holding a large abalone shell from which rose the smoke and smell of sage. Using an eagle fan, she waved it over the crowd and smiled as I walked over to her. I noticed her skirt, a blue fabric imprinted with antlers and decorated with multi-coloured ribbons. Hoofprints edged with beading walked across the skirt.

I looked at the woman, and she looked me in the eye. I felt seen, as if this vaguely familiar stranger knew who I am. Then the old woman smudged me, singing that song I heard years ago when I entered the sweat lodge.

Biingigen, Nokomis-sag, way oh way ha, oh way oh way ha, oh-oh, Biindigen Nokomis-sag, way oh way ha, oh way oh way ha.

7

ZEGAAJIMOWINAN

There's scary stuff in stories, sure, there's stuff that keeps you up at night, there's stuff that makes you watch the darkness you're driving through that much closer. But there's hope, too.

—Stephen Graham Jones, foreword, *Never Whistle at Night*

I HAVE LIVED most of my life in southern Ontario, and I don't recall seeing the northern lights except in photographs. My mother talks about seeing them when we lived north of Thunder Bay. I was a baby then, and the Ojibwe people she lived among, and whose children she taught, had cautioned her about whistling at these lights. These lights are ancestors, they told her, and should be taken seriously, so we don't whistle and attract their attention. Other tribes have prohibitions against photographing them. Some have broad prohibitions on whistling at night at all, whether or not the lights are visible.

On one hand it is a reasonable precaution, as there are all kinds of things out there—from Lakota scouts to predatory animals—whose attention you may not want to attract. As a warning it makes a kind of sense—and it's just a story, right?

One night when my mother, this modern young woman, took me outside, bundled against the cold to see the lights, she whistled. She whistled, and the lights began to shimmer.

The way she tells the story today, it's as if the northern lights turned to look at her, suddenly curious. The lights came nearer, she says, darting and flashing. She grabbed me tight, fled into the house, and never whistled at them again.

There might be more than Lakota scouts and hungry animals lurking in the darkness, the peculiar things that keep us up at night and looking at the shadows a little more closely. They may not be evil—there is hope there as well—but it is probably best if we don't attract their attention unless we know how to respond.

I grew up far away from those kinds of sensibilities, haunted by the unknowns of my own history and embraced by the jump scares of horror movies. The golden age of slasher films is generally thought to have peaked during the 1970s and '80s, while I was in high school, with money earned working at a pizzeria to spend at movie theatres and in bookstores. The years I was in high school brought us Jason, Freddy, Michael Myers, and other villains who became sympathetic the more we learned of their backstory. Those years brought us victims who behaved stupidly and predictably, while we shouted at them from the safety of our theatre seats, throwing hands and popcorn, telling each other they deserved to die if they were going to be like that. These films didn't give us the familiar tropes, the shorthand and patterns, of the slasher genre, but they did seem to make them a permanent and expected part of the experience.[1]

You can't subvert the tropes of the horror genre if you don't introduce them, if you just act like they don't exist. Sure, there's scary stuff in our stories, but through the ways that our stories approach familiar themes, you will see that there's hope too.

In one of our conversations, Jay Odjick talked about introducing and then subverting tropes in his graphic novel *Kagagi*, which was made

---

1 Slasher films have widely recognized tropes or standard features, for example: the weirdo everyone should have listened to, the dangers of splitting up but they do it anyway along with the famous "I'll be right back" that is usually said just before getting killed, having sex inevitably means you're going to die, villains who are fast even though they are just walking and can't seem to die, and so on. Horror more broadly has tropes like the Indian burial ground and the dangerous primitive, which we will get to.

into an animated series. *Kagagi* follows the adventures of a sixteen-year-old boy who inherits the ancient power of the Raven spirit—pretty standard stuff in comic books. Odjick takes the standard stuff and changes it, giving it roots in Algonquin stories and beliefs. His producers challenged him about using a commonplace story arc, the hero rescuing the girl, which he insisted stay in so that he could turn it on its head in a later episode.

Much marginalized horror is about challenging and rewriting that shorthand, because they ultimately gesture to larger social assumptions about who and what is dangerous, who belongs, and who deserves to die. And as happens in contemporary nationalist politics, the answers to those questions typically fall along racial lines. Like Odjick, I will set up the tropes of whitestream horror so I can show you how our horror turns them on their heads.

If horror is the exploration of things that frighten us, then the things that frighten those who have been violently pushed to the margins will be different from the things that frighten those who did the pushing.

• • •

Coming of age as part of a largely unsupervised, feral generation[2] meant that in addition to doing whatever we wanted, we also read and watched whatever we wanted. Feral and unsupervised because our parents were at work and everyone seemed to assume that we were fine on our own for hours at a time. Earlier generations had been unsupervised too, but they had neighbourhoods full of mothers; our neighbourhoods were full of older siblings to follow and younger ones who promised not to tell. I don't know how else to explain the fact that, along with so many of my friends, I was consumed by V.C. Andrews's (unmarked) entire catalogue of gothic horror seeping out from picture-perfect suburban families. But we didn't start with *Flowers in the Attic*; we slipped

---

2 Otherwise known as Generation X.

into it after earlier years with Zilpha Keatley Snyder (unmarked), who wrote in the 1960s and '70s. She was a Newberry Award–winning author who didn't write horror, but she did introduce the preteen market to vaguely occult storylines in the midst of the typical tensions between mothers and daughters. Snyder's books were a contrast to my beloved Nancy Drew, in which even the spookiest situation was inevitably a disgruntled neighbour. With Snyder's books, we were never quite sure if the vaguely occult things actually did happen, as she left it vague and possible.

Horror expands our world *into* dark places. For whitestream audiences, this is understandably terrifying, but what about those of us who have been pushed there? What kind of stories might *we* tell about the things we bump into, the spooky things that are vaguely possible? In his foreword to the dark fiction anthology *Never Whistle at Night,* Stephen Graham Jones (Blackfeet) makes a few observations about what distinguishes Indigenous horror from that of the whitestream.

To illustrate his observations, Jones retells a ghost story, pretty standard fare, about friends driving down a lonely highway at night, when a group of Indians on horseback race across the road and disappear into the night. Except that they don't exactly race *across* the raised blacktop so much as *through* it on their way from one darkness to another. To shift from a ghost story into horror, he says, you'd have one of those riders look the driver straight in the eye. Now you are part of this. Something saw you. Or you could crank it up: The driver looks in the rearview mirror, and one of those Indians is sitting in the backseat. Give the story a Native narrator, and maybe this is justice from beyond the grave. But what if the driver is also Native? And what if that Indian in the backseat takes over the driver, possesses him—which is, as Jones points out, a kind of colonization? But is it colonization if the person being possessed by a long-dead Native is themselves Native? Maybe it's an ancestor. Put us into the story as something other than the thing that haunts you and we're talking about a much different story.

Horror is meant to disrupt places that are normally seen as safe. The rules and tropes of this writing give us a measure of predictability that allows us to navigate unstable terrain. When it becomes a mechanism for *marginalized* storytelling, horror—the destabilizing of places normally seen as safe—is right up our Bad Indian alley.

• • •

Teddy Roosevelt apparently said that he "didn't go so far as to think that the only good Indians are the dead Indians, but I believe nine out of every ten are, and I shouldn't like to inquire too closely into the case of the tenth."[3] Yet in many horror offerings, it's the dead Indians who cause so many of the problems.

This fear of dead Indians remains so universal that after one particularly bad year—when we were beset with plague, wildfires, and exaggerated threats about giant murder hornets—people on social media were questioning the wisdom of building an entire country on an Indian burial ground. Clearly, in modern horror stories, the nine out of ten who are dead are still Bad Indians, while the tenth who survived may yet be a Good Indian if they rescue the central white character before dying or fading into the distance.

A lot of western horror is about restoring order, which means everything and everyone back its place. But Anishinaabe stories, like those of many other marginalized peoples, see balance differently. Balance is layered relationships working together. You can't *have* balance if you insist on borders, and borders require violence to maintain them, which brings us to the place where we first learned about all this: westerns.

In novel and in film, the years of the Wild West are where we first learn about Good and Bad Indians. In westerns, white violence is

---

3 Roosevelt made this remark during a January 1886 speech in New York. Cited in Alysa Landry, "Theodore Roosevelt: 'The Only Good Indians Are the Dead Indians,'" *Indian Country Today,* September 13, 2018, https://ictnews.org/archive/theodore-roosevelt-the-only-good-indians-are-the-dead-indians.

always excused by beginning the story with "secondly," as Mourid Barghouti said in chapter 3, rendering our violence inexplicable. The so-called Indian hater—a stock character from westerns who becomes consumed with rage and kills indiscriminately, like John Wayne in *The Searchers*—makes the violence of other white characters against those same Indians look tame, necessary. The only difference between the Indian hater and the hero is really a difference of scale; both of them kill the Indians and clear the land.[4] Meanwhile, beginning the story with "secondly," rather than what actually happened first, renders the violence of Indians as extreme and savage, making even the Indian hater a sympathetic figure.

Turning to horror: If the thing that goes bump in the night is not an Indian, it is still described in ways that westerns have taught us describe Indians: primitive and savage, inhuman and evil. We might be there as noble savages, another trope, but those characters exist only to transfer their wisdom and spiritual power to the white hero, who inevitably becomes better at wielding our native magic than we are. They are Good Indians who fade into obscurity, having handed over their land and their wisdom.[5]

Kali Simmons (Lakota) and Shaawano Chad Uran (Anishinaabe) talked about this at a conference I attended a few years ago, connecting the horror genre with old westerns, where manly men rescued their women from dangerous Indians, tying American masculinity to scenes of Indigenous genocide.[6] We might not make

---

4 For more on the trope of the Indian hater, check out Seth Bovey's article "Indian-Hating and Popular Culture: The Iconography of John Wayne in *The Searchers*," https://dspacep01.emporia.edu/bitstream/handle/123456789/637/BoveyVol%2030%20Num%202.pdf?sequence=1.

5 Kali Simmons, as yet unpublished essay, "White Men Indian Magic," 2024.

6 Kali Simmons and Shaawano Chad Uran, unpublished paper: "Indigeneity in the Horror Genre" presented at the Native American Indigenous Studies Association conference 2023. Miigwech, Kali and Shaawano, for this revelation in your panel and further conversations. I hope I make you proud grandpa.

movies in the same way now, but if it wasn't for the periodic glimpses of dust-covered, bone-wearing cave dwellers in the 2015 western horror film *Bone Tomahawk*, you'd think the "Troglodytes" our manly heroes (on their way to rescue a kidnapped wife) were talking about were Natives. I mean, we all know that they're talking about Natives, but it's not the 1950s anymore so you can't say that stuff as plainly as John Wayne used to.

Living Indians are clearly bad enough. What about *dead* Indians?

La Llorona is frightening to outsiders, but feminist writers from within the communities where she emerged are reclaiming her. In *Borderlands/La Frontera: The New Mestiza*, queer feminist writer Gloria Anzaldúa (Chicana) examines the stories of her communities and the way that masculine power, machismo, from the late Aztec period to colonial Spain and into our contemporary world, has stripped feminine deities of their power and complexity, reducing them to either virginal/good or sexualized/evil. La Llorona, with her maternal longing and wailing for lost children, becomes a terrifying ghost. In some stories she is said to have drowned her own children in a fit of jealous rage, as in the Greek tragedy *Medea*, or as a sacrifice to the Aztec war god. This is a truly monstrous transformation when you consider the sheer numbers of children who disappeared because of colonial violence. Through the power of the state, our children disappear into mass graves and residential schools, foster homes, and immigrant detention centres. Disappearing beneath concrete while bombs rain down.

There is a song called "Wildflower" sung by Anishinaabe hand drum groups, and the story I was told about that song is related to the residential school era. The first part is sung quietly, as if by mothers urging their children to hide. The second part rises in volume, a wail, as the mothers seek their lost children. When my friend Emely (El Salvadoran) sings this song, I am reminded not only of residential schools but other ways that children are torn from their communities. I think of the mass graves being exhumed in El Salvador, bodies and lives being remembered and re-membered in attempts to identify and then restore them to their families for proper care.[7]

Emely told me about an encounter her uncle had with La Siguanaba, the hideous woman, whose story is also layered with meaning. In the most common version, she was originally a peasant using her charms and magic to marry a Náhuatl, prince. When he was away from home she had affairs, one of which resulted in a child she neglected. Her ambitions and use of magic had tragic consequences. She and her son were cursed, and now La Siguanaba wanders the countryside looking for her lost son and appearing to men who are travelling alone. Her uncle did not see her face (which is good, because according to the story, seeing her face results in madness), but he felt her presence. When he climbed onto his horse to get away, he felt her reach her arms around him. And when she touched the protective charm he wore around his neck, he heard her scream.[8]

La Llorona and La Siguanaba, along with many others, are being revisited by Chicana feminists like Anzaldúa and Theresa Delgadillo (Latina), who sift through the influence of Spanish machismo and gender roles in traditional communities and the way that stories about women have changed over the centuries since Spanish colonization. Anzaldúa and Delgadillo describe the transformation of feminine power and spirituality into a misogynistic caricature, including women blaming themselves for the deaths of their children at the hands of abusive authority.[9] In this context, their wailing and haunting becomes

---

7 Journalist Roberto Lovato (El Salvadoran) has written about the US-sponsored state violence in El Salvador, the mass graves currently being exhumed, and the impacts this has on generations of Salvadoran peoples in his memoir *Unforgetting: A Memoir of Family, Migration, Gangs, and Revolution in the Americas.*

8 Miigwech, Emely, for sharing your uncle's story and your time.

9 Professor Delgadillo discusses this in an NRP segment on La Llorona as a feminist icon, in which she makes the intriguing observation that she sees La Llorona in the character of Bride in the film *Kill Bill*, and now I need to watch that again. https://www.latinousa.org/2015/10/30/la-llorona-as-feminist-icon/.

understandable rather than terrifying. Their wailing becomes a refusal of that instantaneous forgetting that colonial states impose so deftly. Like Ptesáŋwiŋ and Waawaashkeshi'Kwe, they demand respect for their autonomy and refuse to be silenced. The burial grounds left in the wake of Ptesáŋwiŋ, Waawaashkeshi'Kwe, La Llorona, La Siguanaba, and Changing Woman along with other powerful beings are full of mostly white men who caused harm, not tragic Native people who can't even rest when they are dead. So much dominating horror denies marginalized peoples an afterlife and condemns them to haunt white Americans.

In my imagining of Kwe, I take what could be a scary, cautionary, "don't disrespect women or Waawaashkeshi'Kwe is going to get you" story and instead put her at the centre. When she retells her story in the sweat lodge, we are reminded that she had a name: Her father called her Morningstar. When Kwe could be seen as the Good Indian who appears briefly to help the waitress, that offer of tobacco reminds us that Kwe is worthy of gratitude and respect. She doesn't exist in isolation, with no other purpose than to help the hero and smite the bad guys. Similarly, many of the stories from *Deer Woman: An Anthology* are about empowerment and community; the teachings they offer ask us to embody Waawaashkeshi'Kwe ourselves rather than wait for her rescue.

One of these stories, "Asdzą́ą́ Changing," by Tatum Bowie (Diné), presents the Diné story about Changing Woman through a conversation between a grandmother and her granddaughter, who is struggling in an abusive relationship. Changing Woman is the mother of the Diné Hero Twins. Her creative and shape-shifting powers help maintain balance rather than challenge it—as is the more common fear of such power.[10] In the story, the grandmother tells her granddaughter that "Changing Woman didn't get her name by staying the same, and you

10 It is endlessly fascinating to me, having grown up in the evangelical church, how many beliefs and spiritual practices are centred around maintaining balance rather than simply eradicating whatever is defined as evil.

can't change things by letting them stay as they are." Through ceremony and story, the granddaughter is reminded of her own power. Her connection to Changing Woman results in her confronting and then leaving her abusive boyfriend.

Erdrich's novel *Antelope Woman* is not a work of horror, but it does pursue similar themes of violence and captivity that are found there, and it blurs the boundaries between human and other-than-human life. Erdrich presents us with a different kind of Waawaashkeshi'Kwe and gives us a lineage of women who pass on the magical chaos of their ancestor, a woman who ran with and possibly loved an antelope.

The story follows generations of men and women descended from Ozhaawashikmashkodikwe, Blue Prairie Woman, whose infant child, Other Side of the Earth, Matilda, is adopted by Scranton Roy, a Quaker Union soldier who participated in the massacre of her Ojibwe community during the 1860s. While the Roy family is a mix of white and Ojibwe, Blue Prairie Woman's children are also mixed, descended from her own relationship with the antelope. So trauma is part of Antelope Woman's beginnings, but in a different way. The traumas experienced by Blue Prairie Woman and later her daughter Matilda sent them out to the grasslands looking for peace, and they began to run with the antelope.[11] A hundred years later, Klaus, the great-grandson of Roy, kidnaps Sweet Calico, the great-granddaughter of Ozhaawashikmashkodikwe.

The chaos and harms that unfold around Sweet Calico are the result of her kidnapping, but they aren't vengeful. They reflect the imbalance rippling outward from that first stone cast into the water.

---

11 Relations between humans and animals are not unusual in Ojibwe stories; it is part of the blurring between the human and other-than-human worlds and hearkens to a time when we used to understand each other and some animals had the ability to shift their form while remaining who they were. The Ojibwe believe that long ago we understood what animals said, but we withdrew or forgot or just stopped caring, and so they have distanced themselves from us. In *Mean Spirit*, Linda Hogan has several characters who retain this ability to understand what some animals are saying.

Ptesáŋwiŋ and Sweet Calico and all of these women remind us of the importance of consent and respecting the autonomy of others. They remind us that, like whistling at the northern lights or even in the dark, we take without permission or transgress what is sacred at our peril.

• • •

So much horror is about transgression, about unknowable others and the stories we tell about them. In this book, in which we travel with Waawaashkeshi'Kwe through the stories we tell, I would be remiss if I did not stop for a moment to consider Stephen Graham Jones's *The Only Good Indians* and the transgressions that haunt a group of friends.

It was the title and the cover—an elk in profile, seen from the head up with antlers dominating and a single eye looking straight at the reader—that first got my attention. A group of friends, teenagers, hunt on land reserved for elders. They are reckless, and they end up killing several elk, including a pregnant elk cow who refused to die, so one of the friends shoots it several times, killing her and her unborn foal.

Grief and guilt about the losses of identity, tradition, and dead elk track through this book, leaving bloody hoofprints everywhere. This elk, a northern La Lorona wailing for her lost calf, returns a decade later, a spirit presenting as a young girl and then a young woman bent on avenging the loss of her herd and her calf. There is violence against women, something we always need to think about as a mechanism of storytelling. Our women and gender- or sexually nonconforming people are subjected to escalated violence at the hands of all too real systems, so we need to think about the purpose of literary violence. Is the author just being mean for no reason, or does the violence reveal something that couldn't be revealed another way? How is the violence explained, and whom does it serve?

The friends in Jones's book are not good in the conventional sense: Their killing of the elk is destructive, and they transgress tribal law as well as traditional wisdom. But they aren't evil, either. And although they attempt to use traditional ceremonies to save themselves, it doesn't work that way. Ceremony isn't a way to get absolution or avoid responsibility. Ceremony is meant to help you take responsibility, to remind you of who you are. The consequences of their actions ripple out into the relationships around them, as consequences always do. The guilt these characters carry is so palpable it's almost a character itself. And as the survivors struggle to save themselves, the question haunts them: How do you kill something you already killed?

You don't. The final girl—in horror, she is usually the sole survivor who confronts the villain—is the daughter of one of these men who had killed the elk a decade earlier, and it is she who breaks the cycle of violence. Jones relies on these slasher tropes, in this case the final girl, but also subverts them the way that marginalized horror does simply by its context.

In whitestream horror, the final girl is pure. She's the one who hasn't had sex, who follows the rules, who emerges from the carnage bloody but noble and confronts the slasher as no other character can. The final girl is the white hero of western movies, defeating monstrous violence through a mix of morality and righteous violence. But Jones's final girls are not pure; they are complicated, mixed-blood girls who carry complicated mixed-blood ancestors in their spirits. They are La Llorona and Ptesáŋwiŋ and Waawaashkeshi'Kwe and Sweet Calico. They are the feminine tropes of our own stories, who writers like Jones and Anzaldúa seek to restore to wholeness rather than the limited and limiting Madonna/whore femininity of western imagination.

In an unpublished poem by my friend Maya Chacaby (Anishinaabe), "A Love Poem Cross-Cut along the Multicultural Jugular," she uses the language of horror to restore wholeness through complicated ancestors and the relationships formed by those who have been buried and discarded.[12] The lines that captivated me, that still captivate me,

---

12 Unpublished poem, used by permission. Miigwech, Maya: from smart berries to poetry, we are truly stranded together by everything you teach me.

follow a description of Turtle Island with bloody wounds and gaping holes.

> pierced open by the bones of dead Indians
> crushed under Imperial boots, and a thick layer of
> slaved black bodies
> Your ancestors and mine decompose together, resting
> under cement; bulldozed into one discarded heap,
> incised, desiccated by pipelines and garbage dumps.
> our ancestors strand together as filaments
> keeping Turtle Island from breaking apart.

Our ancestors strand together as filaments, keeping Turtle Island from breaking apart: I read those lines one day while working late. I was so moved by their exquisite clarity that I had to find somebody to share them with. I rushed through the office, eventually finding a Black coworker of mine who was also working late, a friend with whom I had many conversations about racist violence and the struggle to belong. These words felt like hope in the midst of horror—an assurance that her ancestors and mine somehow strand like filaments and keep this world together. This world, full of gaping holes, with wounds pierced open and layered with bodies treated like refuse, is being held together by our ancestors, hers and mine.

This stranding and holding by our ancestors is, intentionally or not, a subversion of the Indian burial ground trope. Horror was visited on our ancestors. But rather than acting as a supernatural toxin, the ancestors work together as medicine. They hold creation together despite the toxins introduced by the wemitigoozhiwag, the latecomers whose beliefs drive them to possess.

And maybe *we* aren't the ones coming up from the burial grounds to haunt your cities and towns anyway.

The town of Proofrock in Stephen Graham Jones's *Indian Lake Trilogy* does have a burial ground causing all sorts of mayhem, but it isn't ours. Generations earlier, a reservoir was created, and it flooded a white settlement that became known as Drown Town. Local lore is that the preacher, Ezekiel, told his congregation that if they stayed in the church, God would save them. Except nobody saves them. The waters rise and the people drown, haunting the small fictional town of Proofrock. There's something in the water there, a poison coming from Ezekiel and his church, which infects the community and unleashes cycles of violence, culminating in the final girl of all final girls: Jade Daniels, whose obsession with slasher films helps her to recognize what is happening and know how to respond.

• • •

Lee Francis IV (Laguna Pueblo) and Odjick were both involved in the 2022 graphic anthology *A Howl: An Indigenous Anthology of Wolves, Werewolves, and Rougarou*—Francis as a publisher and Odjick contributing a poem about a young man who allows himself to be bitten to stay with his love. Werewolves are a French creature, but shape-shifting is a common feature of stories told by the people of the lands that became known as the Americas.

I am Caribou clan, which means I am descended from caribou who, seeing how poorly we were doing at being human, took pity on us and became human so that they could teach us. This blurring between human and other-than-human is a common thread in many Indigenous stories. The Anishinaabe believe that there was a time when we shared language and could talk to each other, but for all kinds of reasons they began to withdraw from us, and now we don't understand each other anymore—or maybe it's we who don't understand them. With a creation story like that, it makes sense that shape-shifting would not only be part of our stories but that it would not be terrifying. It's just part of who we are. For the French, however—a European people rooted in a particular kind of Christianity—the boundary between human and nonhuman is fixed and firm. Shape-shifters like the werewolf are a sign of wrongness, a thing to be cured or confronted.

Native Realities, a publishing company owned by Francis, also published *Deer Woman: An Anthology*, a graphic anthology edited by Elizabeth LaPensée (Anishinaabe/Métis) in 2017. Both of these anthologies, *A Howl* and *Deer Woman*, take creatures normally seen as terrifying—all of whom dominate pulp fiction and campy horror—and reclaim them, just as Chicana feminists are reclaiming their stories.

Layered places and shifting between them is part of our cosmology, and stories like "Wowokin" from *A Howl* by Weyodi OldBear (Comanche) remind us of this. OldBear tells the story of Wowokin, a Comanche warrior who died saving his people (saving his people was accidental; Wowokin is not a very good warrior) and who returns to life as a shape-shifting coyote. Living with his coyote pack, he discovers that he has "human medicine," much like people will say that they carry bear or turtle medicine. He is mocked by his pack (he's not a very good shape-shifting coyote either).[13]

Shunned by his coyote pack, Wowokin figures out how to shape-shift into human form and wanders into a sandstorm. He is rescued from certain death by a young woman named Daisy, who is hiding a little boy and a family in her basement. Sheet-clad men arrive, looking for the people that Daisy is hiding, and Wowokin returns to what is now his true form, that of a coyote, to protect the woman and those she is sheltering from the police officers terrorizing them.

OldBear set this story in her family history from the years of allotment. In chapter 3, I mentioned the book *Mean Spirit*, which describes the violence of allotment-era Oklahoma including Indian boarding schools, fraud, and the murders of Osage Indians. This took place alongside the 1921 Tulsa massacre, and it was common to find bodies just

---

13 For the Comanche, warriors could return to this world as coyotes, something that gives me pause as an Ojibwe living near a forested wetland where coyotes howl at night. Miigwech, Weyodi, for your time and conversation helping me understand this and allowing me to share your family story. These connections between Black and Indigenous communities need to be spoken of, and spoken of regularly.

left in fields, or strange fruit hanging from trees.[14] OldBear told me that John Gustafson, the police chief who deputized the white mob who raped, murdered, and looted their way through the African American community of Greenwood during the 1921 Tulsa massacre, worked as private security for many white people who acted as legal guardians of oil-rich Osage people in the years following allotment. A group of Tulsa bankers turned a profit from both tragedies.

Official and unofficial public policy not only gives people permission to enact violence against those whose deaths don't matter; it deputizes them. And so, during this time period, local members of the KKK lynched a Black man to prevent him from inheriting property from an elderly white woman with no other heirs. They were coming for his family as well, so OldBear's ancestors, Edward Hatch Clark and Mary Putsi Parker, hid the family in their root cellar at the Dutch Reformed Mission, where they lived until the threat passed, just as the young woman sheltered a family in her basement and offered help to Wowokin.

These stories of Black and Indigenous relationship are important, particularly now, as anti-Black racism proliferates in our own communities, a zombie virus of scarcity and purity that infects all of us.

• • •

When my oldest son was much younger, I gave him a collection of stories edited by Richard Erdoes (equal parts Austrian, Hungarian, and German) and Alfonso Ortiz (Ohkay Owingeh), titled *American Indian Myths and Legends*.[15] He refers to it off and on, mostly because as an

---

14 The 1939 Billie Holliday (Black) protest anthem "Strange Fruit" began as a poem about the lynching of Black men in the United States. It was written, and then set to music, by a white, Jewish high school teacher from the Bronx named Abel Meeropol. https://billieholiday.com/signaturesong/strange-fruit/.

15 Erdoes's Wikipedia entry refers to an article about him written in 2001 in which he describes himself as "equal parts Austrian, Hungarian and German, as well as equal parts Catholic, Protestant and Jew." https://en.wikipedia.org/wiki/Richard_Erdoes.

adult and parent, he's a little appalled that I gave a book filled with scary stories to a child. I'll admit that I hadn't read it myself, and it likely hadn't occurred to me that there *would* be scary stories in there. At that time, I was building my relationship with my Ojibwe family and the broader Indigenous community. Everything I knew about Indians was still filtered largely through a white lens, and the stories I did know were mostly presented as just-so stories, like "how the chipmunk got its stripes" or "why beavers are small," in which the larger meaning encoded in the stories is ignored or unseen. As with Deer Woman, many of these stories are told in different ways across many communities, and one of them is the story of a rolling, or flying, head. We're going to look at four stories, two traditional stories and two that are reimagined.

American Indian Myths and Legends is filled with stories from tribal groups across what is currently North America, organized into various categories. In the chapter "Ordeals of the Hero: Monsters and Monster Slayers," there is a story about a flying head attributed to the Iroquois, who are more properly known as the Haudenosaunee Confederacy, and dated to a 1902 tale.[16] The flying head is huge and full of sharp teeth. Everything is prey, and everyone is understandably afraid of it. A young mother decides to make a stand (might as well be me, she says), and she tricks it into consuming a pile of red-hot rocks, at which point it flies away.

In her collection *Gii-Nitaa-Aadisooke: Ojibwe Legends from Lac Seul*, Patricia Ningewance (Ojibwe) tells an Ojibwe story of a rolling skull. Before she was a rolling skull, the unnamed woman was a wife and a mother who neglected her home and her children to lay with woodpecker. Her husband found out about it, killed her lover and then killed her, throwing her body into the fire. The father flees, but not before leaving the boys some items they can use to protect themselves. The skull chases the boys, whom she blames for telling their father where

16 This likely refers to the earliest documented version of the story rather than the first time it was told.

she was. The boys create obstacles by throwing the various items their father left for them. She chases them across hills and fields, eventually falling into a deep river.

Nick Medina (Tunica-Biloxi) tells a rolling head story from Wintu and Cheyenne communities in his novel *Sisters of the Lost Nation*, which he imagines as the tale of two sisters, a story within a story about the broader violence targeting Indigenous women and girls and Two Spirit people that we talked about in chapter 4. In Medina's rolling head story, the younger sister refuses to stay home, and after a man injures her, she becomes a skull by consuming first herself and then, in her rage, consuming her assailant, her parents, and eventually everyone she finds. Each loss fuels that rage and leads to more loss. The older sister traps the rolling skull in a hole, much like the rolling skull in Ningewance's story is trapped at the bottom of the river, and then gives the skull a good shake. This restores the victims and finally the younger sister, who learns her lesson about disobedience and the self-destructive rage that often consumes us when we have been harmed by another.

Erdrich revisits the rolling head story in "The Flower," a short story published in *The New Yorker* in 2015, in which she changes the gender and circumstance.[17] Set in the early 1800s, it centres around a young Native woman and the young man who rescues her from an abusive trader. Together they poison him, and as they flee across the country, the trader's rolling head pursues them, bawling and determined. Eventually they find shelter with missionaries, and the girl is sent to a boarding school—which, despite the things she can't get used to, feels safe because she decides it is too far away for a head to roll.

Read through a whitestream lens, these could be cautionary tales—warnings about what happens to unfaithful wives, disobedient children, and Bad Indians. But that's too easy; it reduces them to just-so stories, a kind of Aesop's fable with nothing more to teach us than

---

17 Louise Erdrich, "The Flower," *The New Yorker*, June 29, 2015, https://www.newyorker.com/magazine/2015/06/29/the-flower.

a pithy moral. These are stories about beings that refuse simplistic binaries of good and evil; they invite us into the mashkiig and ask us to think about our relationships to them and each other. We live in a world obsessed with purity, with making individual choices and the mistaken belief that we can and should have clean hands. But we can't. Our complicity is everywhere. The best we can do is look honestly at the relationships that exist between us and what kind of action those relationships call us to. That is the power of Ptesáŋwiŋ and Waawaashkeshi'Kwe, of La Llorona and La Siguanaba, of Sweet Calico and the rolling head. The horror stories told by Bad Indians force us to look at the things about our world we would rather not see. They force us to look beyond the illusions of the stories we've been told and to face the truths that survive in the shadows.

• • •

I appreciate that in so many of our monster stories, the monster isn't actually destroyed. Their power may be diminished for a time, but they continue to exist in some capacity—not just as an existential or material threat but as part of an unseen world that must be lived with, a part of ourselves that should not be severed off and imagined as darkness. This lack of resolution leaves us to deal with the questions about monsters and what they teach us about ourselves rather than simply answering them for us.

It was in a podcast conversation called *Heroes and Monsters* that Algonquin author and comic book writer Jay Odjick talked with me about stories he heard about an unnamed creature of greed and consumption. In Odjick's telling, the original monster was a man who, trapped in a cave with his friends during a blizzard, resorts to cannibalism, which costs him his humanity. As he goes into the countryside, those who survive his attacks are transformed, and they in turn transform others, eventually overrunning the people. The pagwadjininĕ—the little people, whom the Anishinaabe know as memegwesi—agree to help the Algonquin with the fight against these creatures, but it is too much. Many pagwadjinině are lost, which is why we don't see them anymore. Wesakechak, an Algonquin trickster, eventually dispatches all the people the original creature turned, but he doesn't kill the creature itself. He just walks away.

In Anishinaabe beliefs, as in many others, death is just a return to spirit, so killing those who had been transformed might be understood as a mercy. Even if they could be healed, they would have to live with what they had done. By returning to spirit, they are given new purpose and able to shed that guilt.

The monster, on the other hand, is condemned to live with himself, something that Nathan Adler (Two Spirit/Jewish/Anishinaabe) explores in *Wrist*, a book about a family descended from one such monster and the different ways they cope and wrestle with that legacy. When we don't know how everything is meant to play out, we can't be reckless with the lives of others even if they seem monstrous to us.

Odjick commented in that conversation that in losing our culture, the knowledge and rituals for communicating and engaging with the world around us, we lose our stories and pieces of ourselves. Disconnected from their community, stories that are living beings in their own right become caged and reduced to just-so stories: stories warning us not to go outside at night or to stay home when you're told to. By capturing the monsters and locking them away, we let part of ourselves get locked away too. Unlike the flying head or the rolling skull, who are diminished but still free in some way, whitestream monsters are often either destroyed or consigned to a cell or trapped in an underworld. Their captivity tethers them to us, an unacknowledged relationship becoming increasingly distorted and hostile until the rage of those pushed to the margins or made captive erupts in violence—a violence made legible by beginning the story at the beginning.

• • •

One could argue that it was the refusal to see marginalized people at all—an unacknowledged relationship with people whose precarious belonging makes them vulnerable to exploitation and death like the migrants in El Akkad's *What Strange Paradise*, people we may not see but who are nonetheless tethered to us—that provoked the violence of Jordan Peele's movie *Us*, which was about upper and lower worlds. One group, a government experiment in manufactured doppelgangers called the Tethered, live below ground, while the original people live above. Exploited and then abandoned, the Tethered, who appear to have no free will and simply mirror the actions of those living above, take their revenge and come to the surface where they replace those who had, even unknowingly, participated in or benefited from their oppression. People who are violently pushed to the margins are, after all, part of that unseen, unacknowledged world. Whitestream horror tends to take the things they fear about us and turn us into monsters. The horror we write, in some ways, accepts that role but then transforms it into a mirror. Peele doesn't allow us to begin this story with "secondly"; he forces us to begin at the beginning.

The tropes and patterns that whitestream writers use are a kind of shorthand that can help us navigate unfamiliar terrain. But they often do this by relying on racist assumptions about the other, as well as who has access to which spaces, and under what circumstances. It isn't only white-produced horror that does this.

As my son Ben points out, H. P. Lovecraft was racist and not even a particularly good writer, but he did create a unique style of horror.[18] The type of horror he created, weird horror, relies on monsters from a distant past or alternate reality rather than violence or gore. It is useful for stories confronting racism, which is itself a kind of eldritch horror with an ancient past and tentacles that reach into everything. But that ancient past is, coincidentally, where Indians are also placed. Lovecraft's

18 Our faves are often problematic, something we have to acknowledge rather than ignore. And still, when I visited the H. P. Lovecraft store in Providence, Rhode Island, I bought my grandson a Cthulhu colour and numbers book. Get them started early.

past is terrifying and chaotic, and the Indians in Lovecraft's stories tend to bring that chaos into the present. So we have to be careful if we are going to enter those worlds.[19]

Like many others, in 2020, I was transfixed by *Lovecraft Country*, a brilliantly written and produced horror series driven by Black talent in front of and behind the camera that confronted and challenged contemporary racism. Set in the 1950s, the series centres around a young Black man who makes his way across segregated states, looking for his father. Otherworldly mayhem ensues, including one brief story line featuring a magical Indian in the person of Yahima, a Two Spirit Arawak who helps the hero by translating an important document only to be murdered by one of the main characters. The creator and showrunner, Misha Green (Black), apologized for what was widely condemned as a transphobic and anti-Indigenous portrayal of the character.

When we enter into these conversations in the mashkiig, we are going to make mistakes, fail. We need to accept that. The alternative is just a different kind of failure: staying in our part of the mashkiig, concerned only with our own role in whatever the dominant culture offers by way of diversity (to what end?) and inclusion (into what?). That's not how we build the relationships that lead to solidarity. We try, we fail, we try again.

Set in the years shortly after the Mexican Revolution, Silvia Moreno-Garcia's (Mexican-Canadian) *Mexican Gothic* draws on this ancient world of Lovecraftian horror to illustrate the persistence of racist and colonial violence in Mexico that consumes the Native by infecting and transforming the ruling family who rely on it. The heirs of empire who are now building the nations that emerged from that primordial colonial soup often see themselves as innocent or untouched by ancestral crimes, or they refuse to let go of colonial violence even when it is clearly harming them as well. In Moreno-Garcia's gothic

19 Simmons, *White Men Indian Magic.*

novel, the horror is imagined as a fungus that has overtaken a house in a remote village. Colonialism is the ancient horror, reaching forward to transform and consume the present.

Tiffany Morris (Mi'kmaq) also takes us to fungal networks for her novella *Green Fuse Burning*, and to the swamp where Rita finds life amidst death and decay and the character of Lichen Woman, a creation of Morris's imagination and an interesting blurring of the lines between human and plant rather than human and animal. Through Lichen Woman, Rita hears her dead father's voice telling her that "Shadows are sacred, t'us." He says, "They tell us where we've been." The green of this swamp is Rita's favourite colour, a green that is alive and dead all at once.

This place where things are both alive and dead captures for me the essence of the horror written by marginalized people. This world and the shadows it contains are sacred to us. They might be frightening, but they are not to be feared. In my own imagining of Waawaashkeshi'Kwe's beginning, it was fungal networks that carried the story of trauma into the darkness and received instructions for what to do.

Horror is, at its core, the stories we tell about the various ways that the past haunts the present. Horror happens when the things we fear speak with great clarity about ourselves and the worlds we inhabit, or when we build atop sins we refuse to admit. Marginalized writers tell different stories by beginning at the beginning rather than with "secondly," because dead or alive, Bad Indians pick medicine with the things that go bump in the night. We know how to move between worlds and live in layered relationship with the things that scare us, taking them seriously out of respect not terror. Horror tells us who we have been and hint at what might yet be, a profoundly hopeful exercise.

Having confronted the past that haunts our present, we now look toward the future. Toward the possibility that we might even have one.

Kwe

A low rumble starts in the distance. The landscape is barren. Once there had been trees and grass overlooking a beautiful harbour on the southeast coast of what had once been Nova Scotia.

But none of us are who or what we once had been. Locals are calling it Eskegawaage—the "skin-drying place"—again. This is what they called it in the time before Europeans decided it was theirs. Because of decades of space launches, which have blasted concrete dust and other detritus over everything, it is indeed a dry place. Because of the melting ice caps, the ocean levels have risen. The cliffs aren't what they had once been when I was here centuries ago either.

That was me. It was all me. I don't remember what or who I was running from millennia ago, but I just kept running. I ran all the way to this big ocean, down the coast, to where I watched the wemitigoozhiwag land. And then I ran again following the coast and rivers to what would eventually be called Belize. I was happy there.

But sooner or later you have to go home, and although it took a hundred years or more, I followed a song and the smell of sage to a young woman and the sweat lodge where she waited for me. Her friend's T-shirt was emblazoned with that Sabe; you probably call him Bigfoot. Live Laugh Lurk, just like me. Discovery is dangerous, even for us.

After spending time with Animiiki BenesaiKwe, I didn't run so much, but I kept travelling. "Itchy feet," my Nokomis would have said. Itchy hooves. Can't stay in one place for very long.

The Anishinaabe have stories about star people: beings who came to us long ago and whose return we don't really expect but wouldn't be surprised by either. That's another reason to dislike this spaceport and others like them. Not that I oppose people going to the stars; it's a big universe with so many places to explore. But the people going just keep going for all the worst reasons, thinking they own everything they touch and showing absolutely no respect. You ought to respect star people.

Wayne flops on the grass beside me and stretches out. "Hey hey Waawaashkeshi'Kwe." He tugs my braids and gestures with finger guns toward one more ship getting ready to blast off to wherever they are going.

Oceans are rising, forests are burning, and humans are fleeing this place like rats from a sinking ship. They must know the mess they've made if that colony on Mars or wherever they are leapfrogging to from there seems better. Or easier. It always seems easier to start over. I really don't mind if they leave. Little worried about them crossing paths with the star people, but that won't be my problem.

Wayne: I can't believe he calls himself that. But a long time ago some Anishinaabek knew Nanaboozhoo as Wenabozho. After he woke up, he liked it, so he shortened it to Wayne.

Early in the last century, the Anishinaabek and others worked hard to bring back their languages and ceremonies. I did what I could to protect them, finding and dispatching the ones who caused or intended to cause harm, collecting and sharing stories. Holding memories like the rocks I spent so much time with.

I wasn't alone. We often think that we're alone, but we rarely are. The land and waters know what they are doing, and they never stopped creating the life they needed to sustain those they cared for; to get ready for whatever world comes next. The world is full of shape-shifting mystery monsters that people believed in but couldn't ever prove. It was better that way; like I said, discovery is dangerous even for us.

One day, more than two hundred years after he got so mad he laid down and turned to stone, Wayne woke up full of laughter and stories for the people who were ready to hear them. He still makes jokes about how stiff he is, how he "slept like a rock"—things like that. Nobody else makes me laugh the way he does. It must be in the delivery, because those jokes are so very old now.

More people start to gather around, a few with dark hair and flashing eyes. My children, grandchildren. It took years, so many years, for them to understand and forgive me. I left because I had to, but I knew they would be cared for, and when they began to change, I sensed it and I came back to help them understand what was happening, to do for them what nobody else had been able to do for me. My oldest grandson stands beside me.

"Is it the last ship?" Minowe asks.

"The last one leaving from here," I say. The weather has become too unpredictable for future launches to be planned from this spot. There are other spots much farther south and west, but there won't be many more leaving from anywhere really, and most of the people who wanted to leave were already gone.

For a while they tried to round up everyone, say that we had to go, mostly to ensure a cheap labour supply. If you make staying illegal, you can arrest the ones who want to stay and just like that you've got the cheap and expendable labour that colonies need.

That was our rebellion: our refusal to leave the place we were perfectly made for.

We stand to watch the last ship launch, and as the engines fire, one by one we turn our backs on it and go back to camp.

8

DAZHINDAMANG GE-IZHI-BIMAADIZIYANG

I walk backwards into the future with my eyes fixed on my past.

—Maōri proverb

IN ONE WAY or another, most of our traditional stories talk about worlds beginning and ending. They describe the times we went profoundly off-track, lost our collective temper, sacrificed balance, and started thinking of ourselves as the pinnacle of creation instead of the least and most needy part of it. Our stories narrate the ways that we, and the world itself, take steps to restore balance. One of those stories is about a flood. The Anishinaabe creation story includes a flood, a washing of the world by the waters when the worlds zhemnido made kept failing. The idea of Creator trying and failing is hopeful to me; it means that I can try and fail too, and the world we are in is the result of collaboration between nibi and zhemnido. Anyway, this is not that story. This is another story about a different flood that came later. But Nanaboozhoo remembered that earlier story, so he knew what to do.

I told you that Nanaboozhoo walked the earth, and then walked it again with a wolf, who taught him to see and experience the earth differently. By the time that was done, he and that wolf had been through a lot, seen a lot, made a lot of friends and a few enemies. Maybe a lot. You know how it is.

In the flood story told by Patricia Ningewance in *Gii-Nitaa-Aadisooke*, this flood is provoked by Nanaboozhoo's anger after the wolf he travelled with dies from a fall off of a cliff.[1] The wolf, who is his younger brother, landed in the water, and Nanaboozhoo blames the water cougars for his death, so he kills two of them. This has the unfortunate consequence of unleashing water from their bodies, which in turn creates a flood.

Clinging to the top of a tree, or floating in the water clinging to a log (depending on who is telling the story), Nanaboozhoo works with a series of animals to get a handful of mud from the bottom of the flooded world. When my father talked about this story, he said it was a beaver who dove down and got that handful of mud. Most versions attribute this to a muskrat, who also builds dens and lodges. Depending on the storyteller, Nanaboozhoo either blows on the mud or scatters it on the back of a turtle or a log. Either way, he creates the land on which we live from a handful of mud brought up from the submerged land. Working together with water and earth, animals and wind, Nanaboozhoo re-creates the world.

For the Anishinaabe, there is not a single beginning. There are many beginnings, and we are here in the current world. This is something that is found in other traditional stories as well. Many tribal groups believe that other worlds were created before ours, a series of them that failed or ended for various reasons, and that we emerged from the ashes, or submerged depths, of what came before. In the Quechua tradition, every time the world starts over or a new world comes into being, somebody different is the main character; in this world it is humans. Daniel Delgado (Quechua Jew) talked about the Quechua creation story with me a few years ago. It is a story filled with people we no longer know, because they lived before the flood, or now they only come out at night, or for some other reason have shifted to a supporting role.[2]

---

1 Ningewance uses the name Wiiskejaak with Nenaboozhoo bracketed in the title. This book is a collection of stories she was told as a child.

2 You can listen to this conversation from January 2020, "Holding onto Authentic Indigenous Lives with Daniel Delgado," on my blog here: https://www.thousandworlds.ca/daniel-delgado/.

It is, he said, the nature of creation to shift, often in response to the actions of those living within it, and for others to come out on top or perhaps be given a chance. This is sobering, because we know that when this happens, when life is rebalanced, the most vulnerable are the ones who suffer, even though they were not responsible.

Our job, if we are unable to prevent this change by living in such a way that restores balance, is to be ready for whatever world comes next and our new role within that world. Our task is to reach down, as in the Anishinaabe flood narrative, for that handful of mud from the old world, which will help us either build a new world or build a place for ourselves within it. This being ready, this reaching back into the past to collaboratively build a future, is how we imagine ourselves living in the future.

In her book *A Snake Falls to the Earth*, Darcie Little Badger (Lipan Apache) tells a story of layered worlds and reaching to the past through the characters of Nina and Oli. Nina is a sixteen-year-old Apache girl and Oli is a fifteen-year-old cottonmouth snake from the Reflecting World. According to a story left by Nina's great-great-grandmother, which Nina is working to translate from Lipan Apache into English, the connection between these two worlds used to be much greater. The beings from the Reflecting World, spirits whose true form is an animal, are able to shape-shift into human form when they visit this world. They used to visit more frequently, but there are dangers here, and the worlds are becoming distant from each other. The problem, in *A Snake Falls to Earth*, is that ecological catastrophe in this world has consequences in the Reflecting World; if a species becomes extinct here, the associated spirit beings in the Reflecting World also perish. Little Badger gives us shifting perspectives and a mix of traditional and contemporary storytelling to help us imagine what it might be like to live with the layered worlds of the Apache cosmology.

This idea of returning to ourselves, biskaabiyaang, that I introduced in chapter 3 is the hope that we find in marginalized horror and also a persistent theme in the futurisms imagined by marginalized people. The Māori have the most beautiful phrase for this kind of moving forward by returning to ourselves. Kia whakatōmuri te haere whakamua: "I walk backwards into the future with my eyes fixed on my past." This is what we do with our handful of mud that muskrat picks up—with remembering our stories like Nina does, in working to translate her great-great-grandmother's writing. We fix our eyes on the knowledge of our ancestors, and we walk into whatever the future holds, which means that we keep an eye out for the things that future generations may stumble on just as earlier generations kept an eye out for us.

Preparing the path: It's a beautiful way to think about our connections to each other, our responsibilities and care for each other. My youngest son is a rock climber, and as he scales what look like sheer rock faces, he locks in cams and threads them with rope both for himself and those who will come up behind him. He prepares a path, and he relies on the preparation of others, a path made by climbing it.

Speculative fiction is a broad category that includes fantasy, horror, and futurisms. Writing about the genre, Justice (Cherokee Nation) says that "the fantastic is an extension of the possible, not the impossible; it opens up and expands the range of options." Fantastical and futuristic fiction offers us a way to challenge assumptions and expectations of what is real.[3]

Justice also makes the intriguing observation that writing about the future asks us to think about what kind of ancestors we will become. As future generations walk backward into the future, what will they see when they fix their eyes on us?

• • •

Drawing on Afrofuturism, a genre in which the African diaspora imagines its existence through a shared future, Indigenous futurists bend away from linear timelines or futures that exist in isolation from any kind of backstory. The impacts of colonization are part of our stories,

---

3 Justice, *Why Indigenous Literatures Matter*, 149.

and it is our precolonial histories that inform how we imagine otherwise. Relying on our own stories and traditions, we find our place in what is already, for us, a postapocalyptic landscape. Living in a postapocalyptic landscape means that the assumptions and expectations of what is real, extensions of what is possible, will be different from those who are only beginning to imagine the end of their world.

The 2022 film *Prey*, whose producer Jhane Myers is a member of the Comanche and Blackfeet nations, is a perfect example of this. This franchise has a history of Indigenous presence; in the original *Predator* it was Billy, a Native American, who decided to stand up against it. This time, the Predator is stopped by a young Comanche woman whose people have already experienced an apocalypse at the hands of inexplicable invaders and their advanced weaponry. The Comanche's existence in a postapocalyptic landscape extends what is possible for Naru as she faces down one more hunter in a long line of hunters who have tried and failed to destroy her people.[4]

How do we talk about ourselves living in the future? Afro and Indigenous futurisms imagine futures that are wholly ours, rooted in our own ways of knowing and existing, not some homogenous, whitestream future in which we participate. Our futurisms are not a DEI project for nations built on our displacement. They are a way of thinking about possible futures for ourselves, and then making them real.

In *Parable of the Sower* and *Parable of the Talents*, Octavia Butler (African American) develops a belief system she calls Earthseed. It has three primary tenets. We change everything we touch, so the only lasting truth is change. Therefore, God is change. The second tenet is a paradox: The universe shapes God, and God shapes the universe. The final tenet is that the destiny of Earthseed is to take root among the stars.

---

4 Thank you, Max, for reminding me of this excellent movie. Watching the French fur traders get owned by the Predator was pretty great.

Written in 1993, the events of *Parable of the Sower* begin on July 20, 2024, in a United States that has become unstable through climate change, wealth inequity, and a rising Christian nationalism that dominates the political and social world. It sounds far too familiar and prescient. But the signs were all there to anyone paying attention.

The stories centre around a character with hyper-empathy, Lauren Olamina, who had to flee her gated community after it was overrun by people controlled by a dangerous addiction. Olamina's hyper-empathy means that she feels the pain of any harm she sees and can become incapacitated by it. It is rare to find a central character living with disability, particularly one as powerful as Olamina, without it becoming the key to survival. It's a complication that Olamina carries with her and has to navigate as so many disabilities are. Olamina forms the first Earthseed community in *Parable of the Sower*, which is destroyed and scattered during *Parable of the Talents*. But as with the biblical parables being referenced in the titles, this scattering results in the spreading of Earthseed across the country and eventually the world.

It was that last tenet I struggled with as I read Butler's novels. The ideas that God is change and that we shape and are in turn shaped by God make sense. The communities she created are the kind of thing I want to see in the world. And I understood why a Black woman would look elsewhere for a place to truly belong. Our contemporary world of nationalist states increasingly emphasizes the rights of particular "native-born citizens" over foreigners within and without, and it creates escalating numbers of people who are truly stateless. It offers little in the way of safety or welcome to our Black kin. But the idea of space travel—which is what I assumed Butler meant when she wrote about Earthseed "taking root among the stars"—as a central tenet rather than an option wasn't something I felt good about. This world is my home. The land is my ancestor.

One day my son Sam recommended the writing of adrienne maree brown (mixed-race/Black/queer), specifically her book *Fables and Spells*, which is a collection of poetry and short stories in her Emergent Strategy series. In one of those stories, there is an exchange between amb and the dinosaur at the Chicago airport. I have learned that frequent travel means a lot of connecting flights through O'Hare, which does indeed have a large model of a dinosaur in one of the terminals. Overtired and feeling a little loopy during a three-hour layover, amb finds herself talking with Dino, and the short story, made up of these conversations, takes place over several years. We find out that Dino had also known Butler, who was always nice to them, and then Dino and amb have a conversation about Earthseed and our destiny to take root among the stars.

In this short story, called "A Multi-Year Conversation with the Dinosaur at Chicago O'Hare Airport and Other Fossil-Beings," amb tells Dino that she thought that the idea of taking root among the stars referenced space travel—a reasonable assumption, given the focus of protagonist Lauren Olamina on getting to space. But amb says that Butler struggled to write sequels beyond *Parable of the Talents* "because no world she found in her imagination was as right for us as earth. And on earth, we are amongst the stars." She goes on to note, "We may even be celestial to somebody else." "We need to root here," amb says, "Re-root. Choose here." Dino, echoing the many worlds of the Quechua tradition, wonders if perhaps *human* destiny is not the most important thing.[5]

This conversation between Dino and amb inspired me to have Kwe and her people re-root here, choose here, staying behind when the ships take off. Nanaboozhoo has awakened from his slumber and joined the rebellion, which is their refusal to leave. How could they leave this world that created them?

---

5 adrienne maree brown, *Fables and Spells* (AK Press, 2022), 92. If I'm in the right terminal, I make a point of saying hello to Dino when I pass through O'Hare on my way from one place to another. He has yet to respond, or maybe I just haven't figured out how to listen to him.

So often we imagine ourselves on other worlds, colonizing them and terraforming them to suit our needs. But what will it say about the ancestors we are if we create a world that future people want to escape?

• • •

Then again, there is also no shame in leaving a place so unsafe that staying is no longer an option. Sometimes, in speculative fiction and in life, survival does look like leaving. Sometimes, when things get so bad that Mars (or wherever people are leapfrogging to from there) seems better, maybe leaving is the right thing to do.

If you look at the stories of marginalized people—both the ones that are true and the ones that are "all lies, from beginning to end"—you see that many of them contain stories of migration and movement. The Anishinaabe story of themselves as a people describes movement from the place of our creation to the east coast and then back, to the mashkiig and lands around the Great Lakes.

We return to Weyodi OldBear, who explores a future migration in her book *As Many Ships as Stars*, about a large group of Comanche who, in the horse-stealing tradition of their ancestors, steal a spaceship to escape an earth that is increasingly impossible to live in and take to the stars.

As I read this book, I saw how deeply OldBear rooted these spacefaring Comanche in their own history—just as she did with Wowokin, the coyote who becomes a human in her short story that appears in the anthology *A Howl*. The Comanche emerged as a tribe after a split within the Shoshone and then moved down through the Great Plains into what became central Texas. They welcomed distant relatives, the Náhuatl, who traveled up from what became Mexico to get away from the Spanish invaders and together formed their own society. There are stories about Comanche stealing horses from the Spanish and becoming accomplished riders and traders, incorporating new technology into their lifeways.

Weaving together these two parts of her history, OldBear's spacefaring Comanche become increasingly reliant on their old stories to help them navigate new social situations. Lacking a *place* to root their belonging, they root themselves in their *stories*. In the worlds of OldBear, these Comanche become more themselves while they are in space.[6]

Similarly, in *Thor: Ragnarok*, Taika Waititi (Jewish/Māori) reminded all his kin that Asgard was not a place; it was a people. I'm not diminishing the importance of land. As Gloria Anzaldúa writes, "The land was Mexican once/was Indian always/and is./And will be again."[7] But it is a belonging born of knowing, not of ownership, which is why even when we don't have our land—and many of us don't—we can still root ourselves in the knowing contained in our stories.

In a nice bit of synergy, OldBear's spacefaring Comanche stumble across a succulent plant that gives them the ability to fold space and travel tremendous distances. They call the plant, altered by that familiar science fiction mechanism of radiation, a "deer star plant," because the altered shape looks like antlers. The plant becomes another kind of Deer Woman, looking out for her people as they travel the stars.

If we stay who we are, OldBear told me in a conversation, tech can enhance us. It always has. A few weeks earlier, I had spoken with a cohort of Indigenous university students taking a course in AI development. The invitation was a little baffling, as I admitted to the organizers that I learned everything I know about AI from watching *Terminator* and *The Matrix*. These are not bad or even unreliable sources, but as I thought about the topic and tried to pull some remarks together, I knew that this group didn't need me there to talk about potential harms. They could watch the British speculative fiction series *Black Mirror* like the rest of us for that.

---

6 Personal communication with Weyodi OldBear.

7 Excerpt from *Borderlands/La Frontera: The New Mestiza.* Copyright 1987 by Gloria Anzaldúa. Reprinted by permission of Aunt Lute Books, www.auntlute.com.

What they needed, and why I was asked, was our stories. Whatever ways we travel or imagine ourselves into an alternative past, present, or future, we must be rooted in the stories that contain everything we need to know about worlds beginning and ending. This does not mean codifying old stories and asking ourselves "what would Nanaboozhoo do?" Because you don't always want to do that! We need to remain rooted in stories so that we know ourselves better.

In her book *A Short History of the Blockade: Giant Beavers, Diplomacy, and Regeneration in Nishnaabwin*, Simpson tells that story about the giant beaver I mentioned last chapter and uses it to reflect on contemporary political and social practices. In particular, she uses it to analyze the use of blockades as political strategy and the value of building alliances. When she describes the conflict between the beaver and Nanaboozhoo, she locates it on social media, which gave me an idea for the remarks I would give to these students.

I often tell the story of the deer abandoning the Anishinaabe, as it is a rich story filled with much we can learn about governance and diplomacy, about resurgence and reconciliation. This time I followed Simpson's lead, and after I gave a very brief sketch of the story as I first learned it, I said this wasn't the only time we broke up, and I told the students about an entirely fictitious time that the Anishinaabe decided to start their own global social media platform.[8] Of course, things go sideways, and the deer abandon the Anishinaabe a second time. We aren't going to DEI ourselves into a different world if we have no intention of changing those structures that create and maintain marginalization. From the Nuremberg trials to Truth and Reconciliation

---

8 To be clear, this is completely fictitious. As far as I know, the Anishinaabe have not created their own global social media platform, although studies about community-run platforms show much better outcomes in terms of positive self-image and community building than global platforms—which, unsurprisingly, trend toward colonial practices that cause harm. Marginalized communities have to be cautious in how they use and curate these global spaces.

Commissions, various inquiries, and far too many DEI projects: People talk about racism as an individual failing rather than looking at the ways that structures and systems encourage and empower certain individuals at the expense of others. This is why western audiences can cheer for the rebellion in *Hunger Games* and *Star Wars* while living in the middle of a Capital City run by Palpatine. And as marginalized peoples, we can get caught up in that too, doing unto others the very things we hate.

Imagining ourselves in the future is an opportunity to imagine an end to colonization and the nationalisms that sprung from it, rather than just the end of the world. To imagine ourselves in something other than an ongoing manifest destiny, in space or here on earth.[9] Speculative fiction is a place where we can examine these systems and imagine something different.

In her book about spacefaring Comanche, OldBear, intentionally or not, mirrored the time the deer abandoned the Anishinaabe. Both groups needed to sing their own songs, and listen to their own stories and remember who they are so that they could come back together in a good relationship. The Comanche took that ship, went off on their own, and rooting themselves in the knowing of their stories they returned to themselves. Biskaabiyaang.

The Anishinaabe have old stories about star people who visited us. Other stories tell us that after we pass on, we join our ancestors in the stars, not some happy hunting ground of whitestream imagination. You'll recall the story I told you about my mother whistling at the northern lights in the last chapter. Perhaps in sending the Comanche to the stars, OldBear sends them to the right place to return to themselves. To go beyond the plains of their homeland and into the stars, where creation began and their ancestors wait.

---

9 "Rethinking the Apocalypse: An Indigenous Anti-futurist Manifesto," *Indigenous Action*, March 19, 2020, https://www.indigenousaction.org/rethinking-the-apocalypse-an-indigenous-anti-futurist-manifesto/.

This is what I emphasized for the cohort of AI students: that as they build futures for themselves and their communities, they should root themselves in their own stories. That way, whatever they build will be connected to their communities. We talked about the inevitability of change. We talked about how our community shapes us and how our work shapes our community. And we talked about our destiny to take root among the stars.

Chelsea Vowel (Métis) explores how emerging tech could be situated within wholly Métis communities in her collection of short stories, *Buffalo Is the New Buffalo*. The title is a response to the notion that "education is the new buffalo," a phrase coined by Blair Stonechild (Saulteaux) in 2006. That phrase is now widely used to describe the way that Indigenous peoples can, *if they control education systems themselves*, become self-reliant through education the same way they had been self-reliant through buffalo.[10] Vowel takes exception to this, wondering why we can't look ahead to a world once again populated with buffalo or bison. Education is useful, yes. But can't *buffalo* be the new buffalo?

Two particular stories in Vowel's collection intrigued me: "âniskhôhôcikan" imagines a translator in the form of an implanted nanotechnology enabling children to hear only in Cree, and "I, Bison" considers what happens to a young woman, Angie, whose brain is mapped and uploaded to a construct. Neither of these stories idealize technology, even while they propose it as a solution to real-world problems. The parents in "âniskhôhôcikan" wrestle with the knowledge that unless they speak in Cree, their children will never actually hear their real voices, because what the children hear (when the parents speak English) is the translator. Facing linguistic extinction, they ask themselves: Is

10 This is an important distinction. The phrase is often disconnected from the need for Indigenous people to control their education and just applied broadly. But an education rooted in the stories that allow colonialism to continue won't sustain us. We need to control our education. Freedom Schools run by Black and Indigenous people are an example of life-giving education rooted in the community.

knowing that their children will never actually hear their real voices a sacrifice worth making? Some languages have few, if any, first-language speakers, and others are re-creating their languages from resource material. Do we *have* decades and generations to develop the linguistic skills that this technology would develop in a single generation? As it is, some of our languages are growing, but most are diminishing, and with the possible exception of Hawai'i, none of them have the financial investment needed to create a generation of language speakers.[11] We have so much language tech available to us, and yet our languages continue to diminish. Vowel imagines what kind of tech Cree people might create to counter that trend.

Angie, one of the main characters in "I, Bison," has a history of trauma and unstable mental health that results in self-destructive and often violent outbursts. This short story sets up a contrast between her experience of disability as an individual problem that must be accommodated, punished, or healed and the possibility that it is instead something created by trauma and compounded by a disabling society. It also considers the spiritual impact of such technology; can our spirits move on if our mind is mapped and uploaded, held captive in a server farm somewhere?

The scientists leading the mind-mapping project think that the upload of Angie's mind to the construct was a failure, because when they enter the construct, all they see is herd of bison. But it turns out that the protagonist, Angie, whose mind has been uploaded, is present as part of that bison herd. While aspects of her mental health struggles are still present—she still has the anxiety and anger she struggled with—they don't have the same impact or consequence, because the social life of the herd is organized differently than the world we exist in. She is free, just part of the herd.

11 For more information on the revitalization of Hawai'ian language, you can check out this website from the University of Hawai'i: https://www.uhfoundation.org/saving-hawaiian-language.

At the behest of Angie's mother, who is worried that Angie's spirit won't be able to move on if she remains uploaded in the construct, her friend Gus figures out a way to access the construct. She finds Angie, who then pleads with Gus to leave her be. Angie asks Gus to tell her mom that she isn't there, tell her that the experiment was a failure. The scientists think she isn't there, after all, and discovery would be dangerous.

These are unquestionably Métis stories. This doesn't make them illegible to those outside of that community, but sometimes words or social norms in the stories will elude other readers. Vowel does offer explanations and footnotes, as well as brief reflections on what each story is intended to work through. Like so much Indigenous horror, these stories of Indigenous futurism remain unresolved. "I, Bison" and "âniskhôhôcikan" leave us with questions rather than answers. But those questions are posed within our worlds and our priorities, remembering relations with land and other-than-human relatives.

• • •

The postapocalyptic novel *Moon of the Crusted Snow* and the sequel *Moon of the Turning Leaves* by Waubgeshig Rice (Anishinaabe) do not offer explanations or translations. Set in a northern Anishinaabe community, these books follow the community along an alternative future in the aftermath of something that happened down south that turned off their electricity and phones. In the first book, we have no idea what happened. The community is already somewhat isolated by their location, but with power and communication systems shut down, their isolation is complete.

Yet the book manages to avoid the claustrophobia typical of these stories. Their isolation becomes a kind of flourishing. Instead of being isolated from the world by the loss of electricity, telephone, and regular supply shipments, we find that it was these very things that had isolated this Anishinaabe community from themselves. Cut free from barriers created by western life, the community initially struggles but then begins to flourish. Story, language, and ceremony become central. By the time of *Moon of the Turning Leaves*, which is set about ten years later, story, language, and ceremony are just part of how the community exists. The Anishinaabe were never an arctic people, as the elder Aileen notes; they had been pushed north. In the second book the community begins their journey south, toward the place where their ancestors had once lived. Each novel ends with a return to the woods, and to themselves.

This draws me back to the conversation with Delgado about Quechua creation stories and multiple worlds, about the lessons we gain from our traditional stories of worlds ending and beginning. Our job is to be ready, to be prepared for the world that comes next. Although this community is not without struggles, they have language speakers and elders to lead and teach ceremony. The Anishinaabe language used by the characters is not translated in Rice's books—a deliberate choice, as I noted before, one that emphasizes the need for language reclamation by isolating the reader from the things being said. Once again, through Rice's books we find that what is isolating for western audiences is actually freeing for the Anishinaabeg.

Aileen, one of the elders in *Moon of the Crusted Snow*, tells Evan, the protagonist, that we don't have a word for *apocalypse*—and that the world isn't ending anyway. The world actually ended for us a long time ago, she says, when the settlers arrived. We've been adapting and surviving ever since. This doesn't mean that it is easy. Throughout both books, the Anishinaabe characters come up against white people who are also freed from the legal constraints of the society built for them, and they use that freedom to take by force what they believe they are entitled to.

I once made a list of all the various dystopic futures in the movies we watch: plagues, zombies, evil corporations, authoritarian governments, drought, floods. Looking at that list confirmed for me that all of these apocalypses—with the possible exception of zombies—are things that marginalized peoples around the world have already experienced.[12]

We have been diminished but not erased. The apocalypse is, from our perspective, something that began to roll over us five hundred years ago. And the things that whitestream fiction imagines as a dystopic future describe the past and present that settlers have inflicted on us. It's only scary when it happens to them, I guess.

That means that the futures *we* imagine can be filled with utopic vision. Standing at the edge of one apocalypse, we look outward where a thousand worlds struggle to be born. This is something that Lee Francis IV (Laguna Pueblo), the founder of the Indigenous comic-con IndigiPopX, is excited about: publishing books and comics exploring a thousand alternative timelines, vectoring out from wherever we stand. A thousand possible futures, any one of which could become a place we inhabit, a path we make by walking together.

Even when we celebrate whitestream science fiction, we do it on our own terms, transforming broadly familiar stories and characters through our own languages and artwork. The Star Wars franchise has been hugely popular throughout Indian Country, where many Indigenous peoples see themselves as part of the rebellion against empire. In 2021, the first film of the Star Wars franchise, *A New Hope*, was dubbed in Navajo; and in 2024, it was dubbed in Anishinaabemowin. Throughout 2020, when *The Mandalorian* began streaming, beaded and painted representations of "baby Yoda," in the easily recognized formline art of the Haida or the woodlands style made famous by Norval Morriseau, proliferated, and he was immediately adopted as one of our own. Johnnie Jae (Otoe-Missoria/Choctaw), whose artwork is worn by the young man keeping fire in the flash fiction before chapter 5, says that

---

12 Okay, but the Pentagon really did come up with CONOP 888, Counter-Zombie Dominance, as a training scenario for junior officers. According to Wikipedia, it was a useful training tool that avoided the political risks of using a real country, which tells you something about how the United States views the enemies they invent.

the character of Grogu (baby Yoda's real name) resonated so deeply and immediately because of the similarity with residential schools and child welfare. We recognized the stolen child, and saw ourselves in the care and protection of the Mandalorian.[13]

When I spoke with that AI cohort, I used Anishinaabe stories, because those are my stories. And I encouraged students to look at their own stories to see what they could pull forward. Several students commented that I had made them see their own stories differently, one student saying that I made him want to go home and ask his grandparents to share stories with him. Using our own stories to imagine the past, present, and future differently encourages others to do the same and reminds us that our stories do have something to say about space travel, nanites, and AI. Rabbi Danya Ruttenberg (Jewish American) often says that every generation has to read Torah with an eye to what it has to say to them in the moment in which they live. This is true for all of us. The stories that Ananzi brought down from Nyame, the ones that we just thought up (whether they are true or lies from beginning to end): We need to look at them to see what they say to us now, in this moment, and how they can guide us into imagining ourselves in the future.

Cherie Dimaline (Métis) demonstrates this beautifully in the young adult novel *The Marrow Thieves*, a world where white people have lost the ability to dream. The solution lies, literally, in the bones of Indigenous people. In an echo of residential schools and Indian hospitals, Indigenous peoples are rounded up and have their marrow extracted to be given to white people so that they can dream again. In the midst of climate change and authoritarian political systems, the characters, all Indigenous, create a mobile community. Unable to stay long in one place where they can root themselves, they find themselves connected and rooted through Story, with a capital S. Story is a character in its

---

13 Emily Blake, *Why Some Indigenous People See Themselves in Star Wars Icon Baby Yoda*, January 12, 2020, https://www.cbc.ca/news/canada/north/indigenous-baby-yoda-1.5420189.

own right, both as a way to remember and recount history as well as dreams and connection, which is something that the broader society has lost.

Walking backward into the future, with a handful of mud that contains everything we need to know about how to imagine new worlds rather than just reforming old ones: This is the way.

• • •

Chosen family, rebuilding community, and the importance of story are part of *Moon of the Turning Leaves*, the sequel to Rice's *Moon of the Crusted Snow*. This time the Anishinaabe language spoken is understood by all the characters, although it is still not explained to the reader. Where *Crusted Snow* was the story of the characters withdrawing like the deer, in *Turning Leaves*, they have returned to themselves and are ready to send out a scouting party to see what is out there, if they can expand their community. The future they have built is rooted deeply in who they are, through their stories and Anishinaabe language. Similarly, the community being built in *Marrow Thieves,* a community of Cree, Anishinaabe, and Métis people, is rooted in Story and Cree language, which is hinted at but not actually spoken until one of the characters is dying. Stories and language are the collective memory of a people, so of course they are what we must root ourselves in.

Memory is at the core of "The Generation Chip," a short story by Nadia Afifi (Palestinian) in the anthology *Thyme Travellers*, edited by Sonia Suliaman, who was one of the storytellers in the discussion about oral storytelling during that year of Indigenous reading, alongside Rice and Christie. In this story, after the death of their grandmother Hind, three siblings are given chips that Hind made at a Mind Clinic. One contains her memories, another her recurring dream, and the third contains paths not taken: the alternate futures had she made different choices.

The siblings have to decide what to do with the information in these chips. To Salim, the eldest, it seems obvious: Give the memory chip to the historical society and discard the others as irrelevant junk science. The sister, Mahel, agrees. But for Kamel, who received the paths-not-taken chip, it is more complicated. He has seen a series of alternate futures that explore various paths, including their grandmother's life with her true love, a young woman from her hometown. Hind, it turns out, did not love their grandfather the way they had thought she did.

When I think about Justice's question—about the kind of ancestors we might be—this story comes to mind. What story would my memories put alongside my dreams and regrets, tell my grandchildren about me? Afifi, the author, didn't write a story about the siblings combing through Hind's social media to decide what to archive and what to delete in order to tell her story; she imagined a way of extracting memories three specific ways.

The solution proposed by Salim—ignoring the grandmother's recurring dream and the paths not taken—seems reasonable but also troubling. On their own, the grandmother's memories might benefit the larger community, but without the information contained in the recurring dream and paths untaken, they don't tell the whole story of who she was. Salim's rejection of these other pieces of knowledge, the dreams and possible futures, is much like the way Indigenous ways of knowing are rejected by broader society. Indigenous knowledge, which is often rooted in relationships between things rather than seeing the thing in isolation, is not seen as "scientific"; it is not "rigorous." Salim saw a greater good of historical information. Kamel saw his grandmother.

Extracting memory like marrow to provide us as individuals or communities what we need has costs. Silvia Moreno-Garcia (Mexican-Canadian) explores this in her speculative short story "A Shadow in Amber," from the anthology *Sword Stone Table*. Her story about memory and the connections it forms is a retelling of "The Lady of Shalott," a poem by Tennyson about a woman with a mysterious curse who was unable to even look at Camelot, let alone travel there.

Moreno-Garcia's unnamed heroine lives on the top floor of a sky-scraping apartment building, rarely leaving because of the violence in the city below. Her contact with the outside world comes through injecting and then experiencing the memories of others, opera mostly, until Delgado, the man who brings the vials of memory, provides her with a memory of a young man cliff diving. She never learns his name (privacy reasons, Delgado explains), so she calls him Lancelot and becomes immersed in the memories of his life: cliff diving, motorcycle riding, and the exquisite intensity of his love for the wife of his best friend. She knows that memories offer few insights into a person. They are brief moments, shadows trapped in amber that can be experienced and examined but leave so much out, just as the siblings in "The Generation Chip" learned, and she longs for more. We feel her desperation in the days between Delgado's visits, a desperation that echoes Salim's frustration that Kamil won't consent to simply releasing the memories. Give me what I need, she says.

When Delgado tells our lady in the tower that Lancelot died, a banal pedestrian death at that, just 2 weeks after he collected the memories she has already experienced, she falls into despair. He has always been out of reach, a ghost caught in a vial.

There is a meme: We are our ancestors' wildest dreams. We are the future that they imagined. We are Salim, Mahel, and Kamil, and perhaps the lady in the tower as well. What do we do with the memories our ancestors have left us, the futures they imagined? Running our fingers along photo albums and scrolling the social media pages of those who have passed on. Replaying the moments the way we might worry a sore tooth or press on a wound. It is so hard to let them go, as Angie begged Gus to do in "I, Bison."

The Anishinaabe have a practice of adding "ba" to the names of those who have passed on, often not speaking their name at all for a year, maybe more. Speaking their names might draw them back, confuse their journey into the west. Erdrich, in her updated conclusion to *Books & Islands in Ojibwe Country*, wonders if it is not something more than that—if the refusal to say their name is perhaps a decision to hold onto the memories themselves. Their name can be a kind of distancing, an idealized memorial, so instead we experience life with them again and again through the things we remember, and we do this with others who knew them too. Putting our memories together, we see our ancestors as whole people with dreams and regrets, and in that way walking backward into the future together.

Diaz talks about this as well in an interview that is included in the book *We Are the Middle of Forever: Indigenous Voices from Turtle Island on the Changing Earth*. You speak *around* the name of those who have died, she says; you talk about things they have done or places they have been. You immerse yourself in the person, in the loss, rather than maintaining the distance offered by their name.[14] Her poem "Grief Work" describes grief work as a thing we do together; rather than try to escape the pain of grief and loss, we allow ourselves to be washed clean by it. We go to where there is love, she writes, to the river. Pulling ourselves beneath the waters, she says, we are rearranged.[15] We immerse ourselves in the memories of our ancestors, in their language and dreams, in the stories they told about the lives they didn't have. This is the power of writing from the mashkiig: being able to immerse ourselves this way in the rivers of our ancestors without concern for who might be watching, curtains or branches twitching furtively.

• • •

We conclude with a story about the Tuktuaapik, a caribou-being known to the Inuit. The Inuit are a circumpolar people, and the Tuktuaapik is one of many such beings that exist in worlds beyond the borders we've drawn around ourselves. Caribou are large animals, and for a time,

---

14 Jamail and Rushworth, *We Are the Middle of Forever: Indigenous Voices from Turtle Island on the Changing Earth* (New Press Books, 2022), 285.

15 "Grief Work," Natalie Diaz. Copyright 2020 by Natalie Diaz. *Postcolonial Love Poem* (Graywolf Press, 2020), 93.

various species of caribou covered more than half of what is currently Canada, reaching from the north shores of Lake Superior, where my paternal family live, and up past the arctic circle. Known as reindeer in Eurasia, caribou cover the northern Scandinavian countries and across much of Russia to the northern Pacific coastline. Communities throughout the circumpolar region and the lands just south are connected by stories about caribou, reindeer, and the beings who take shape in things we might recognize, like the Tuktuaapik.

The Indigenous comic anthology *Moonshot* is published by Inhabit Education Books, an Inuit-owned publishing company. Their third volume, which Odjick introduced us to in our conversation about graphic novels, is edited by Elizabeth LaPensée, who also edited the *A Howl* and *Deer Woman* graphic anthologies, and Michael Sheyahshe (Caddo). It contains a piece of speculative fiction about the Tuktuaapik called "Waterward" by Sean (Scottish/Mohawk) and Rachel (Scottish/Inuk/Cree) Qitsualik-Tinsley. This caribou-being is a witness to an Inuk woman's distress and desperation as she seeks to be freed from what she finds an intolerable life.

After ensuring that her husband has left for a hunting trip, Pairivaa packs up her infant triplets into her amauti and walks a great distance to a lake that her father has told her about. There she intends to ask the lake-masters to grant her wish that she could be free again. Free of her husband, free of her children, she wants to go back to her life as it used to be.

Anyone who has read a story about wishes knows that there is a price to be paid, and Pairivaa understands this. Welcomes it. The Tuktuaapik comes closer, crouching, and watches her. Pairivaa sees una and is initially confused, thinking that the caribou-being represents the beings of the lake.[16] The Tuktuaapik demurs, referring to the beings of this lake as "those who devour." They are the raw essence of life, eating

16 Like many languages that emerged in these lands, Inuktitut is not gendered. Instead of saying he or she, they say una, which means "this person, here."

and birthing throughout eternity, the Tuktuaapik says—a single being despite appearing to be many.

At that point Pairivaa recognizes the Tuktuaapik and dismisses una to focus on her need to be free. The Tuktuaapik persists, wanting her to be certain of the price to be paid. But Pairivaa reminds una of the principle of noninterference: that is, people make their own choices, and we have to respect them, respect their isuma, their autonomy. This is the first gift of Ptesáŋwiŋ and is something valued broadly in the societies that emerged from the lands that became the Americas. It is how we are able to live in layered relationship instead of hard borders.

Do the children not also have isuma, the Tuktuaapik asks? No, Pairivaa responds, they do not. They are her children, extensions of her, which gives her the right to decide what to do with them. Although she appears to believe she was sacrificing her children, the parts of herself that were keeping her tethered to this life she never wanted, in the end it is Pairivaa herself who pays. It is her hands and head that are offered, and then taken by the creatures of the lake, not her babies.

The story ends with Tuktuaapik gathering the infants in caribou wrappings and holding them close. Isuma was respected; una had watched while Pairivaa destroyed herself. And, throwing their spear into the waters, the Tuktuaapik itself was granted a wish, which was to have children of their own.

In the present we often feel trapped by events in the past; bearing the consequences of decisions made by others, we fall into despair. Rooted in that kind of vision of the past, our future looks dismal, dystopic. We may not have access to beings with the power to grant wishes, but we are too often willing to sacrifice the most vulnerable among us, those to whom we are tethered through relations of kin or of power, as if that will set us free.

Like Pairivaa, Hind, the grandmother in the short story "The Generation Chip," also wrestles with a life that was not what she would have chosen. In the end, through the paths not taken, Kamel and his siblings come to understand her: She may not have chosen her husband, but she did choose them.

"Waterward" might be a horror story, an Inuit tale of ancient beings. But it invites us to think about the ways our view of the past limits the futures we imagine and the desperate paths we may take as we imagine something other.

People tend to idealize the past. So does walking backward into the future simply mean longing for a past that never was? Are we fixing our eyes on ancestors in all their complexity, as people with dreams and regrets? Or do we idealize them too, marking their names while granting them nothing more than a two-dimensional memory—a handful of lines on a meme to be shared around social media? In the words of Diaz: Dare we sink into the grief and allow ourselves to be washed clean by the very things that ache us?[17]

This is, I think, what Butler means when she says in the *Parable* books that we shape God and are shaped by God. We transform and are transformed, but only by refusing to escape our grief.

Seven generations forward means seven generations back, and each one of us is in the midst of seven generations, part of an infinite web of relations stretching across time in as many dimensions as our imaginations can come up with. We truly are in the middle of a world gone mad, a world that has forgotten who they are and why they do anything at all.

Bad Indians turn to the mashkiig, but not to extract what it might teach us so that we can rescue what is not worth saving. Having pushed aside the detritus and burned what no longer serves us, if it ever did, we make room for new ideas. We take seriously that life that surrounds us and return to ourselves through histories told by those with a stake in collective futures. Bad Indians refuse hierarchies and boundaries in favour of the connections we find outside the colonial centres and

---

17 Natalie Diaz, "Poet Statement on Grief Work," accessed November 13, 2024, https://poets.org/poem/grief-work.

immerse ourselves in the swamp, and in relationship with the others we find there. Holding onto each other, we sink into the mashkiig and rekindle our connections with the beings who know such things, allowing them to transform us into something new. We take each other by the hand, and together we walk backward into the future. Remembering the first rule of Bad Indians book club: Always carry a book.

BAAMAAPII

Dear Mom,

The trouble with writing a book about books is that there are just so many of them. Every revision of *Bad Indians Book Club* has me adding books I forgot to include or something I just finished reading, and I know that I'm leaving out peoples' favourites. So if they've read this far and I haven't mentioned some book or author who would have been perfect, well, I'm sure it is, and they are. But I'm already way over the word count. That's the trouble with teaching me to love books, which you did. There's just so many of them.

Some of my earliest memories are about books. The Heidi series is part of those memories. I think those stories helped me feel connected to you. Knowing that you had lived in Switzerland as a small child (the idea of mother as child is baffling to a little kid), I might have imagined that they were about you in some way. I remember paging through the Childcraft Series and a multivolume set of Disney stories. I remember the time you took my Nancy Drew books from me; I don't remember what I had done, but it must have been serious to warrant that kind of consequence. I hope it was worth it.

Dading, my grandmother, also loved books. And her mother too. I come from a long line of women who found ideas and questions and moments of peace in the writings of others. I come from a long line of women who have used books to communicate and teach, and I find myself pressing books into the hands of others, just as you and Dading pressed books into mine. My boys are storytellers, all three of them, and more than one book has been pressed into my hands by each of them.

Throughout the book I have introduced people according to how they introduce themselves, an abbreviated kind of introduction that gives readers an idea of where they are writing from. For you I would write Vicki (German Ukrainian), but that actually says so little about you. Even if people know that you are German Ukrainian and living in Canada, which is much different from being German Ukrainian living in Germany or Ukraine, it says nothing about how you came to be here. You and your siblings came here as "Displaced People," not the more contemporary language of "Refugee." I think I like that term better: Displaced People. My father's people were Displaced too. It feels like a place of connection between you in a way that Refugee does not. On the other hand, displaced sounds so passive, like somebody just scootched you aside. For your family and my father's, it was much more violent than that.

Was being a nurse the way you had dreamed it when you read those Cherry Ames books? I don't imagine so. They were pretty idealized even for the 1960s. That's a kind of danger in books that people rarely talk about: We get introduced to a thousand possible worlds, and then none of them look like what we've imagined, what we were told they would be. This is why relationships are so important: to remember that books and people go together.

I think about how you entered this place, how you built relationship with the land and people, how you welcome others. I am at best a reluctant gardener, but your ability to coax life and food from the ground is magical. Your capacity for generosity in relationships and curiosity about people astounds me. I look at my boys and I see pieces of you. Each of them nurturing or gathering life from the earth and then feeding the people who gather around them. Travelling and collecting stories, caring about those our society would rather leave behind. They listen to stories, not just from people but from the places where they find themselves. Because what was Max doing on that rock in the water if not listening to the lake? Ben teaches Charlie to listen, but the stories Ben tells mean that he must also be listening to Charlie carefully, and Sam always notices things about places and people with particular insight.

You taught us all this. To love stories along with the books and people who contain them. To be curious. To look beyond the labels written on top of us to the connections between us. To see what people bring rather than where they belong.

You dared us to be Bad Indians and to make our own paths by walking them, pushing aside the detritus and making space for new ideas. You knew that the world was alive in ways we could not understand and encouraged us to be the kind of people that the land wants back. It was Indian land once, and will be again.

You taught us to pick up history as a living weapon against those for whom we are nonpersons, so that we could tell the stories that need to be told, refusing to accept other people's versions of us. You reminded us to listen to the water for what it might teach us, and to centre the voices of those who are pushed to the edges. You taught us that we are not atoms in the universe but stories, worlds held together by the connections between us.

Sometimes somebody asks me: What radicalized you? What made you believe that a better world was not only possible but inevitable, and that we should work together to bring these new worlds into being?

I tell them that you did. You made me believe that anything was possible.

Thank you, Mom.
Baamaapii.

MIIGWECH

***The trouble with gratitude is much like the trouble with books; there's just so much of it and the more I start identifying the people I am thankful for, the more I notice the layers of communities that helped me to craft this, helped me to become the person who could craft this. Some of it is scattered through the book, I hope you noticed your names.

My Podcast Friends. Kerry, without whom none of this would have even been possible. Thank you for helping me find my inner mystic. To all of the participants of these conversations, to Jenessa who moderated the chat so faithfully and Robin who stepped in when Jenessa participated in the discussions, thank you so much for your time and generosity. I have learned so much from you in the things you taught me and the ways you pushed me.

My Native Community. Online and offline, drum circles and sister friends, teachers, and kwewag. I am so grateful for each of you investing in me and allowing me to invest in you. I hope you see yourselves in these pages, in the ways that you have influenced and changed me. Okie, you picked me up and kept me safe. Shine bright, Moon Tree Woman. Forever grateful for friends like Frances, Nicole, Robyn, and Joy, always up for the best kind of trouble.

My Comrades. People I organize with and show up for. I believe in you; I believe in us. I believe in a world where a thousand worlds can exist together without borders inside us or around us. I believe that the land can be free, that it is the only way that we can be free. I believe that we can be the kind of people that the land wants back. People like Harsha and Kelly, Kit, Kerry, Khadija, and Leigh. You trust me with your communities and your backs. Please know that I've got you in whatever capacity I have.

My Reading Posse. A writer is only as good as the people they trust with often embarrassingly bad drafts. To those of you who cheerlead, add emphasis (dung beetles ARE badass), offer suggestions, and make corrections to things I have misremembered, I am so grateful. Renee, Kali, Linda, and Taté, early readers like you have made this book so much better. Miigwech.

Valerie, I am once again thankful to have you editing my words and asking questions. Sometimes I forget that my readers don't know what's going on in my head. Rob, having you as my agent has been the happiest of accidents. Thank you for everything you do.

I am so grateful for Gary's endless patience, cooking, tidying up, fixing everything, driving into town to pick up things I forgot, road trips with side quests, for never once rolling his eyes when more books arrived in the mail or when I wanted to stop in one more bookstore, and then building me the bookshelves to hold them all. I will forever walk backward into the future with you. Ben, Angela and Charlie, Max and Sam. You are so much better at all of this than I am. I am so grateful that you chose me, and the best moments in my life are when somebody I meet asks me if I'm your mom.

NOTE ABOUT THE COVER

Wanada Parker Page, whose likeness is depicted on the front cover, was born in Indian Territory sometime in or around 1882, to Quanah Parker and his principal wife and comrade in arms, Weckeah OldBear. Her mother's third surviving daughter, Wanada Parker Page was, like many Comanche girls, initially named after her mother. She was struck down by an unknown illness in early childhood, however, and was unable to stand without the use of crutches. Her parents were advised to rename her Wʉnʉrʉ, anglicized as Wanada, a name meaning literally Stand Up, implying strength and bravery. She would need both when she was sent to Carlisle Residential School as soon as she healed. There she excelled academically and was renamed Annie.

Upon graduating from boarding school, her first act was to reclaim the name her parents had given her, Wanada. Her second was to step into the role of secretary and translator for her father, leader of the Comanche Nation. Her father was an intelligent man who was fluent in Spanish as well as his native Comanche but often frustrated by his understanding of English. Wanada traveled with him across the country, translating for him in both political and business negotiations and writing reams of letters on his behalf, many as part of the fight against the "Opening Up" or taking of the joint Kiowa-Comanche-Apache Reservation. She also helped him, as translator, to avoid being used by various Christian sects to endorse any particular church or Christianity, to which he never converted. All correspondence bearing the signature of Quanah Parker is the work of his daughter Wanada.

Her father, a man as interested in his personal appearance as his daughter Wanada, employed a white seamstress to keep the two of them dressed in the latest styles when she accompanied him. When she was home she was known to throw formal balls attended by people from as far away as Georgia and Tennessee. Fiercely beautiful and fiercely intelligent, Wanada was married twice and appreciated the company of men almost as much as they appreciated her. At the age of thirty-eight, Wanada starred as Red Wing, the romantic rival of Esther Lebarre, a sixteen-year-old Comanche girl, in the silent film *The Daughter of Dawn*. She gave birth to no children, though she managed to keep a banana tree alive in a house without electricity. She was rumored to have been sterilized without consent at an Indian Hospital facility.

As time went by, in the traditional Comanche way, Wanada served as grandmother and great-grandmother to the descendants of her sisters and brothers. She survived to the age of seventy-eight, passing on in 1970.

—Weyodi OldBear

THE PODCASTS

1. Clearing Space for Story

Panelists for Ambe:[1] **Foundations:** Daniel Heath Justice (Cherokee Nation), Janet Marie Rogers (Mohawk/Tuscarora), Joy Henderson (Black/Lakota); Ishkenikeyaa Waawaashkesh (Anishinaabe), Robin McBurney (canadian), and Neil Ellis Orts (queer Texan/German descent)

Recommended Books

Why Indigenous Literatures Matter, Daniel Heath Justice (Cherokee Nation)

Janet Marie Rogers (Mohawk/Tuscarora) read poetry selections[2] from her own catalog of works.

Panelists for Being Indigenous: Joy Henderson (Black/Lakota), Ann Marie Beals (Black/Mi'kmaq), Jesse Wente (Anishinaabe), and Seán Carson (Nêhiyaw/Anishnaabe/Otipêmisiwak)

---

1 Eagle-eyed readers may note that Ambe is spelled differently than in my first book, *Becoming Kin,* where each chapter ends with a call to action (Aambe). There are some attempts at standardizing the spelling in Anishinaabemowin (Anishinaabe language), and the difference reflects my own learning.

2 This was an attempt at weaving poetry into the discussions. We also had poets for two other panels, Memoir and History, but it wasn't a practice I maintained, mostly because I don't read a lot of poetry. Another gap.

Recommended Book

Unreconciled: Family, Truth, and Indigenous Resistance, Jesse Wente (Anishinaabe)

2. Science and Nature Writing

Collapsing our discussions "Surrounded by Relatives" and "Harvest Time"

Panelists for *Ambe: We Are Surrounded by Relatives*: Daniel Heath Justice and Chanda Prescod-Weinstein (Black/Jewish), Neil Ellis Orts (queer Texan/German descent), Celeste Smith (Ohnkweonwe), and Ben Krawec (Ojibwe Anishinaabe)

Panelists for *Ambe: Harvest Time*: Dr. Jonathan Ferrier (Michi Saagig Nishinaabe), Mayam Garris (Black/Queer), Ben Krawec, and Ziya Tong (Earthling)

Recommended Books

Braiding Sweetgrass: Indigenous Wisdom, Scientific Knowledge, and the Teachings of Plants, Robin Wall Kimmerer (Potawatami)
Gathering Moss: A Natural and Cultural History of Mosses, Robin Wall Kimmerer
Badger, Daniel Heath Justice
Raccoon, Daniel Heath Justice
Undrowned: Black Feminist Lessons from Marine Mammals, Alexis Pauline Gumb (Black)
The Disordered Cosmos: A Journey into Dark Matter, Spacetime, and Dreams Deferred, Chanda Prescod-Weinstein
Salmon and Acorns Feed Our People: Colonialism, Nature, and Social Action, Kari Marie Norgaard (non-Native/white)
Indigenous Food Sovereignty in the United States: Restoring Cultural Knowledge, Protecting Environments and Regaining Health, Devon A Mihesuah (Choctaw) and Elizabeth Hoover (unmarked), et al.

3. History

Panelists for *Ambe: History*: Nick Estes (Lakota), Cheryl Savageau (Abenaki/French Canadian), Tiya Miles (Black), Khadija Hammuda (Libyan), and Seán Carson (Nêhiyaw/Anishnaabe/Otipêmisiwak)

Recommended Books

An Indigenous Peoples' History of the United States, Roxanne Dunbar Ortiz (settler)

Our History Is the Future: Standing Rock versus the Dakota Access Pipeline, and the Long Tradition of Indigenous Resistance, Nick Estes (Lakota)

The Heartbeat of Wounded Knee: Native America from 1890 to the Present, David Treuer (Ojibwe)

All Our Relations: Indigenous Trauma in the Shadow of Colonialism, Tanya Talaga (Anishinaabe)

The Ties That Bind: The Story of an Afro-Cherokee Family in Slavery and Freedom, Tiya Miles

Crossing Waters, Crossing Worlds: The African Diaspora in Indian Country, Tiya Miles

Mother/Land, Cheryl Savageau, particularly the piece "I Wrote about Indians Again Today"

1491: New Revelations of the Americas before Columbus, Charles C. Mann (unmarked)

Property and Dispossession: Natives, Empire, and Land in Early Modern North America, Alan Greer (unmarked)

4. Stories about Refusing Patriarchy

Panelists for *Ambe: Refusing Patriarchy*: Nick Thixton (white/Jewish/and queer), Taté Walker (Mniconjou Lakota/Two Spirit storyteller), Seán Carson (Nêhiyaw/Anishnaabe/Otipêmisiwak), Robyn Bourgeois (Nêhiyaw iskwew), and Angela Gray (Black)

Recommended Books

Halfbreed, Maria Campbell (Metis)
Hood Feminism: Notes from the Women That a Movement Forgot, Mikki Kendall (Black)
Split Tooth, Tanya Tagaq (Inuk)
The Beginning and End of Rape: Confronting Sexual Violence in Native America, Sara Deere (Mvskoke)
Reproductive Justice: The Politics of Healthcare for Native American Women, Barbara Gurr (settler)
FIERCE: Essays by and about Dauntless Women: Various, Taté Walker contributor
A Two-Spirit Journey: The Autobiography of a Lesbian Ojibwa-Cree, Ma-Nee Chacaby (Anishinaabe)
How We Fight White Supremacy: A Field Guide to Black Resistance, Akiba Solomon (Black) and Kenrya Rankin (Black), added by panelist Angela J. Gray

5. Memoir

Panelists for *Ambe: Memoir*: Ernestine Hayes (Tlingit) and Demita Frazer (African American), Jenessa Galenkamp (Métis), and Joy Henderson (Afro-Lakota)

Recommended Books

Heart Berries: *A Memoir*, Terese Marie Mailhot (Niaka'pamux)
Native: Identity, Belonging, and Rediscovering God, Kaitlin Curtice (Potawatomi)
How We Get Free: Black Feminism and the Combahee River Collective, Keeanga-Yamatta Taylor (African American)
In My Own Moccasins: A Memoir of Resistance, Helen Knott (Dane Zaa)
From the Ashes: My Story of Being Indigenous, Homeless, and Finding My Way, Jesse Thistle (Métis)
The Tao of Raven: An Alaska Native Memoir, Ernestine Hayes (Tlingit)
One Native Life, Richard Wagamese-ba (Anishinaabe)
A Mind Spread Out on the Ground, Alicia Elliot (Tuscarora)

Chapters 6, 7, and 8 draw on multiple panels and podcast interviews, each of which contributed in various ways to all three chapters.

***Ambe* Panels:**

All We Are Is Story: Finding Our Way Home with Richard Wagamese-ba: Shelagh Rogers (Métis), Daniel Delgado (Jewish/Quechua), Jenessa Galenkamp (Métis), and Dalton Walker (Anishinaabe)

The Stories We Tell: Waubegshig Rice (Anishinaabe), Sonia Sulaiman (Palestinian), and Kesha Christie (Afro-Caribbean)

***Medicine for the Resistance* podcast interviews:**

The Losses that Sustain Us with Omar El Akkad (Egyptian/Canadian)
African Storytelling with Kesha Christie (Afro-Carribbean)
Transformation, Tradition, and the Way Forward with Daniel Heath Justice (Cherokee Nation)
Indigenous Futurisms with Zainab Amadahy (Afro-Indigenous: Black/Tsalagi/Seminole)
The End of Colonialism with Lee Francis IV (Pueblo Laguna)
Esu, Gedde, the Clown and the Trickster with Mosa McNeilly (Black Canadian)
Finding Drew Hayden Taylor with Drew Hayden Taylor (Anishinaabe)
Heroes and Monsters with Jay Odjick (Algonquin)
Poetry as Resistance with January Marie Rogers (Mohawk/Tuscarora)

6. Fiction

Recommended Books

Anything by Richard Wagamese-ba (Anishinaabe)

7 and 8. Horror and Speculative Fiction

Graphic Novels: Jay Odjick (Algonquin), Lee Frances (Pueblo Laguna), Neil Ellis Orts (queer Texan/German descent), and Anrya Foubert (French Canadian)

Recommended Books

Kagagi, Jay Odjick (Algonquin)
A Howl: An Indigenous Anthology of Wolves, Werewolves, and Rougarou, ed. Elizabeth LaPensée (Irish/Anishinaabe/Métis)
Moonshot: The Indigenous Comics Collection, AH Comics
Moon of the Crusted Snow, Waubgeshig Rice (Anishinaabe)

BIBLIOGRAPHY

Adler, Nathan Niigan Noodin. *Wrist*. Kegedonce Press, 2016.

Agger, Helen Olsen. *Dadibaajinn: Returning Home through Narrative*. University of Manitoba Press, 2021.

Ahmed, Sara. *Living a Feminist Life*. Duke University Press, 2017.

Anzaldúa, Gloria. *Borderlands/La Frontera: The New Mestiza*. Aunt Lute Books, 1987.

Akiwenzi-Damn, Kateri, et al. *This Place: 150 Years Retold*. Highwater Press, 2019.

Barghouti, Mourid. *I Saw Ramallah*. Anchor Books, 2003.

Becker, Rachel. "The World's Largest Dam Demolition Has Begun. Can the Dammed Klamath River Finally Find Salvation?" *CalMatters*, August 31, 2023. https://calmatters.org/environment/2023/08/klamath-river-dams-demolition/.

Begley, Chris. *The Next Apocalypse: The Art and Science of Survival*. Basic Books, 2021.

Benally, Klee. *No Spiritual Surrender: Indigenous Anarchy in Defense of the Sacred*. Detritus Books, 2023.

brown, adrienne maree. *Fables and Spells*. AK Press, 2022.

Butler, Octavia. *Parable of the Sower*, reprint edition. Grand Central Publishing, 2019.

———. *Parable of the Talents*, reprint edition. Grand Central Publishing, 2019.

Byrd, Jodi. *The Transit of Empire: Indigenous Critiques of Colonialism*. University of Minnesota Press, 2011.

Byrne, Monica. *The Actual Star: A Novel*. Harper Voyager, 2022.

Carruthers, Charlene A. *Unapologetic: A Black, Queer, and Feminist Mandate for Radical Movements*. Beacon Press, 2018.

Childs, John Brown. *Trans-Communality: From the Politics of Conversion to the Ethics of Respect*. Temple University Press, 2003.

Coates, Ta-Nehisi. *The Message*. Penguin Random House, 2024.

Danticat, Edwidge. *Create Dangerously: The Immigrant Artist at Work.* Vintage Books, 2011.

Deb, Siddhartha. *Twilight Prisoners: The Rise of the Hindu Right and the Fall of India.* Haymarket, 2024.

Delgado, Daniel. "Are Jews Indigenous? A Quechua Jew Weighs In." Life Is a Sacred Text, May 6, 2024. https://www.lifeisasacredtext.com/indigenous/.

Devaney, Rachael. "'Overstepping.' Plymouth Town Committee Makes Decision on Land Acknowledgement Request." *Cape Cod Times,* August 19, 2024. https://www.capecodtimes.com/story/news/2024/08/19/plymouth-herring-pond-wampanoag-land-acknowledgment-ferretti/74799128007/.

Diaz, Natalie. *Postcolonial Love Poem.* Gray Wolf Press, 2020.

Dimaline, Cherie. *The Marrow Thieves*. Dancing Cat Books, 2017.

DiPrima, Diane. *Pieces of a Song: Selected Poems.* City Lights Books, 2014.

Drucker, Peter. *Management Challenges for the 21st Century.* Harper Collins, 2009.

Dunbar-Ortiz, Roxanne. *Loaded: A Disarming History of the Second Amendment.* City Lights Books, 2018.

El Akkad, Omar. *American War*. McClelland & Steward, 2018.

———. *What Strange Paradise*. McClelland & Stewart, 2021.

Erdoes, Richard, and Ortiz, Alfonso, eds. *American Indian Myths and Legends.* Pantheon, 1985.

Erdrich, Louise. *Antelope Woman: A Novel.* Harper Pernnial, 2016.

———. *Books & Islands in Ojibwe Country.* Harper Perennial, 2003, 2014.

Evans, Mari. *Black Women Writers (1950–1980): A Critical Evaluation.* Anchor Doubleday, 1984.

Fiddler, Thomas. *Killing the Shamen*. Penumbra Press, 1981

Fox, Keolu, and Chanda Prescod-Weinstein. "The Fight for Mauna Kea Is a Fight against Colonial Science." *The Nation,* July 24, 2019. https://www.thenation.com/article/archive/mauna-kea-tmt-colonial-science/.

Freeman, John. "California Book Club: Deborah A. Miranda." YouTube, November 16, 2023. https://www.youtube.com/watch?v=DflbCJL8PsY&t=449s.

Garcia, Tess. "Latine vs Latinx? What Young People of Latin American Descent Think of These Terms." Teen Vogue, October 12, 2022. https://www.teenvogue.com/story/latine-vs-latinx-what-young-people-think.

Gelderloos, Peter. *The Solutions Are Already Here: Strategies for Ecological Revolution from Below.* Pluto Press, 2022.

Gibson, Marion. *Witchcraft: A History in Thirteen Trials.* Simon & Schuster UK, 2024.

Gilmore, Ruth Wilson. *Abolition Geography.* Verso, 2022.

———. *Golden Gulag: Prisons, Surplus, Crisis, and Opposition in Globalizing California.* University of California Press, 2007.

Graham Jones, Stephen. *The Only Good Indians.* S&S/Saga Press, 2021.

———. *My Heart Is a Chainsaw (The Indian Lake Trilogy: Book 1).* Gallery/Saga Press, 2021.

———. *Don't Fear the Reaper (The Indian Lake Trilogy: Book 2).* S&S/Saga Press, 2023.

———. *The Angel of Indian Lake (The Indian Lake Trilogy: Book 3)* S&S/Saga Press, 2024.

Grande, Sandy. *Red Pedagogy: Native American Social and Political Thought.* Rowman and Littlefield, 2004, 2015.

Gross, Lawrence. *Anishinaabe Ways of Knowing and Being.* Ashgate Publishing, 2014.

Gumbs, Alexis Pauline. *Undrowned: Black Feminist Lessons from Marine Mammals.* AK Press, 2020.

Gurr, Barbara. *Reproductive Justice: The Politics of Health Care for Native American Women.* Rutgers University Press, 2014.

Hawk, Shane, and Van Alst Jr., Theodore C., ed. *Never Whistle at Night: An Indigenous Dark Fiction Anthology: Are You Ready to Be Un-Settled?* Random House Canada, 2023.

Hogan, Linda. *Mean Spirit.* Ivy Books, 1991.

Hurston, Zora Neale. *Dust Tracks on a Road.* Amistad, 1995.

International, Amnesty. *A Human Response to Discrimination and Violence against Indigenous Women in Canada,* 2004. https://www.amnesty.ca/sites/amnesty/files/amr200032004enstolensisters.pdf.

Jacobs, Lara A. *Indigenous Voices: Critical Reflections on Traditional Ecological Knowledge.* Oregon State University Press, 2025.

Jamail, Dahr, and Stan Rushworth. *We Are the Middle of Forever: Indigenous Voices from Turtle Island on the Changing Earth.* New Press, 2022.

Joerstad, Mari. *The Hebrew Bible and Environmental Ethics: Humans, NonHumans, and the Living Landscape.* Cambridge University Press, 2019.

Jones-Rogers, Stephanie E. *They Were Her Property: White Women as Slave Owners in the American South.* Yale University Press, 2020.

Juster, Susan. *Sacred Violence in Early America.* University of Pennsylvania Press, 2018.

Justice, Daniel Heath. *Badger.* Reaktion Books, 2015.

———. *Raccoon.* Reaktion Books, 2019.

Justice, Daniel Heath, and Jean M. O'Brien. *Allotment Stories: Indigenous Land Relations under Settler Siege.* University of Minnesota Press, 2022.

———. *Why Indigenous Literatures Matter.* Wilfred Laurier University Press, 2018.

Kairos. "Missing and Murdered Indigenous Women and Girls Timeline." https://www.kairoscanada.org/missing-murdered-indigenous-women-girls/inquiry-timeline.

Kimmerer, Robin Wall. *Gathering Moss: A Natural and Cultural History of Mosses.* Oregon State University Press, 2013.

King, Tiffany Lethobo. *The Black Shoals: Offshore Formations of Black and Native Studies.* Duke University Press, 2019.

Krisha, Swapna et al., eds., *Sword Stone Table: Old Legends, New Voices.* Vintage, 2021.

LaPensée, Elizabeth, Allie Vasquez, Patty Stonefish, Rebecca Naragon, Weshoyot Alvitre, eds. *Deer Woman: An Anthology.* Native Realities Publishing, 2017.

La Pensée, Elizabeth, et al., eds. *A Howl: An Indigenous Anthology of Wolves, Werewolves, and Rougarou.* Native Realities Publishing, 2022.

La Pensée, Elizabeth, et al., eds. *Moonshot: The Indigenous Comics Collection* (Volume 3). Inhabit Education Books, 2020.

Le Carré, John. *The Looking Glass War.* Penguin Group, 1965.

Liboiron, Max. *Pollution Is Colonialism.* Duke University Press, 2021.

Little Badger, Darcie. *A Snake Falls to Earth.* Levine Querido, 2021.

Lorber, Ben, and Shane Burley. *Safety through Solidarity: A Radical Guide to Fighting Antisemitism.* Melville House, 2024.

Lovato, Roberto. *Unforgetting: A Memoir of Family, Migration, Gangs, and Revolution in the Americas.* Reprint edition. Harper Perennial, 2021.

Machado, Antonio. *There Is No Road.* White Pine Press, 2003.

Maracle, Lee. *I Am Woman.* Press Gang, 1996.

McKittrick, Katherine. *Dear Science and Other Stories.* Duke University Press, 2021.

Medina, Nick. *Sisters of the Lost Nation.* Berkley, 2023.

Michigan State University, Department of Plant, Soil, and Microbial Sciences. "Upsettingly, Michigan Does Not Have the Largest Fungi on Earth, Humongous Fungus." November 14, 2018. https://www.canr.msu.edu/news/upsettingly-michigan-does-not-have-the-largest-fungi-on-earth-humongous-fungus.

Miranda, Deborah A. *Bad Indians: A Tribal Memoir.* Heyday, 2022, 2024.

Moreno-Garcia, Sylvia. *Mexican Gothic.* Del Rey, 2020.

Morris, Tiffany. *Green Fuse Burning.* Stelliform Press, 2023.

Morrison, Toni. *Beloved.* Knopf Publishing Group: Older Edition, 1987.

Mura, David. *A Stranger's Journey: Race, Identity, and Narrative Craft in Writing.* University of Georgia Press, 2018.

Murdoch, Isaac. *Serpents and Other Beings.* Kegedonce Press, 2022.

———. *The Trail of Nenaboozhoo and Other Creation Stories.* Kegedonce Press, 2019.

Ningewance, Patricia. *Gii-Nitaa-Aadisooke: Ojibwe Legends from Lac Seul.* Mazinaate, 2018.

Odjick, Jay. *Kagagi.* Arcana Studio, 2011.

OldBear, Weyodi. *As Many Ships As Stars.* Android Press, 2024.

Orange, Tommy. *There There.* Knopf, 2018.

———. *Wandering Stars.* McClelland & Stewart, 2024.

Parker, Robert Dale. *The Sound the Stars Make Rushing through the Sky: The Writings of Jane Johnston Schoolcraft.* University of Pennsylvania Press, 2007.

Parks, Sara, Shayna Sheinfeld, and Meredith J. C. Warren. *Jewish and Christian Women in the Ancient Mediterranean.* Routledge, 2022.

Peacock, Thomas, and Marlene Wisuri. *Ojibwe Waasa Inaabidaa: We Look in All Directions.* Minnesota Historical Society Press, 2002.

Powell, Katrina M. *Beginning Again: Stories of Movement and Migration in Appalachia.* Haymarket, 2024.

Prescod-Weinstein, Chanda. "Book Review | Dear Science and Other Stories, by Katherine McKittrick (Duke University Press, 2021)." *Catalist Journal,* 2021. https://catalystjournal.org/index.php/catalyst/article/view/36952/28911.

Rice, Waubgeshig. *Moon of the Crusted Snow.* ECW Press, 2018.

———. *Moon of the Turning Leaves.* Random House Canada, 2023.

Ruttenberg, Rabbi Danya. "Jews and Colonialism." Life Is a Sacred Text, September 16, 2024. https://www.lifeisasacredtext.com/colonialism/.

Savageau, Cheryl. *Mother/Land.* Salt Publishing, 2006.

Sharma, Nandita. *Home Rule: National Sovereignty and the Separation of Natives and Migrants.* Duke University Press, 2020.

Simpson, Leanne Betasamosake. *A Short History of the Blockade: Giant Beavers, Diplomacy, and Regeneration in Nishnaabwein.* University of Alberta Press, 2021.

———. *As We Have Always Done.* University of Minnesota Press, 2017.

———. *Theory of Water: Nishnaabe Maps to the Times Ahead.* Penguin Random House, 2025.

Smiles, Niiyokamigaabaw Deondre. "To the Anishinaabeg of the Future." *ACME: An International Journal for Critical Geographies,* 2024.

Sulaiman, Sonia. *Thyme Travellers: An Anthology of Palestinian Speculative Fiction.* Roseway Publishing, 2024.

Talaga, Tanya. *All Our Relations: Finding the Path Forward.* House of Anansi Press, 2018.

———. *Seven Fallen Feathers: Racism, Death, and Hard Truths in a Northern City.* House of Anansi Press, 2017.

Taylor, Astra. *Remake the World.* Haymarket, 2021.

Tennant, Zoe. "Our Stories Give Us a Lot of Guidance: Daniel Heath Justice on Why Indigenous Literatures Matter." *CBC,* April 9, 2020. https://www.cbc.ca/radio/unreserved/why-stories-matter-now-more-than-ever-1.5526331/our-stories-give-us-a-lot-of-guidance-daniel-heath-justice-on-why-indigenous-literatures-matter-1.5527999.

Thomas, Kai. *In The Upper Country*. Penguin Canada, 2024.

Tong, Ziya. *The Reality Bubble: How Science Reveals the Hidden Truths That Shape Our World.* Penguin Random House, 2019.

Trask, Haunani-Kay. *From a Native Daughter.* University of Hawai'i Press, 1993, 1999.

Treuer, David. "How Do You Prove You're an Indian?" *New York Times,* December 20, 2011. https://www.nytimes.com/2011/12/21/opinion/for-indian-tribes-blood-shouldnt-be-everything.html?ref=todayspaper.

Twitty, Michael W. "Dear Disgruntled White Plantation Visitors, Sit Down." *The Bitter Southerner*. Accessed November 13, 2024. https://bittersoutherner.com/dear-disgruntled-white-plantation-visitors-michael-twitty-cooking-gene.

———. "Dear Disgruntled White Plantation Visitors, Sit Down." *Afroculinaria*, August 2019. https://afroculinaria.com/2019/08/09/dear-disgruntled-white-plantation-visitors-sit-down/.

———. *The Cooking Gene: A Journey Through African American Culinary History in the Old South*. Harper Collins, 2018.

Ulrich, Laurel Thatcher. *A Midwife's Tale: The Life of Martha Ballard Based on Her Diary, 1785–1812*. Vintage Books, 1990.

Vowel, Chelsea. *Buffalo Is the New Buffalo.* Arsenal Pulp Press, 2022.

Wagamese, Richard. *Ragged Company*. Anchor Canada, 2009.

———. *Starlight*. McClelland & Stewart, 2018.

Walcott, Rinaldo. "Diaspora against the Nation-State." *Briarpatch*, April 8, 2024.

Walker, Taté. *The Trickster Riots.* Abalone Mountain Press, 2022.

Willis, Ann. "The Klamath Dam Removals: A Story of People and Possibility." American Rivers, September 9, 2024. https://www.americanrivers.org/2024/09/the-klamath-dam-removals-a-story-of-people-and-possibility/.